5/17/18

To: Jody Parker

The Sawners Of Chandler

A Pioneering Power Couple in Pre-Civil Rights Oklahoma

By Hannibal B. Johnson

*Best wishes always,
Jody. Thanks for
your friendship and
support.

Hannibal B. Johnson*

EAKIN

D1226119

Copyright © 2018
By Hannibal B. Johnson
Published By Eakin Press
An Imprint of Wild Horse Media Group
P.O. Box 331779
Fort Worth, Texas 76163
1-817-344-7036
www.EakinPress.com
ALL RIGHTS RESERVED
1 2 3 4 5 6 7 8 9
ISBN-10: 1-68179-118-8
ISBN-13: 978-1-68179-118-0

Acknowledgments

No man, who continues to add something to the material, intellectual and moral well-being of the place in which he lives, is left long without proper reward. — Booker T. Washington

Special thanks to Melvin Chatman for his meticulous research on the lives of George and Lena Sawner,[i] whom he re-discovered while writing his family memoir, *Chandler: The Ellis Family Story*,[ii] in the late 1990s. Mr. Chatman, a Chandler native and hometown historian, lent his considerable knowledge, wisdom, and personal connections to this project. He shared detailed archives, including family memorabilia.

Strong ties bind Mr. Chatman to the Sawners. His grandparents, Whit and Maggie (Riley) Ellis, became dear friends of George and Lena Sawner, so close that the Ellises named their youngest son George Sawner Ellis. Mr. Chatman's mother, Ann Ellis, was one of the ten Ellis children who studied under the tutelage of Mrs. Sawner at Chandler's all-black Douglass School.

In addition to their sisterly bond, Maggie Ellis and Lena Sawner shared a strikingly similar child-rearing philosophy. Maggie Ellis applied it to her ten-child household. Lena Sawner, with no biological children of her own, employed it on the scores of young ones who passed through the doors of Douglass School. Both women believed in family unity, faith without fanaticism, academic achievement, oratory (diction and enunciation), and gratitude.[iii]

The Ellis children never forgot the family-centric, achievement-without-excuses philosophy shared by their mother and Mrs. Sawner; the lessons instilled at home were reinforced at school. They realized the anchoring, centering role of family, but they also credited some measure of their individual and collective successes to Mrs. Sawner's unshakable belief in their limitless potential.

Through the passage of generations, the Ellises internalized an anything-is-possible mindset they credited largely to Lena Sawner. Like indelible ink, Mrs. Sawner's uncompromising insistence on excellence through rigor and her unflappable devotion to the students at Douglass School could not be erased from their psyches. That each of the ten Ellis children taught school at some point in his or her life-

iii

time is a testament to Mrs. Sawner's potent influence. *Chandler: The Ellis Family Story*, chronicles the life and times of this tight-knit Oklahoma family profoundly influenced by George and Lena Sawner.

Mr. Chatman conceived and championed an effort to secure broad recognition of George and Lena Sawner. He offered presentations at The Lincoln County Historical Society Museum of Pioneer History ("LCHS Museum of Pioneer History") in Chandler and the Ralph Ellis Library in Oklahoma City. He contacted Langston University, Oklahoma State University, the University of Oklahoma, and the Oklahoma Historical Society in hopes of generating a groundswell of popular support for according the Sawners their historical due. By 2008, Mr. Chatman's work began to pay dividends. This book builds upon that work.

Thanks to the staff of LCHS Museum of Pioneer History, including Jamie Sullenger and V. Diana Kinzey, for their invaluable assistance. The LCHS Museum of Pioneer History, the repository of a treasure trove of historical materials and artifacts, helps bring the Sawners' story to life. Its accommodating staff made visits pleasurable and productive.

Thanks to Jan Vassar, a Sumatra, Indonesia-born Chandler and Oklahoma historian with layers-deep knowledge of Lincoln County. Ms. Vassar shepherded the reclamation of the too-often-overlooked African American narrative that is part and parcel of that county's history. She shared insights gleaned from her background as a researcher, writer, editor, and reporter with stints at newspapers, television stations, nonprofit entities, and the Sac and Fox Nation that helped define and refine this book.

Ms. Vassar, a current Chandler resident, still encounters locals who remind her of the special character of her hometown. That difficult-to-describe hallmark manifests in a noticeably cordial, respectful sense of shared community displayed by both black and white Chandlerites, a number of whom maintain longstanding, deeply-rooted relationships across racial lines. Ms. Vassar credits George and Lena Sawner with laying the foundation upon which this spirit of interracial comity rests.[iv]

Jeanette Haley, longtime curator of the LCHS Museum of Pioneer History, deserves special mention. She accepted, processed, and made available to the public materials contained in the Sawner collections. Ms. Haley promoted the curation of black history documents and artifacts generally, recognizing the dearth of such materials and their importance to a full telling of pioneer history. Among other projects, she compiled lists of the separate schools and Negro cemeteries in Lincoln County now found in the black history files at the LCHS Museum of Pioneer History. Jamie Sullenger, a later conservator, leveraged Ms. Haley's work, creating exhibits and programs and continuing to encourage the collection of information about African American participation in the Lincoln County narrative.

Special thanks to Von Dosta McCormick, the daughter of Grace and Henry McCormick. The elder McCormicks lived in the Sawner house after Lena Sawner died in 1949. George Sawner predeceased her in 1924.

In 2010, Von Dosta McCormick discovered original documents relating to Lena Sawner's teaching career and George Sawner's membership in a prominent, nationwide African American business group inside a closet in the house. Ms. McCormick presented these historical treasures to Jan Vassar, then a member of the board of directors of the Oklahoma Historical Society, which currently houses the documents. Copies are available in the Sawner files at the LCHS Museum of Pioneer History.

Thanks also to Victor Brown, Bernice Caldwell, and George Sawner Ellis (the last surviving child of Maggie and Whit Ellis), all former Douglass School students and admirers of Mrs. Sawner, for sharing their crisp recollections of the school and its iconic leader. Thanks to Phil Boyd of Chandler Public Schools, James Dunavant of Langston University, and Larry O'Dell of the Oklahoma Historical Society for providing leads and other information.

I offer a note of special appreciation to those who read and critiqued the manuscript for this book at its various stages, including Melvin Chatman, George Sawner Ellis, Dwight Eskew, Vanessa Adams-Harris, Arlene Johnson, Jan Vassar, and Steve Wood.

Table Of Contents

The Sawners of Chandler
A Pioneering Power Couple in Pre-Civil Rights Oklahoma

By Hannibal B. Johnson

Lena Lowery Sawner, *circa* 1922, and George W.F. Sawner, *circa* 1900

Introduction

If there is no struggle, there is no progress. Those who profess to favor freedom, and deprecate agitation, are men who want crops without plowing up the ground, they want rain without thunder and lightning. —Frederick Douglass

The United States of America today seems not simply generations removed, but worlds apart, from the good ole U.S.A. of 1900. At a backward glance, life at the turn of the twentieth century looks formidable indeed.

A delve into the data from 1900 reveals concentrated wealth amidst widespread privation. Then, the United States' 76 million people comprised the wealthiest economy in the world, with a *per capita* annual income averaging, in present-day dollars, about $5,000 — on par with Britain and Australia, twice that of France and Germany, and quadruple that of Japan and Mexico. Still, issues of wealth distribution and income inequality plagued the country. Most Americans lived in relative poverty.

1

Electricity lit three percent of American homes. Household plumbing remained a luxury for most. Thirty-three percent of American homes offered running water, fifteen percent sported flush toilets, half of all farm households lacked indoor plumbing altogether and had no outhouse.

Most Americans lived within a mile of where they worked. They walked virtually everywhere. Only one urban household in five owned a horse.

Half of all Americans lived in spaces that averaged more than one person per room. Many took in lodgers.

Life expectancy at birth stood at only forty-seven years. Infant mortality rates soared. Of every 1,000 babies born, 140 died in their first year, succumbing to garden-variety ailments like flu, pneumonia, typhoid, gastritis, and whooping cough.

Illiteracy burdened ten percent of the population. The average adult functioned at the eighth grade level. Only seven percent of students completed high school.

Men dominated the workaday world, routinely working to the point of physical exhaustion. They typically logged sixty-hour workweeks spread over six days. Two-thirds of men over age sixty-five worked full-time jobs. Few earned pensions.

Women made up eighteen percent of the paid workforce, concentrated in piecework fields like textiles, apparel, shoes, and canning. At home, women spent some forty hours a week on meal preparation and meal cleanup, seven hours on laundry, and an equal number of hours on housecleaning. The average housewife baked a half a ton of bread—about 1,400 loaves—a year.[v]

This portrait of the life of the "average American" at the turn of the twentieth century only hints at the brutal hardships faced by those who overwhelmingly fell below the median in virtually every conceivable gauge of general well-being. In 1900, life for the marginalized, the forgotten, and specifically, the African American, proved particularly precarious:

> [N]inety percent of African Americans still lived in the Southern US in 1900—roughly the same percentage as lived in the South in 1870. Three-quarters of black households were located in rural places. Only about one-fifth of African American household heads owned their own homes (less than half the percentage among whites). About half of black men and about thirty-five percent of

black women who reported an occupation to the [1900] Census said that they worked as a farmer or farm laborer, as opposed to about one-third of white men and about eight percent of white women. Outside of farm work, African American men and women were greatly concentrated in unskilled labor and service jobs. Most black children had not attended school in the year before the [1900] Census.[vi]

Juxtaposed against this grim assessment of black life at the turn of the twentieth century, the lives of George and Lena Sawner shone like the blazing sun on an oven-hot August day in Oklahoma. Educated, professional, and economically stable—well-off by most standards—the Sawners lived the American dream, accompanied, periodically, by nightmarish reminders of the realities of race. The couple owned a home, rental property, stocks, businesses, and two cars. They hobnobbed with local, state, and national dignitaries. They vacationed in faraway places like Montreal, Canada.[vii]

A 1918 article in the *Tulsa Star* newspaper painted an idyllic portrait of this audacious, authentic Oklahoma couple.

[Mrs. L. L. Sawner] represents one of the most cultured women in our Race, and the only lady principal of a High School in our State. She is the wife of Hon. G. W. F. Sawner, a cotton buyer who has more than made good in the cotton business. Mrs. Sawner has enjoyed many educational advantages, and is one of the best prepared women we have. She has worked zealously in the Liberty Loan, War Saving, War Fund and Red Cross drives. She is patriotic in every sense of the word. The people of Oklahoma have honored her many times, both in the educational, fraternal and other professions, and each time this polished woman has demonstrated her ability along all lines, which means the betterment of humanity. Her school work in the state easily puts her in the front ranks as an instructor, and many young people in the state have received their training through this lady. She travels extensively, and enjoys a large acquaintance throughout the country. Her husband has made good accumulating this world's goods, and is one of our best fixed men. These people are truly leaders, and have the confidence and respect of all. They are great entertainers, and when one visits their palatial home, he never forgets the hospitality this excellent couple extend. The [Tulsa] Star is pleased to claim them as friends, in fact, they are friends to every worthy enterprise, operated by our Race.[viii]

The Sawners excelled in their respective spheres and claimed the social, political, and economic accoutrements commensurate with their successes. Material trappings and stature aside, the Sawners never severed their roots.

Despite their undeniable attainments, the Sawners, like other African Americans in Oklahoma, often swam against the current, regularly battling waves of bigotry and intolerance. Reminiscent of the Jim Crow South, the political waters in Oklahoma, particularly as they cascaded over racial matters, became increasingly contaminated.

Like Chandler's dike in a raging racial storm, the Sawners helped restrain a relentless torrent of racism, at least in one small corner of one rising state. Together and separately, these transformational figures with Oklahoma moorings and oceans-wide achievements buoyed the lives and boosted the fortunes of generations of Oklahomans.

In an era of unceasing anti-black sentiment and vicious racial violence, the *café au lait*-colored duo could have "passed" for white.[ix] Indeed, strangers often perceived them as being of the Caucasian persuasion. They regularly left railroad conductors nonplussed, wondering why on Earth a distinguished *white* couple would be sitting, willingly, in the Jim Crow car amongst common Negroes.

Fair-skinned, stringy-haired George Sawner bore unmistakable European physiognomy and, as a result, withstood a barrage of challenges to his racial identity.[x] In a 1919 newspaper article discussing Mr. Sawner's visit to Boley, Oklahoma, America's premier all-black town, the writer noted: "Hon. G.W.F. Sawner of Chandler was in the city a few days around with friends and chums. He is the only white man accorded absolute privilege in Boley."[xi]

Despite plausible deniability, Mr. Sawner opted into his blackness and thus out of a life of white privilege. In so doing, he encountered all manner of hardships attendant to the life of a black man in a white supremacist era. Fully aware of the struggles that lay ahead, he roundly embraced his racial identity and toiled tirelessly to improve the lot of his African American kin.

George Sawner fashioned himself a renaissance man. He traveled in orbits sparsely inhabited by African Americans of his era. In fact, he penetrated social and political circles impervious to most, irrespective of race.

He worked closely with leaders of commerce. He hobnobbed with Oklahoma Territory (later, Oklahoma) leaders. He knew the likes of Booker T. Washington and W.E.B. Du Bois, nationally known black intellectuals and "race men."[xii] He practiced law. He accepted an appointment to a gubernatorial commission charged with improving tempestuous race relations in Oklahoma. He earned national stature among black business moguls. He owned shops, cotton gins, and farms. He served as a director of a black-owned bank and a realty and investment company.

Mr. Sawner matched the breadth of his ventures with the depth to which he undertook them. In all he did, he emerged as an energetic, results-oriented leader laser-focused on achievement.

Upon George Sawner's death in 1924, a *Chandler News-Publicist* necrology described this indefatigable Oklahoman as "one of the most unique and influential characters in this section of the state and one of the most trusted and outstanding men of his race in Oklahoma."[xiii] His former law partner, W.H. Twine, eulogized Sawner as "[a] magnificent and manly man, a pioneer who led his people to success in the early days of Oklahoma[;] A patriot who never faltered in his duty to his country."[xiv]

Press comments accompanying Mr. Sawner's *Chandler News-Publicist* obituary included remarks captioned "Good-bye, George":

> The whole state of Oklahoma stands bowed in grief this week because of the passing . . . of G. W. F. Sawner. Seldom, if ever, do you find a man who led the vigorous active life as did Mr. Sawner who can lay down and die without an enemy. Seldom, if ever, do you find a man who can live in a community for almost half a century and leave behind him as he passes into the grave an unspotted record.
>
> . . .
>
> George Sawner believed in his race. He trusted all humanity. Many financial reverses came to him just before he was called to his reward, but he died with a smile. We shall never forget the last evening spent with him, just a few short days before he passed away. Wasted physically, weak in the fatigue of age and yet that buoyancy of spirit, that never fading thought of race betterment was uppermost in his mind.[xv]

Mr. Sawner earned the moniker "pioneer" not just by virtue of his singular passion for African American uplift, but for his industriousness and professionalism. Few could match his business acumen and triumphs and, among African Americans, fewer still.

George Sawner proved anything but typical. He took as his bride a similarly unconventional woman, Lena Lowery. The couple settled in Chandler shortly after the turn of the twentieth century.

While the aphorism "behind every great man there is a great woman"[xvi] might have been applied to the dynamic duo during their years together, a variation on that theme seems more accurate: *Alongside* every great man there is an *equally great* woman. Both George and Lena Sawner fed off the symbiotic relationship they shared. Together, they blazed trails along thought-to-be-off-limits portions of the Oklahoma prairie.

Just as surely as George Sawner earned the label "Renaissance man," Lena Sawner exhibited a similar jack-of-all-trades endowment, setting herself apart as educator extraordinaire, intercultural ambassador, and philanthropist. Despite her near-regal bearing, voguish coiffure, and impeccable dress, Mrs. Sawner declined to arrogate herself above others. She valued style, but exalted substance.

Lena Sawner never showed an imperious nature. Instead, she counted as companions the sister virtues of grace and humility. A God-fearing woman, she elevated only Him, but, through precept and example, she lifted those whose paths she crossed.

Mrs. Sawner relished her African ancestry. Comfortable in her own skin, she conceded nothing on account of race. She instilled her dare-to-dream, sky-is-the-limit philosophy in generations of black children who faced a barrage of attitudinal and institutional challenges to their individual and collective sense of self-worth.

For Mrs. Sawner, the gravitational pull of family proved irresistible. Her world spun on its axis—namely, her husband, George —until his demise decades before hers. Thereafter, her life revolved around a constellation of children, the sons and daughters of other black Chandlerites. She bore no biological children, but Chandler's black children *were* her children, the bright and shining stars in the Sawner galaxy.

Chandler's Negro school, named for statesman and abolitionist Frederick Douglass, served as Mrs. Sawner's studio. As with students in segregated schools throughout the land, Douglass School pupils made due with shopworn materials and supplies, often hand-me-downs and castoffs from Chandler's white schools.

Despite the physical and material shortcomings evident at Douglass School, Mrs. Sawner handcrafted Negro education, beginning with only a half-dozen students. With a sculptor's dexterity, she fashioned young minds for generations.

She educated black children. She fought for black teachers. She stood up for civil rights. She challenged internalized and externalized oppression—black self-doubt and white racism—with her own form of soul force: personal excellence. She built bridges across the racial divide. She agitated, but in a most lady-like fashion. Above all, she made an enduring difference in the lives of legions.

As an educational artisan, she designed a model by which to shape and mold her students. In so doing, she recast not only Chandler, but also communities well beyond its borders.[xvii]

Mrs. Sawner happened upon the Chandler scene in 1902, fittingly, the birth year of a triumvirate of artistic legends: poet Langston Hughes; photographer Ansel Adams; and author John Steinbeck. Like these arts icons, she used her passion and gifts to instruct and inspire. She set in motion an evolution at Douglass School that, by the end of her long tenure in 1934, yielded a highly regarded educational institution with virtuosic teaching talent and a corps of students and alumni brimming with the self-confidence that comes through preparation and opportunity.

Mrs. Sawner's diplomacy ranks with that of another famous black woman from another era, quick-witted Sojourner Truth.[xviii] A pro-slavery Southerner approached the former slave, abolitionist, and social activist following her lecture in Cincinnati, Ohio, in 1853. With a noticeable air of condescension, he offered a snide rejoinder to her well-received address: "You were wrong in everything you said. Why, without slavery, the Negroes would starve to death. They were made to be slaves. As far as I am concerned, you made no more impression than a flea-bite."

Sojourner Truth delivered a polite but trenchant reply. "I am sorry to hear that," she purred, "but perhaps, with God's help, I can keep you scratching!" Sojourner Truth having parried the acerbic thrust of her overmatched opponent, the verbal jousting ended.[xix]

Like Sojourner Truth, Lena Lowery Sawner understood that mild agitation—just enough to keep them scratching—could yield profound behavioral change. Mrs. Sawner chose education as her *modus operandi* for that discomposure. She churned out confident, capable, and competent black students, a certain irritant to those who bought into the black inferiority myth. She advanced the cause of race relations in Oklahoma at a most inhospitable time for African Americans.

Mrs. Sawner did not live to see the dawn of public school integration. Still, in her own inimitable way, she had already been to the mountaintop, seen the Promised Land,[xx] and prepared the precious black children of Chandler to get there, with or without her. Her legacy extends well beyond geographic boundaries of Chandler, Oklahoma, and the temporal boundaries of her educational career. No matter our place along the color line or within the two worlds she traveled:[xxi] one black; the other white—separate and unequal, we are all better for Lena Sawner having lived.

Outside Chandler and Oklahoma, this educational architect remains largely unknown. Like a would-be queen queued up for her coronation, Mrs. Sawner still lingers in the backcourt, awaiting ascension to her throne among the assemblage of legends and luminaries who shaped the course of the African American experience. Lena Sawner and her king, George Sawner, should surely be counted among Oklahoma's African American royalty and, indeed, among *Oklahoma's* royalty.

Because George Sawner predeceased Lena Sawner by twenty-five years, she spent about twice as much time in Chandler as did he. Moreover, as an educator, Mrs. Sawner directly and deeply touched the lives of hundreds of impressionable students, their families, and community members.

Her individual legacy, though perhaps more profound and palpable than that of her husband, cannot be wholly separated from that of the Sawner union. George Sawner's social, political, and economic standing no doubt contributed to his wife's triumphs, both during his lifetime and after his death.

Mr. Sawner taught through living. Mrs. Sawner lived through teaching. He, a business tycoon, lawyer, and civil rights advocate; she, an exceptional teacher, school leader, and philanthropist.

The Sawners were particularly well-suited for their roles of race ambassadors. George Sawner needed transracial relationships to further his commercial ventures and broaden political interest in the enhanced civil rights he championed on behalf of all African Americans. Lena Sawner needed to establish positive relations across racial lines to further her educational mission. Her prominent role as a teacher and school leader in the white-dominated, albeit separate-but-equal, public education arena made white allies all but essential.

The Sawners navigated upstream against the swift current of racial animus that meandered through the state. Throughout their journey, they earned respect on both the black and white banks of the great and raging river of race. They became role models for black Chandlerites. They served as cultural ambassadors to Chandler's white community, largely composed of families from "free states" (*i.e.*, states that outlawed slavery prior to the Civil War).[xxii] Both their African American and white contemporaries saw George and Lena Sawner as leaders—as exemplars of Negro excellence.

The Sawners' leadership and constructive engagement helped make Chandler, by comparison to other towns in Oklahoma and elsewhere, a relative oasis of racial understanding in a world fraught with racial strife. Though by no means a utopia, Chandler represented a level of progressivity, placidity, and promise on matters of race unusual for the times, and notably aberrant in Oklahoma.

Well over a century ago, in the early 1900s, the Sawners stood up and stood out. This erudite, connected, politically-savvy pair gave life a go in a western outpost, the erstwhile Oklahoma Territory, and later, in America's forty-sixth state. In the process, George and Lena Sawner paved the way for future generations and countless individuals who, sadly, may never know the Sawner surname.

We too often forget the crafty cragsmen like Mr. and Mrs. Sawner—the men and women who chip away at society's jagged edges so that future generations experience a smoother climb up a less steep hill. It is never too late to honor them through remembrance.

This is the story of a remarkable duo that emerged as a profound force for race relations in a small Oklahoma town. *The Sawners of Chandler* chronicles the life and times of this under-the-radar Oklahoma power couple, George and Lena Sawner. It is the saga of a before-their-time pair who refused to be constrained by external societal boundaries and barriers or limited by internal misgivings and self-doubts.

Chapter One: Wonders of the West

"While waiting for a Moses to lead us into the Promised Land, we have forgotten how to walk."
— Wendell Johnson

From: United States Census 1900, https://familysearch.org/learn/wiki/en/United_States_Census_1900

Oklahoma once ranked as a wonder of the West, a destination discovery romanticized in rhetoric resonant with black audiences. Persons of African ancestry first traversed modern-day Oklahoma with Spanish explorers in the 1500s. They later accompanied the Five Civilized Tribes[xxiii] (the Choctaw, Seminole, Cherokee, Muscogee (Creek), and Chickasaw), forcibly resettled from the Southeastern United States in the 1830s and 1840s.[xxiv] Still later, propaganda propelled the great black migration that came as part of the post-Reconstruction black diaspora from the South in the 1880s and 1890s.[xxv] At each turn in the unfolding saga of this once-remote refuge, race remained relevant.

Oklahoma's congenital struggles with race formed the backdrop for the Sawners' remarkable lives. The Sawners were *who* they were because they were *where* they were.

On November 16, 1907, Oklahoma and Indian Territories merged into the present-day State of Oklahoma. Prior to that time, Oklahoma Territory, the western half of this land of the red people,[xxvi] captured the imaginations of restive Americans, both black and white.

Oklahoma Territory[xxvii] first opened for general settlement on April 22, 1889. Like predators in the wild, Oklahoma Territory newcomers foraged for new beginnings and, more specifically, economic opportunities, in these "Unassigned Lands."[xxviii] Corporate interests like the railroads saw Oklahoma Territory as fertile field for market expansion and revenue-generation and as a new profit center.[xxix]

With increasing frequency, African American migrants from the Deep South escaped the straightjacket of Southern political, economic, and social domination. Oklahoma Territory, once home to several Indian tribes,[xxx] ranked among the most desirable of destinations.[xxxi] The fascination with Oklahoma Territory was more than mere wanderlust. Widely perceived by non-Indians to be undiscovered, uninhabited, and unspoiled, this wonder of the West held virtually unlimited promise. For forlorn African Americans, tall tales about this faraway Eden grew to utopian proportions. Imaginations ran wild.

Imagine an all-black state in the land of the red people.

A place of possibility and promise:
Civil rights,
Economic opportunity,
Social equality —
Right here in Oklahoma.

A place with black leadership:
A governor,
An entrepreneur,
A booster —
Right here in Oklahoma.

A place of relative peace:
A safe place,
A just place,
A more perfect place —
Right here in Oklahoma.

Imagine.
Imagine.
Imagine.

Imagine an all-black state in the land of the red people.[xxxii]

"I's glad I came to Oklahoma"—postcard, *circa* 1907, touting the Oklahoma Promised Land.[xxxiii]

John Booker, African American pioneer and participant in the 1891 land run.[xxxiv]

The Booker brothers, sons of John and Mary Booker, 1918; left to right: Andersen Booker, Thomas Booker, Mercer Booker, Frank Booker, and John Booker.[xxxv]

A special July 1, 1907, census captured the demographic impact of the Oklahoma allure. On that date, the population of Oklahoma Territory stood at 733,062; that of Indian Territory, 681,115. Those numbers reflected a dramatic seven-year increase in population of 334,731 (84 percent) for Oklahoma Territory and 289,055 (78.9 percent) for Indian Territory. The population of Indian Territory more than doubled from 1890 to 1900; that of Oklahoma Territory in the same period more than quadrupled. Oklahoma Territory boasted the largest, and Indian Territory the second largest, population increase between 1890 and 1900 of any state or territory in the United States.[xxxvii]

Oklahoma Land Run of '91
A Lincoln County Centennial Salute

Reproduction of the October 3, 1891, *Harper's Weekly* depicting the Land Run of 1891 through the eyes of artist W.A. Rogers.[xxxvi]

The demographic stew that fed Oklahoma's rapid expansion often simmered and occasionally boiled over. African American aspirations clashed with entrenched notions of white supremacy in a land once reserved for the American originals.

Like just the right blend of salt and pepper added to this ingredient-rich mix, George and Lena Sawner lent a sense of balance, earning the trust and respect of all whom they met. The Sawners played a pivotal role in the business, education, and political spheres in nascent, racially-challenged, Oklahoma. They walked the racial tightrope that spanned the yawning chasm of difference and distrust between, primarily, black and white Oklahomans. Largely on their account, Chandler remained calm amidst the storms of racial tumult that battered Oklahoma and the nation. The Sawners' lives and the unusual town that hosted them offer lessons for the ages.

Who were the Sawners' contemporaries? What was the state of race relations in American during the Sawner era? How and why did race relations in Chandler differ from those in other Oklahoma communities? The answers to these questions lie, at least in part, in post-Civil War developments and migrations.

Swept up in the winds of social change after the collapse of Reconstruction, African Americans blew into the Oklahoma Territory with gale-force energy. This alien acreage beckoned like a sultry siren. And she would prove just as beguiling.

African Americans, dreamers who fantasized about an all-black state within the Oklahoma Territory, faced a rude awakening. Deferred and ultimately discarded, this longing for a cocooned, all-black existence grew out of a yearning for black self-actualization. African Americans simply wanted a place where they, too, could live out, unmolested, the promise of this "sweet land of liberty."[xxxviii] Some saw it, or at least romanticized about it, in the lands of the untested Oklahoma Territory.

Even as this ultimate reverie faded, another vision, almost as intriguing and even more enduring, took shape. This latter dream morphed into reality. A number of new, all-black towns and settlements sprang up all across Oklahoma Territory and Indian Territory.

The founding of these all-black towns and the imaginings of an all-black state helped lay the foundation for African American progress during the twentieth century.[xxxiv] The epic tale of Oklahoma's all-black town movement is a quintessentially American narrative.

Cherokee   Choctaw   Muscogee
                          Creek

Chickasaw   Seminole

Gallery of the Five Civilized Tribes; portraits drawn/painted between 1775 and 1850.[xl]

Five Civilized Tribes Museum in Muskogee, Oklahoma.[xli]

Picture it: An all-black state founded by nineteenth century "Negroes" pining for social, political, and economic rights denied them in a schizophrenic America. The Constitutional idealism embodied in words like "freedom," "justice," and "equality" simply did not square with the realities on the ground. Escape to an all-black state seemed a palatable—even desirable—solution. As envisioned, an all-black state would be a gap-filler between American aspirations and African American actuality.

The prospect of an all-black state captured the attention of the nation. In 1890, amidst a groundswell of support among African Americans, United States President Benjamin Harrison took note of ascending ambitions among African Americans in Oklahoma Territory.

While efforts to establish an all-black state in Oklahoma Territory fell short, all-black towns like Boley, Clearview, Langston, Red Bird, Rentiesville, and Taft emerged on both sides of the territorial dividing line. So, too, did centers of music, culture, and commerce in segregated urban communities like "Deep Deuce" in Oklahoma City and the "Greenwood District" in Tulsa (a.k.a., "Negro Wall Street" and, later, "Black Wall Street"). The economically fragile and politically precarious all-black towns and their similarly vulnerable urban kin

mushroomed. Though imperfect, they became islands of opportunity, laboratories for entrepreneurship, and sanctuaries from social and
political subjugation.

African Americans sought solace in Oklahoma. Their ensuing
push for an all-black state and the resultant consolation prize—the
all-black towns—reconfigured the American landscape.

Prior to the opening of Oklahoma Territory, all-black towns inhabited by persons of African ancestry with tribal connections sprang up
in then-Indian Territory (the eastern part of present-day Oklahoma).
Formed around 1850, Tullahassee (meaning "old town"), one such
"Native" town, served as a mission for the Muscogee (Creek) tribe.
These towns would soon be contrasted with all-black towns populated with "state Negroes," late nineteenth century and early twentieth
century migrants primarily from the Deep South.[xliv]

For African Americans, the national milieu—social, political, and
economic desperation—impelled the movement north and west.
Post-Civil War America, despite the end of slavery, remained a forbidding place. In 1877, federal troops stationed in the South to protect newly freed black Americans withdrew. The removal of this national command and control foreshadowed a reversion to the *status
quo ante*. White Southerners reasserted themselves with a vengeance,
their near-stranglehold on power virtually unchecked. Disempow-
ered black Southerners choked on the swill of unrelenting white racism. African American social, political, and economic gains made
during Reconstruction dissipated like the fog at sunrise.

With their hopes dashed, many African Americans migrated
north, often to Kansas. In *The Exodus of 1879*, writer John B. Van Deusen homed in on three primary reasons black citizens bolted from
their Southern discomfort: (1) a sense of personal insecurity; (2) economic discontent; and (3) attractive propaganda.[xlvi]

Sentiments for separate black colonies continued to gain traction
as the resentments and recriminations of white Southerners intensified. Respite-seeking African American "Exodusters" founded dozens of all-black towns in the wake of Reconstruction, most of them
north and west of the traditional "Black Belt,"[xlvii] the Deep South
areas where the African Americans maintained a numerical predom-
inance.

Black Southern migrants formed cloistered frontier communities.
They believed in themselves. They clung to hope. They trusted the
process.

These beleaguered American idealists made their play for the

Exodusters in Nicodemus, Kansas, 1885.[xlviii]

rights of American citizenship, self-governance, and economic self-sufficiency. Against what appeared to be long odds, they trusted the house; they bet on the capacity of the country, over time, to embrace them as equals, as fully formed citizens.

S.L. Johnson, a black Louisianan, in a 1879 letter to Kansas Governor John St. John, noted: [i]"I am anxious to reach your state . . . because of the sacredness of her soil washed by the blood of humanitarians for the cause of freedom. [xlix]

Nicodemus, Kansas, emerged as the destination of choice for a host of early black pilgrims, including native New Yorker Edward Preston McCabe, an 1878 arrival from Chicago. Kansas voters elected the charismatic Republican to the post of State Auditor in 1882 and again in 1884.[l]

McCabe ventured into Oklahoma Territory on Monday, April 22, 1889, for the first opening of its Unassigned Lands. The crack of a gunshot pierced the allergen-rich, spring air at noon that day, heralding the promise of a new life for him and tens of thousands of other intrepid souls. From that awe-inspiring beginning, McCabe established the all-black town of Langston in 1890. Not long thereafter, President Harrison rewarded the Republican stalwart with an appointment as Oklahoma Territorial Auditor.[li]

In Langston, McCabe took to land speculation, creating the Mc-

Cabe Townsite Company. He founded the *Langston City Herald*, one of several black-owned Oklahoma newspapers that agitated for civil rights and equality for African Americans. He secured a $500,000 pledge from William Waldorf Astor to support the construction of modern-day Langston University, founded in 1897 as Colored Agricultural and Normal University.[lii]

Ever industrious, Mc-Cabe built a business on boosterism. He printed promotional circulars and hired paid agents—cheerleaders— to tout Oklahoma Territory among African Americans in

Edward Preston McCabe[liii]

the South. This fervent advocate, feverish propagandist, and fearless defender sired the black town movement.

In 1890, McCabe met with President Harrison, reportedly to discuss sculpting an all-black state from within Oklahoma Territory. This idea triggered impassioned reactions from people like George Sawner, who quipped: "Surely McCabe . . . realizes the folly of a distinctly Negro state, ruled by Negroes. McCabe knows it is impossible to keep the white man away from Negroes." Sawner added, "Negro supremacy is not the desire of Negroes or McCabe, but they do wish one state at least, in the union, where the Negro will have an equal chance in the race of life with other men."

By some accounts, McCabe, the advocate-in-chief for the creation of a black safe haven, kept his eyes on the real prize: an Oklahoma governorship in a new, all-black state. The President offered a listening ear, and then took the proposal for this Negro proving ground under advisement.

Some white Americans supported the concept of an all-black state, albeit contemptuously. They saw it as an opportunity to deal with the "Negro problem," not unlike forced Indian removal decades earlier had, theoretically, dealt with the perceived "Indian problem."

The Langston City Herald (Langston City, Oklahoma Territory), Vol. 5, No. 1, Ed. 1, Saturday, April 27, 1895.[liv]

Like Indians on a reservation, African Americans, too, could be cor-ralled and controlled. An all-black state, these anti-black elements reasoned, would diminish the prospect of black/white social inter-course and quell black demands for social equality and economic parity. This isolationist approach would be tantamount to a near-final solution.

Despite the dubious embrace of the all-black-state proposal in some quarters, others chafed at notion of a concentrated, self-con-trolled black enclave. An article in the *New York Times* on March 1, 1890, proclaimed: "If the black population could be distributed even-ly over the United States it would not constitute a social or political danger. But an exclusively or overwhelmingly Negro settlement in any part of the country, is, to all intents and purposes, a camp of sav-ages."[lvii]

Undeterred by his critics and the failure of the all-black state movement, McCabe focused his energies on creating all-black towns in Oklahoma. He masterminded a Southern strategy.

McCabe, through both written accounts and personal ambassa-dors, painted idyllic portraits of Oklahoma for folks in need of a fan-tasy. It paid off. He and other Oklahoma boosters lured droves of forlorn African Americans to his would-be Shangri-La, a place that seemed to offer much of what segregated America withheld. Black hamlets, villages, and towns populated by these seekers coated the prairie landscape.

Unification of Oklahoma Territory and Indian Territory—Okla-homa statehood—loomed on the horizon. Black settlements existed on both sides of the geographic divide.

As these all-black enclaves emerged, sundown towns multiplied. The latter communities telegraphed a clear message to African Amer-icans: "Open-by-day, off-limits-after-dusk." Oklahoma towns like Norman, Marlow, and Okemah signaled their hostility toward Af-rican Americans, proscribing residency and discouraging extended visits. All-too-frequent signs made the message clear: "Nigger, don't let the sun go down on you here." Indeed, the *Oklahoma Guide*, a newspaper out of the Oklahoma Territorial capital of Guthrie, report-ed in 1905 that "[a]n Indian [Territory] judge climbed a telegraph pole and tor[e] down a sign which read, 'nigger don't let the sun go down on you.'" The paper followed the account with a rhetorical question: "Could you find an [Oklahoma Territory] Judge that would do the same?"[lix]

Race mattered mightily at the conception and birth of America's forty-sixth state. Democrats controlled pre-statehood Oklahoma. Most African Americans favored the Republicans, the "Party of Lincoln." Neither party embraced African Americans as fully vested American citizens.

At the November 1906 Constitutional Convention in Guthrie, the Territorial Capital, the convention's elected leader (and later, Governor of Oklahoma), William H. "Alfalfa Bill" Murray of Tishomingo, pandered to the racist sympathies of his colleagues.[ix]

Similarly, on September 13, 1907, Roy E. Stafford, editor of the *Daily Oklahoman*, penned a white supremacist broadside that captured the Zeitgeist:

GIVES JUSTICE TO BOTH THE RACES

Negro Must Be Made to Know His Place—Should Have Equal Privileges But Entirely Separate

(By Roy E. Stafford.)

Give the negro a chance by making him understand that a line is drawn between the white and the black races.

Educate him entirely in a school that is presided over by negroes and whose pupils are all negroes.

Give him entirely equal advantages of railway passenger facilities, but separate him from white passengers.

Provide a waiting room for him at every railway station in the new state, and make all appointments equally as good as those given the white race.

Permit him to better his moral and his financial condition, but let him realize always that he must not hope for social equality with the white man.

This is my attitude toward the negro.

. . .

Let's avoid a return to the reign of the Klu [sic] Klux Klan.

Let there be no unnecessary oppression.

Give the negro a chance, by teaching him that he is a negro.

He is not as intelligent as [a] white man. He will never be as intelligent as a white man and why not let him understand as much NOW.

Elect democrats to Oklahoma's first legislative bodies and they will pass a Jim Crow law.

They will give the negro all the rights and privileges accorded white people—

But—

THEY WILL BE SEPARATE.[lxi]

Pre-nuptial exuberance and electricity swept across the terrain as the Twin Territories[lxii] prepared to tie the knot. *The Guthrie Daily Leader* characterized the mood on statehood-eve:

> The city will be in gala attire early on the morrow for the big historic event which takes place at noon…. Every train arriving this afternoon brings large crowds; the hotels are now filled to the brim and the streets are thronged with visitors waiting for the morrow when their long dream becomes a reality, and citizens of the twin territories, upon the reading of the President's proclamation conferring on Oklahoma the right of self government [sic], will set up a wil [sic] tumult of joy, cannons will echo, rifles will crack, steam whistles will shriek out approbation, and all the bells in the city will uproariously proclaim the glad tidings.[lxiii]

Then, the auspicious day arrived. On statehood day, November 16, 1907, symbolic nuptials between a white man and an Indian woman, intended to reflect Oklahoma and Indian Territory, respectively, followed the reading of the Presidential statehood proclamation.

> The reading of the proclamation was followed by one of the most interesting and unique features of the inaugural ceremonies. It was a mock marriage wherein Young Oklahoma, a handsome young bridegroom, was united to Miss Indian Territory, a dusky Indian maiden. In the absence from the city of Congressman-elect Bird S. McGuire, who was to have been the bridegroom, this important post was acceptably filled by C.G. Jones of Oklahoma City, who, while not so good looking as Mr. McGuire, perhaps, performed his part admirably. The bride was represented by Mrs. Leo Bennett, wife of the U. S. marshal at Muskogee, and one of the most beautiful women of Indian blood in the new state. After an eloquent proposal by Mr. Jones, and an acceptance by William A. Durant, a Choctaw Indian, on behalf of the bride, the ceremony was performed by Rev. W.H. Dodson of the First Baptist Church at

The Daily Oklahoman, November 17, 1907 (Oklahoma Statehood Day)[ixv]

Guthrie. This feature was greatly appreciated by the crowd, which applauded loud and long.

Rev. Dodson offered a fervent prayer on the union, and then Judge Dale raised his hand for silence as Mr. Haskell and Leslie G. Niblack, a Guthrie newspaper man, stepped forward simultaneously. Facing Mr. Haskell, with one hand uplifted, and open bible held in the other, Mr. Niblack, recently commissioned a notary public, administered the oath and immediately afterward Governor Haskell signed the official papers. [lxiv]

The widespread sense of Pollyannaish exuberance accompanying the staged unification of white and red at statehood left little room for black optimism. As the territorial newlyweds tied the statehood knot, prospects dimmed for African Americans in the soon-to-be Sooner State. Oklahoma careened toward the ditch of Southern oppression out of which African Americans had only recently crawled. Even the all-black towns could not fully insulate African Americans from the fetid waters of racism that seeped through the imagined Promised Land.

Oklahoma's founding fathers wrote black second-class citizenship into the state's early legal framework, including its constitutional and statutory law. The Oklahoma Constitution defined "Colored" and "Negro" as any person with any African descent—the "one drop" rule, *aka* the "rule of hypodescent."[lxvi] Non-blacks, including Native Americans, became, in effect, honorary white citizens, thus escaping the burdens associated with blackness and gaining access to the trappings of white privilege.

Consistent with the race-based Constitutional regime and harmonious with past practice in pre-statehood Oklahoma Territory, the Oklahoma Legislature created separate schools for white and "Colored" children.

> When Oklahoma became a state, November 16, 1907, the prevailing attitude of its citizens toward separation of the races in schools of Oklahoma Territory had been right well developed, and was increasingly accepted by a large majority. In 1901 after a decade of trying various laws, there was enacted a separate school law that satisfied most white patrons sufficiently well to be continued, with few changes, through remaining territorial years and into statehood.[xlvii]

Once again, *any* black blood consigned its bearer to inferiority in the eyes of the law and, by extension, in the minds of most non-black Oklahomans.

Jim Crow (segregation) laws proliferated. The first bill passed by the newly minted Oklahoma Legislature, Senate Bill Number One, segregated rail cars and rail car facilities. The law withstood a legal challenge from E.P. McCabe, the father of the all-black town movement and the pied piper of the black state initiative.[lxviii] The United States Supreme Court's *Plessy v. Ferguson*[lxix] precedent had by then ensconced "separate but equal" as the law of the racialized land. Legal and extralegal disabilities for African Americans mounted.

In 1908, McCabe left Oklahoma for Chicago, where he gradually drifted into obscurity. He died a pauper in 1923, and is interred in the Topeka, Kansas, cemetery.[lxx]

The proud Americans who labored under weight of blackness in a white-dominated, color-conscious Oklahoma did not do so without protest and challenge. Champions emerged. People rallied. Battles ensued.

W.H. Twine (1864 - 1933),[lxxi] a Kentucky-bred lawyer, trained at all-black Wilberforce University in Wilberforce, Ohio, found his way to Oklahoma Territory in a late 1800s land run. He taught school in Chandler, then moved first to Guthrie, and finally to Muskogee. As editor and publisher of the leading black-owned newspaper in Indian Territory, the *Muskogee Cimiter*, Twine relished his role as a warrior in the battle for black civil rights. Dubbed "The Black Tiger," he became the first black lawyer admitted to the Federal Bar in Indian

Territory.[lxxii]

After passing the Oklahoma Territory bar examination on October 31, 1891, Twine organized the territory's first black law firm with partners George Sawner and E.I. Saddler.[lxxiii] Already a celebrity on the home front, Twine catapulted to national prominence. Taft, one of Oklahoma's all-black towns, originally bore the name "Twine, Indian Territory" in his honor (*circa* 1903). Twine welcomed Booker T. Washington to Muskogee in 1905.

Like E.P. McCabe and so many other late nineteenth century and turn-of-the-twentieth-century African American leaders, Twine affiliated with the Republican Party. A staunch civil rights advocate, he challenged segregation at every turn. He also represented indigent clients whose causes he deemed important and just. Despite his best efforts and those of like-minded, similarly talented African Americans, nothing could stop Oklahoma's rapid trajectory into the depths of racial depravity.

The *Black Dispatch* in Oklahoma City drew attention to this frontal assault on black civil rights. The paper's editor, Roscoe Dunjee, excoriated white citizens who took pleasure in the pain and suffering of African Americans, be it through the denial of Constitutional rights or the wholesale rejection of black humanity. Dunjee even updated W.E.B. Du Bois, the black intellectual steeped in the civil rights advocacy work of the National Association for the Advancement of Colored People (N.A.A.C.P.), on the denial of voting rights in the nation's premier all-black town, Boley.[lxxiv]

Iverson "I.W." Lane, the mayor of all-black Red Bird, challenged the restrictive registration requirements of which Roscoe Dunjee complained to W.E.B. Du Bois. In 1939, the United States Supreme Court found that Oklahoma's draconian voter registration provisions, like the "grandfather clause" it overturned decades before in the *Guinn* case,[lxxv] effectively disenfranchised black voters, and thus violated the Fifteenth Amendment.[lxxvi]

Moral matters turned mortal. For African Americans, the stakes in Oklahoma, as elsewhere, escalated beyond civil rights and civil liberties to the right to life itself. The new state of Oklahoma shared in the racial violence rippling through the America of the early twentieth century, the zenith of white-on-black savagery: whipping parties,[lxxvii] lynchings, and white-led mass actions, commonly mislabeled as race riots.

Race continued to limit life prospects for Oklahoma's African Americans for years to come. Some gave up on the Oklaho-

Stonewall Finance Company
INCORPORATED
208 EAST SECOND STREET
OKLAHOMA CITY, OKLAHOMA

CAPITAL STOCK $25,000.00

3/8/28

Dr. W. E. B. Dubois
New York City, N.Y.

Esteemed Friend: -

I have just returned from Tulsa where I held
a conference with Judge Franklin E. Kennamer,
of the Northern federal district of Oklahoma.
Judge Kennamer must soon face charges in
the Congress of the United States, brought
by certain Klan, bootlegging and anti-Negro
influences in this state. I am enclosing
herewith copies of the Tulsa World, which
indicate in part the nature of the charges,
but you could never determine the exact
background from which the charges spring,
unless I relate the position Judge Kennamer
has taken with regarding to Negroes.

Since statehood the Negores of Okfuskee
County, in and near Boley, have never voted.
Upon the elevation of Judge Kennamer to the
bench, he immediately began to slam state
officials in jail who refused to allow Negroes
their suffrage privileges. I personally raised
last year a fund to assist in the appeal of
the state of Oklahoma against a decision of
Kennamer's (which we won) and a case wherein
we had to spend more than $3,000.

Because of this decision more than 700 blacks
vote in and around Boley. The whites in
the county have countered with a petition
to Congress to take them out of Kennamer's
district and place them in the Eastern
district, where they will be under Judge
Robert L. Williams, former governor, when
the vicious registration law of Oklahoma was
passed.

Stonewall Finance Company
OKLAHOMA CITY, OKLAHOMA

This bill, which would slice Okfuskee county out of Kennamer's district is now before the senate judiciary committee, both white and colored Republicans have protested against its passage.

The immediate emergency has to do with the impeachment charges now filed against the Judge. It happens that Congressman Dyer, of St. Louis, is the vice-chairman of the house judiciary committee. The thought just occurred to me that a letter from you to him, covering the facts, as herein set out might be illuminating to Mr. Dyer to the extent that he would give our man a clean bill of health. I know, of course, that the case will be determined, in a sense, but at the same time, you know as well as I do that court procedures many times prevent the entrance of facts that would show a lack of good faith in a cause of action.

I am hoping that you will be spurred to immediate action in getting in touch with Mr. Dyer and any other members of the house judiciary committee, who might be interested in our cause. Every court town in Judge Kennamer's district has passed resolutions of confidence, and there is not a litigant who has appeared before his court whose name is signed to any of the affidavits before congress.

Thanking you for the interest I know you will take in this matter, and assuring you that I will appreciate an immediate reply, I am

Very friendly

Roscoe Dunjee

The Black Dispatch Publishing Company

PUBLISHERS OF "THE BLACK DISPATCH"
A PAPER WITH A POLICY AND A PURPOSE

POST OFFICE BOX 1694
OKLAHOMA CITY, OKLAHOMA

5/18/28

Dr. W. E. B. DuBois
69 5th Ave.
New York City, N.Y.

Esteemed Friend;

I was away when your letter came just as you
were away when mine came to your office some
time ago. I learned, through press reports,
that you were out of New York, before your
letter came, and therefore understood your
silence.

The matter with reference to Judge Kennamer,
has been most satisfactorily adjusted,
charges have been dropped entirely, and for
this reason, I have not written you sooner.

I am enclosing herewith an editorial
appearing this week in the Black Dispatch. I
think that the Negroes of Chicago, and the
nation should be informed as to the character
of man William Harrison is. It would be a
calamity to the Negroes of the nation should
he be elevated to the position he now seeks.

I believe you know something of his record
in the case we carried from Oklahoma, and
the selfish and baneful attitude he assumed
in that matter. Turn on the light, DePriest
may have his faults, but I believe he would
take an upstanding position in favor of the
[program] for which the N. A. A. C. P. and
the Negroes of the nation desire.

                    Very Friendly

                    Roscoe Dunjee

ma-as-Promised-Land fantasy. Having endured bitter disappoint-
ments, some returned to the South, frustrated by the unholy alliance
between the new American sister—Oklahoma—and Mr. Jim Crow.
Some struck out north to Canada. Others fled south to Mexico. In
1913, a charlatan named "Chief Sam" even organized a "Back to Africa" movement from the all-black town of Clearview. Interested parties bought shares in Chief Sam's company, essentially purchasing
safe passage via ship to Africa. Those who embarked on the journey
discovered poor planning, rickety vessels, and harsh conditions in
Africa. His perfidy revealed, one-time true believers, left dejected
and destitute, abandoned the return-to-the-motherland camp.[lxxviii]

As in the country as a whole, lynching became a *de facto* mechanism of social control in Oklahoma. Between 1907 and 1915, Oklahoma vigilantes lynched at least fifteen African Americans.[lxxix]

To be sure, lynching targeted specific individuals, typically, an
African American male accused of a crime or a social infraction involving a white "victim." But, lynching aimed principally to strike
fear in the hearts and minds of the group to which its targets belonged—an early example of domestic terrorism. The unmistakable
takeaway from these acts of barbarism was: Know your place and
stay in it![lxxx] Often after a lynching, black families would be driven
from town. Oklahoma came increasingly to mirror the Southern cru-
cible from which so many African Americans had recently leapt.

The May 1911 murders of a mother and her child in Okemah, a
town a mere fifty-mile drive southeast of Chandler, is emblematic
of this extralegal onslaught of racial brutishness, though atypical in
terms of its victims. Okemah, just outside the all-black town of Boley,
is also the birthplace of folk music standout Woody Guthrie.[lxxxi] Even
amidst the horrors of thousands of incidents of racial mayhem, the
slayings of Laura Nelson and her teenage son, L.W., stand apart as
particularly brazen, boorish, and barbaric.

A local lawman, Sheriff Deputy George H. Loney, confronted
L.W. Nelson about stolen goods in the Nelson home. L.W. Nelson
allegedly shot and mortally wounded Sheriff Loney. Authorities arrived on scene to arrest the Nelson boy. Laura Nelson intervened,
attempting to protect her son. Officials subdued the pair and took
them into custody.

A lynch mob seized Ms. Nelson, barefoot and clad in a floral print
dress, from the jail, dragged her six miles to the Canadian River,
raped her, and hanged her from a bridge as leering white townsfolk

The lynching of Laura Nelson and her son, L.W., May 25, 1911, Okemah, Oklahoma[lxxxiv]

bore witness. They hanged L.W. alongside his mother.

Photographs of the gruesome scene soon surfaced and circulated.[lxxxii] *Without Sanctuary—Lynching Photography in America*[lxxxiii] documents the chilling image of those two black bodies, mother and son, swaying from a small town Oklahoma bridge as anonymous onlookers gaze downward at the hangmen's handiwork.

The ghastly scene in Okemah recalls that haunting 1939 Billie Holliday song, *Strange Fruit.*[lxxxv]

No poplar trees. No Southern breeze. But Oklahoma bore its share of that strange fruit, not all of which swung from trees, bridges, or lampposts.

More evidence of the curious crop came some ten years later in Tulsa, a boomtown dubbed "The Magic City" for its incredible oil-catalyzed metamorphosis from dusty outpost to urban hub. Teeming white mobs exploded in an orgy of vitriol and violence, annihilating Tulsa's black community with a punishing onslaught of bullets and burnings.

The Roaring Twenties,[lxxxvi] a widely-heralded period of immense social, economic, and cultural change in America and beyond, ranks among America's darkest periods in terms of racial violence against African Americans. F. Scott Fitzgerald's celebrated 1925 novel about the Roaring Twenties, *The Great Gatsby*,[lxxxvii] explores wealth, decadence, idealism, rapid social change, and other broad 1920s-centric

State Committee

FOR

J. C. "JACK" WALTON

FOR

GOVERNOR

I. W. YOUNG Chairman

OKLAHOMA CITY, OKLA.

October 12th. 1922.

Dear Madam:

The National Federation of the Negro Women's Clubs has started a crusade on their knees in support of the Dyer Anti-Lynching Bill. This is very commendable and should succeed.

In further support of the Anti-Lynching crusade would it not be a good idea to use your ballot also against this menace to our life and happiness?

Ought we not vote for men and measures that have been proven friendly to our causes rather than those which have promised but never fulfilled?

In consideration for the many big things that Hon. J.C. Walton as Mayor has done for the Negro in Oklahoma City may we not expect your support for him for Governor of this state?

We recommend him to your thoughtful and intelligent consideration and ask you to vote for him as a just and liberal man rather to vote for a Lily-White republican who says he doesn't want your vote. The result is with you. Think, decide act for your race's best interest.

Respectfully yours,

Walton for Governor Committee

_____

Chairman.

November 9th. 1922.

The election of the Hon. J. C. Walton as
Governor of this state on last Tuesday, to my
mind, has a double significance:

1st. It demonstrates that the White man
is no longer a victim of the appeals to race
prejudice made by the demagog politician, and
has awakened to his own interest.

2nd. That the Negro has broken the
crysalis of political sentimentality that has
bound him in the past, and has emerged a full
fledged thinker and is following the lead of
his friends.

Both of those circumstances prodage
greater things for both races and a greater
Oklahoma.

Correspondence courtesy of the Oklahoma Historical Society.

themes. Few popular period works chronicled the hard truths and painful realties of race in general and blackness in particular.

Early in the twentieth century, the black community in Tulsa— the "Greenwood District"—became a nationally renowned entrepreneurial center. Legendary African American statesman and educator, Booker T. Washington, reportedly dubbed the community "The Negro Wall Street" for its now-famous entrepreneurial energy and enterprise. The 1921 Tulsa Race Riot, a relentless white assault on "Black Wall Street," obliterated the Greenwood District.[lxxxviii]

Conditions for African Americans in Oklahoma descended to a frightening new low in the early 1920s. Jack Callaway Walton, a progressive Democrat who would become Oklahoma's fifth and shortest-tenured governor, seemed to offer some hope of calming increasingly turbulent race relations.

Walton waged a short-lived war on the resurgent Ku Klux Klan, which had gained a greater foothold in Oklahoma following the 1921 Tulsa Race Riot. The Oklahoma Legislature impeached and convicted Governor Walton, who held office from January 8, 1923, to November 19, 1923, on corruption-related charges. Objections to Governor Walton's aggressive efforts at purging the anti-black Klan played into his demise.[lxxxix]

Though some African Americans abandoned Oklahoma, others persevered. Arguably, the all-black towns blossomed in spite of—or perhaps *because of*—the rapid segregation of Oklahoma, and became the legacy of E.P. McCabe.[xc]

A number of the all-black towns sprang up near Freedmen's allotments—lands awarded to persons of African ancestry with blood, affinity, and/or treaty ties to one or more Native American tribes. A minority of members of each of the Five Civilized Tribes enslaved persons of African ancestry. Emancipated after the Civil War, these "Freedmen," together with other free persons of African ancestry living among the Five Civilized Tribes, sometimes pooled their allotments to create black enclaves.[xciii]

Despite a promising beginning, the all-black town movement peaked between 1890 and 1910, just as the American economy transitioned from farm-based to industrial. African Americans founded more than fifty all-black towns and settlements in Oklahoma between 1865 and 1920. The Recession of the late 1920s and the Depression of the 1930s decimated many of them.

The fate of Oklahoma's all-black towns, though, would not be the end of the story for black Oklahomans. The African American experience in early Oklahoma extended beyond the all-black towns and into predominately white communities like the Sawners' hometown of Chandler, Lincoln County, Oklahoma.

Boley, Oklahoma, historic marker.[xci]

Town Council of Boley, Oklahoma, America's premier all-black town, *circa* 1910.[xcii]

Chapter Two: Life in Lincoln County

No man can put a chain about the ankle of his fellow man without at last finding the other end fastened about his own neck.

— Frederick Douglass

Map of Oklahoma Counties[xcv]

Lincoln County, Oklahoma, African American pioneers, 1891 land run: left to right, B.T. McCall, John Booker, Rev. S.R. Glover, and Pink Manning; photo *circa* 1950.[xcvi]

Pride in their blackness undiminished, George and Lena Sawner straddled the early twentieth century color line with exceptional adroitness and aplomb. The Sawners cultivated progress and promise in Chandler, their fruitful, privileged lives rife with self-awareness and social obligation. They sowed seeds of racial progress that scattered throughout Lincoln County and the rest of the state. Many of those seeds lay dormant for years, even decades, but most would ultimately germinate.

Chandler, the direct outgrowth of a land opening in Oklahoma Territory, came into being on September 28, 1891, a few days later than first anticipated. Soldiers blocked the town's projected September 22, 1891, opening on account of an unfinished survey.

At noon on the town's modified date of birth, gunshots rang out. Thousands of settlers dashed up a steep hill, the gateway into the 320-acre town site that once comprised part of the Iowa, Kickapoo, and Sac and Fox lands. The seekers claimed 2,208 free lots in this as-yet-undeveloped space in Lincoln County.[xcvii]

Legendary Route 66[cii]

Town planners strategically located Chandler at the geographic center of the county, proximate to Indian Spring, a reliable water supply (formerly, "Doran's Spring"). Now a city green space called Indian Spring Park, this wellspring sits on the southeast edge of town.[xcviii]

Location, though strategic, became a major liability for Chandler, at least for one moment in time when Mother Nature unleashed her unbridled fury. On May 30, 1897, a tornado ripped through town, mangling physical structures and killing several residents. A next-day news account recounted the utter devastation wrought by the terrible twister.[xcix]

This near-annihilation experience rattled the town to its core. Chandler emerged bloodied, but unbowed. Townspeople rallied and development continued. By the early 1900s, several rail lines passed through Lincoln County, the first of which, a 103-mile Oklahoma City-Sapulpa stretch of the Frisco Railroad, began operations in Chandler in 1898. Other railway service meandering through Lincoln County in the early 1900s included recognizable railroad lines like the Santa Fe, the Rock Island, the Missouri-Kansas-Topeka, and the Fort Smith-Western.

In addition to ready rail service, Chandler boasted automobile accessibility. The town sits along one of the nation's premier thoroughfares, Route 66, an original highway within the U.S. Highway System and a still-iconic presence. Chandler is proximate to the two largest cities in Oklahoma, forty-eight miles east of Oklahoma City and seventy-eight miles west of Tulsa.

Early on, enthusiasts and boosters hawked a too-good-to-be-true portrait of Chandler. An early 1900s advertisement for City Drug Store trumpeted the town as Xanadu-on-the-plains, a picture perfect place for commerce and community.

Chandler, the County Seat

Chandler is the permanent county seat, the principal business point, and the central point of Lincoln County. With such a county to support it, and with an energetic and progressive class of people to guard its welfare, Chandler is already a most desirable home city and prosperous business center, and is destined to rapid and substantial growth in the immediate future.

Here are some points to remember in regard to Chandler:

Two railroads, with ten passenger trains a day, giving easy connections with all parts of the country; fine municipal water works system, and good electric light plant; natural gas at low cost; splendid school; six churches with resident pastors; nearly a score of lodges; post office of the first class with nine mails a day and eight rural mail routes; 90-ton cotton seed mill and five cotton gins; ice plant; principal streets paved; ten miles of brick and cement sidewalks; two first class weekly newspaper[s] and three strong baking institutions; court house that cost $127,000; good city government and reasonable tax rate for new [county]; selected by the national government as the permanent rifle range for national guard and by the state as the permanent encampment and maneuvering ground for state troops; adjacent to the lands to be reclaimed by the celebrated Deep Fork drainage project; best telephone exchange in the state, and long-distance connections with everywhere; healthful location and wholesome moral atmosphere; the leading cotton market of the leading cotton county in Oklahoma; is not now and never had been a boom town, but, instead one whose prosperity rests upon the solid foundation of agricultural prosperity; prices of property comparatively low, with certainty of early increase; offers splendid opportunities for numerous manufacturing enterprises; extends as cordial welcome to strangers, with inducements for them to become permanent residents; all the advantages of a live town in a good county where the agricultural development has only begun.[ciii]

Early twentieth century Chandler exuded a certain vibrancy and hopefulness. Filmmaker J.B. "Benny" Kent[civ] captured a bit of that *joie de vivre* in his film, *Early Days*. Chandler footage in the Kent film includes a fair in 1911, shoppers and pedestrians on Chandler streets in 1912, military troops, the nineteenth anniversary cake for Jacob's Store in 1915, a Victory Parade in 1916, and an undated, noticeably mixed-race, crowd scene.[cv]

Like the surviving film footage, many vestiges of Chandler's pioneer past still exist, including still-used downtown buildings constructed in the early 1900s. Hardware used by cowboys to tether their horses while they frequented saloons remains imbedded in cement curbs of some downtown stores. Hundred-year-old red bricks stamped with "Chandler OT" ("OT" meaning Oklahoma Territory) adorn homes, shops, and even several streets.[cvi]

Chandler is the hub of Lincoln County, a jurisdiction named for the "Great Emancipator," President Abraham Lincoln.[cvii] In a rare, if not unique, election, voters chose "Lincoln" over two other proposed county name options, "Sac and Fox" and "Springer."[cviii]

The thirty-two current towns and communities in Lincoln County include the following (an asterisk denotes incorporated towns): Anderson, Agra*, Arlington, Avery, Carney*, Chandler*, Clifton, Davenport*, Dudley, Emsey, Fallis*, Fowler, Ingram, Jacktown, Kendrick*,

Meeker, Merrick, Midlothian, Midway, Parkland, Payson, Prague*, Rossville, Sparks*, Soonerville, South Village, Stroud*, Tryon*, Warwick*, Wellston*, Wildhorse, and Wilzetta.[cix]

As previously mentioned, in the late 1880s, thousands of Americans, African Americans among them, migrated to Oklahoma. Black migrants came from all areas of the country, but mainly from the Southern states, aiming to chart a new course in largely uncharted territory.

The failure of the post-Civil War Reconstruction, unrelenting oppression, political powerlessness, and economic woes, coupled with attractive and aggressive propaganda, impelled the black Southern diaspora. A number of these seekers eventually found their way to Oklahoma, and to Lincoln County.

White settlers outnumbered black seekers in Lincoln County. Nonetheless, the relative flood of black migrants triggered mudslides of white newcomer resistance, centered on the unsettling prospect of black saturation and domination.

Black immigrants threatened white hegemony or, perhaps more precisely, they were perceived as posing such a threat. These darker denizens might, for example, somehow wrest control from white citizens in the social, political, and economic spheres. Moreover, black success, real or perceived, challenged widely-held white supremacist notions, and thus the psychological well-being of white settlers.

This perceived "Negro problem" would only come to fruition if a critical mass of African Americans assembled. In Lincoln County, about ten percent of the new migrants claimed African descent,[cx] arguably not a critical mass, but nonetheless a ratio sufficient to stoke fear, resentment, and hostility among apprehensive white residents.

In the early 1900s, more black carpetbaggers trickled into Lincoln County[cxi] from places near and far: Arkansas, Kansas, Texas, Louisiana, Alabama, and Mississippi. Anxious white settlers telegraphed a "keep out" message to blacks contemplating settlement in the county's rapidly expanding town sites. In response, African Americans colonized rural areas.

African Americans set up residence in all quadrants of Lincoln County except the northeast. Most gravitated toward the comfort of rural enclaves, tapping into the knowledge and skills borne of their agrarian roots. These callow Negroes, like so many other settlers, often lived in pre-modern dwellings such as log cabins and dugouts, earthen shelters formed from holes dug in the ground or into hillsides.

State Negroes, black émigrés from various states, sometimes butted heads with black locals, known as "Natives," persons of African descent with biological, cultural, and/or affinity ties to the Five Civilized Tribes. Still, white residents continued to be the greatest source of friction for all persons of African descent.

Throughout the span of Lincoln County history, numerically-predominate white residents wielded enormous power and privilege. Still, black minority would not be cowed; black voices refused to be silenced. Finding their niche proved daunting for black Lincoln County pioneers, the vast majority of whom lived in rural areas. They faced all manner of trials and tribulations (*e.g.*, poverty, poor health care, and food insecurity), but they pressed on, all the while insisting upon a modicum of self-determination.

The "Negro problem," this black immigrant conundrum, posed fundamental issues of belonging and engagement: Where would *they* live? How would *they* earn a living? Where would *they* find schooling and worship opportunities? What role would *they* play in the local political system? How would *they* relate to their white neighbors and, conversely, how would their white neighbors relate to *them*?

This focus on the black migrants as "alien" and "other"—this "us-versus-them" dichotomy—came at the expense of attention to shared humanity. This dynamic would shape race relations for decades.

African Americans in Lincoln County gravitated toward segregated living arrangements, organizing informal black communities in part to escape the harassment and hostility they too often faced in the greater society. These settlements—small, *ad hoc*, groups of people, typically 75 to 300 in number, living in the same area (usually several square acres or square miles), and sharing common goals and beliefs—leveraged the synergy of collective social, economic, and political alliances and alignment.

The informal black communities in Lincoln County shared at least four of the five following characteristics: (1) Black residents occupied ninety percent or more of homes in the community; (2) the community supported at least one critical institution (*e.g.*, school[cxii], church, or cemetery); (3) residents and outsiders named the community; (4) community members took ownership of and expressed pride in their environs; and (5) founders established the community prior to 1930.[cviii]

Though Lincoln County boasted no *formal* all-black towns,[cxiv] the existence of twelve *informal* black communities suggests a passion for opportunity and equality among Lincoln County's African American progressives akin the fervor that fueled Oklahoma's all-black towns. The Lincoln County informal black communities were to all-black towns as modern-day developing nations are to developed nations. The all-black towns—places like Boley, Clearview, and Langston— operated on a higher plane, maintaining institutions, building infrastructure, and achieving external recognition at levels unmatched and unmatchable by these less formal settlements.[cxv]

The faces of African Americans in Lincoln County.[cxvi]

Ten of the twelve informal black communities included white settlers peaceably co-existing among black residents.[cxix] Each informal black community dealt with racial challenges differently. Some chose affirmative advocacy. Some chose industriousness and personal excellence. Some chose quiet accommodation. Elements of all three approaches characterized "The Bottom," the informal black community located within the Chandler city limits.

Black settlers, primarily farmers, began to arrive in rural areas in and around Chandler prior to 1889. The United States Census figures illustrate fluctuations in Chandler's black population over time: 1900 – 1,621; 1910 – 86; 1920 – 263; 1930 – 351; 1940 – 419; and 1950 - 389.[cxx] The average percentage of black residents for these census periods: 11.6 per-

The informal black communities in Lincoln County included, from east to west:[cxvii]

1. Key West
2. River Bend
3. DeGraffenreid
4. Black Alley
5. Glover's Settlement
6. Chandler: The Bottom
7. Payson
8. Rock Springs
9. Kickapoo
10. Sweet Home
11. Dudley
12. Fallis

Map of informal black communities in Lincoln County, Oklahoma, 1889 - 1954[cxviii]

cent[cxxi] of the total population. The 1900 census indicated an average of 3.25 persons per black-inhabited dwelling. Part of the explanation for this relatively low number may lie in an African American response to the aforementioned "Negro problem." African Americans may have simply slowed their pace of growth to accommodate white fears.

Pinpointing the hub of Chandler's black community proved challenging in the early 1900s. Unlike some similar communities, Chandler never enacted a sundown law.[cxxii] Africans Americans could (and did) live in all sectors of town, not simply work in select areas, only to have the welcome mat pulled from under their feet at dusk. The absence of a *de facto* nightfall curfew applicable to African Americans helps explain how George and Lena Sawner and others of their hue wove themselves into the quilted fabric of everyday Chandler life early in the twentieth century.[cxiii]

Most African Americans in Chandler resided in one part of town, the southeastern part, from 8th to 15th Streets, on the east side of Manvel Avenue, in the area called "The Bottom."[cxxiv] It included about twenty houses, several churches, and a cotton gin.

"The Bottom" describes the particular geography of the area. From a south-looking-north vantage, the scoop-shaped earthen void that inspired the name of the community is readily apparent.

Two white families lived in The Bottom. The patriarch of one of those families, Ray Shafer, worked as an auto mechanic by day and operated a makeshift garage in his backyard. He built the family home with rocks he hauled from a nearby quarry.

Donna Sue Shafer, his eldest daughter, recalled living in harmony with black neighbors and experiencing a happy and otherwise mostly unremarkable childhood. She remembered being the occasional "lonely only," the one white person in a particular place at a particular time. Ms. Shafer's childhood experiences at Mingo's Movie House became one such "lonely only" occasion.

The two principal movie houses in Chandler barred African Americans. Ever-industrious black Chandlerites arranged for an alternative cinematic experience. For many years, Douglass High School permitted two black entrepreneurs from Shawnee to use its auditorium for a once-a-week movie showing. The practice ended shortly after Lena Sawner left Douglass in the early 1930s. Mingo's Movie House at 15th Street and Allison Avenue filled the void.[cxxvi] Mingo's became the area's 1930s segregated cinema, screening films on Friday and Saturday nights.

Donna Sue Shafer in front of the home of Ray Shafer, 2004.[cxxvii]

William Mingo, a county agricultural extension agent, ran the theater, a crude, temporary facility with planks over a large ditch running parallel with 15th Street. Mr. Mingo later conceived and created a mobile movie theater that traveled to other parts of Lincoln County.

In addition to the Shafers, the Jacksons, another white family, called The Bottom home. Little Eileen Jackson became a friend and playmate of Ann Ellis, the mother of Chandler historian, Melvin Chatman.

A number of churches served Chandler's black residents. Some remain: Bethel African Methodist Episcopal (A.M.E.) Church; Mount Calvary Baptist Church; Central Baptist Church; and Central Methodist Episcopal Church (Lane Chapel).[cxxviii]

Lena Sawner patronized Bethel A.M.E. Established in 1899, the congregation relocated to its present location, 1304 South Allison Avenue, in 1904. In 1943 to 1944, the presiding elder, W.D. Miller, combined the church's membership with that of Rock Springs A.M.E. Church, adding about ten families to the church rolls. In 1947, Bethel A.M.E. added a dining hall, "Sawner Hall," funded with revenues generated from a statewide church campaign and a significant contribution from the venue's namesake, Lena Sawner.

Though flush with worship opportunities, The Bottom suffered from a void of employment options. Most black Chandlerites labored in the cotton fields. Some pursued professional and entrepreneurial opportunities. A few women and men taught school. Evangelism offered a career path for select men.

For women, and most especially, black women, teaching ranked among the prime career opportunities during the early twentieth century. Preaching, an available vocational path for black men, often provided only part-time work.

When cotton production in Lincoln County slowed, itinerant black laborers followed the crop to other cotton-centric states, returning to Chandler at season's end. Cotton-picking wages supplied the sole source of annual cash income for many black families.

In Lincoln County, the towns of Chandler and Fallis afforded black businesses the rare chance to operate side-by-side with white-owned establishments on the towns' respective main streets. Chandler's first black-owned commercial venture, The Peevey House, opened around the turn of the twentieth century and located in The Bottom near the corner of Allison and 15th Streets, housed travelers arriving from the railroad station a few hundred yards away.

Another inn, The Franklin Hotel, later named The McKinney Hotel, occupied space just east of the 9th Street Bridge and Allison Avenue. Most other black businesses operated from storefronts on Manvel Avenue between 12th and 13th Streets.

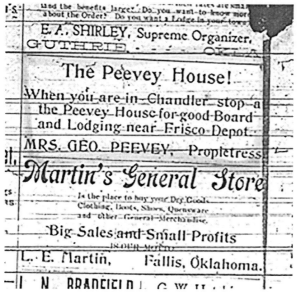

Advertisement for The Peevey House in the *Fallis Blade*, June 2, 1901.[cxxix]

In Chandler, respectful relationships between blacks and whites, progressive as measured by the prevailing laws and customs, evolved. Black enterprises seized upon opportunities for business success. Social integration existed at the margins.[cxxx] George and Lena Sawner helped create and sustain the culture of openness and hospitality that characterized early Chandler.

Local white citizens credited Lena

Sawner and her work at Douglass School with fostering positive race relations and overall tranquility in the community:

> To Mrs. Sawners [sic] goes a great deal of the credit for the fine spirit of co-operation which exists between the two races in Chandler. Her students were taught citizenship and usefulness and many of the fine [N]egro men and women who have graduated from higher institutions of learning received their inspiration from Mrs. Sawner.

> She numbered as her friends prominent persons of both races in Chandler and in the state of Oklahoma.[cxxxi]

Vintage Chandler, Oklahoma, *circa* 1900.[cxxxii]

Chandler earned a reputation as an incubator for black industriousness. Opportunities seemed as rich as the red earth beneath their feet, liberties as widespread as the dusty prairie air, possibilities as plentiful as the expansive Oklahoma sky. Chandler dodged the thickest of the racial thorns and thistles that so often plagued early twentieth century life.

Beyond Chandler, Lincoln County escaped the most brutal form of racial violence against African Americans. Lynching, domestic terrorism waged against African Americans, often with law enforcement complicity and/or dereliction, plagued turn-of-the-century America, and continued largely unchecked for decades thereafter.

Chandler historian Jan Vassar scoured old newspapers, reviewed printed and oral histories, conducted interviews, and examined various online sources in a no-holds-barred effort to answer a single question: Did a lynching ever occur in Lincoln County? She discovered two "near-lynchings." She ran across an event that may have been misinterpreted as a lynching, but found no instance of a documented lynching in the county.[cxxxiii]

Race relations in Chandler not only exhibited a similar absence of overt hostility, but also evidenced a level of civility unmatched in many communities. Black and white Chandlerites showed one another outward signs of respect, often referring to one another, as appropriate, with a polite "Sir" or "Ma'am."[cxxxiv] Friendly trans-racial relationships characterized most aspects of life. Children of different races played together. Long-term friendships developed across racial lines. People embraced a *laissez-faire*, "live and let live" philosophy. Other evidence abounds of black/white co-existence, even amicability, in racially mixed neighborhoods, an integrated central business district (albeit one that constricted black access to only one or two blocks of a multi-block commercial area), and a forward-looking, yet segregated, black school widely hailed by Chandler's white elite.

Over time, single-race public schools, particularly, *de jure* segregated public schools like Chandler's Douglass School, fell into disfavor, in part because of the educational disparities they reflected and perpetuated. Twentieth century public schools became a vehicle through which to accomplish systemic societal integration.[cxxxv]

The Chandler school system remained racially divided until the United States Supreme Court declared separate educational facilities inherently unequal, and therefore unconstitutional, in its 1954 *Brown v. Board of Education*[cxxxvi] decision. Other Lincoln County school systems used the desegregation of Chandler High School as a model for executing what elsewhere became a difficult, contentious process. In some of the adjacent county towns, resistance to dismantling traditional racial separation in schools mounted, and unifying these school systems took years to effect.

Racial incidents, though rare, sometimes occurred. Around the time of World War I (1914 – 1918), some white Chandlerites attempted to naturalize a known destabilizing force: the Ku Klux Klan. Though the fledgling Chandler Klan launched marches and night rides, the black community never considered the Klan an existential threat. Indeed, Chandler historian Jan Vassar noted that the Klan in Lincoln County seems to have been primarily anti-Catholic in orientation.[cxxxvii]

Black Chandler residents sometimes stumbled upon the Klan connections of their white neighbors. During one Klan horseback parade through the town's main street, a black observer recognized one of the masked men. The black man reportedly shouted, "Mr. Gladson: What you got that sack over your head for? Everybody knows who you is!"[cxxxviii] Leaving aside issue of facial and body recognition that could thwart concealment, Klansmen could scarcely mask their identities from the black laborers who routinely laundered and pressed their pristine white garments.[cxxxix]

Ora Ellis recalled a terrifying encounter with Klan nightriders in 1919. Then a four-year-old, Ellis remembered how the horses and riders, by the light of torches, cast eerie shadows on the landscape as white-hooded figures astride majestic equine specimens occupied the middle of Manvel Avenue.[cxl] Despite such occasional spectacles, the Chandler Klan never gained a foothold—another testament to the town's temperate racial climate.

Overall, Chandler's black, white, and Native American denizens managed peaceably to coexist, together, but worlds apart. Though not totally devoid of racial issues, race-based concerns never dominated social intercourse in Chandler.

Black, white, and Native American Chandlerites lived mostly separate lives. Then, and to a lesser extent, now, these population pockets gravitated toward their own places of worship and social activities. Their separation in the educational sphere only magnified the social distance.

Even in death, racial separation persisted. The town's cemeteries, Oak Park Cemetery (white) and Clearview Cemetery (black), technically desegregated in 1954. It would be decades, however, before Chandler's departed souls rested together in a racially desegregated burial ground. The first black interment in Oak Park Cemetery came in 1985. Since then, few white persons (spouses of black persons) have been laid to rest in the black cemetery (*i.e.*, Clearview Cemetery), and few black persons have been buried in the white cemetery (*i.e.*, Oak Park Cemetery).

Notwithstanding these still-relevant racial separation measures at death, those among the living have long enjoyed opportunities for trans-racial engagement. African American shops could be found throughout Chandler, but converged in the 1100 block of Manvel Avenue, the town's main street: the Whit Ellis Restaurant (1907 – 1932); the Columbus Irvin Barber Shop, located at the same site as the Whit Ellis Restaurant; the Brown Hotel (*circa* 1940s); the Dave Reed Restaurant (*circa* 1940s); and the McKinley Hotel, located near the

Ninth Street bridge (*circa* 1950s).[cxli] The Sawners' investment property along this stretch sat adjacent to the Laurel Gas Station near 12th Street on Manvel Avenue. The Brown family leased the building, operating a business at street level while living upstairs.

Manvel Avenue in Chandler, Oklahoma, looking north from 11th Street (*circa* 1900)[cxlii]

Whit Ellis Restaurant, Monrovia,[cxliii] in Guthrie, Oklahoma, 1906.[cxliv]

Whit Ellis Restaurant, 1115 Manvel Avenue, Chandler, the first black business on the town's main street, 1911.[cxlv]

Whit Ellis' Restaurant, 1115 Manvel Avenue, Chandler, 1922.[cxlvi]

Whit and Maggie Ellis Family, Chandler, 1928: Back row, left to right, Hasko Vintrez Ellis, James R. Ellis, Wade Ellis, Sr., Cliff Ellis, Whit Ellis, Jr., and Roberta Ellis; Front row, Ora Herbert Ellis, Sr., Whit Ellis, Sr., George Sawner Ellis, Maggie Ellis, Margret Ann Ellis, and Francis Edwin Ellis.[cxlvii]

Ellis family home, 206 West 12th Street, Chandler, Oklahoma (1952).[cxlviii]

Chandler, *circa* 1924.[clix]

Willis "Jutes" Summers on Manvel Avenue (a.k.a., "Main Street") with unidentified woman, 1918; Photo taken in front of Whit Ellis's final restaurant. The side of the original restaurant, 1115 Manvel Avenue, is visible to the right and behind the two photo subjects.[cl]

The Summers Family, Chandler, 1923--Back row (left to right): Willis ("Jutes"), Sel-phia, Eugene, Fred, and Lowery: Front row (L-R): Maggie, Minnie, Thelma, Uncle "Gum" (Henry Summers' brother), Geraldine, and Maedella.[cli]

South side of the Sawner building on Manvel Avenue; (left to right) Earnes-tine Fry (daughter of Hattie Young); Jewel Gray; husband of Jewel Gray (kneeling in front of her); and Myrtle Estes Brown, *circa* mid-1940s.[clii]

Ellis "Piggy" Charles, *circa* 1935. Piggy lived in The Bottom and ran a speakeasy out of the front of his home during the Great Depression.[cliii]

Members of Chandler's all-black amateur baseball team, *circa* 1947: (left to right) Lonnie "Dog" Summers, Ed Brown, and Sharon Talley. Between 1930 and 1933, "The Chandler Team" proved to be one of the top teams on the colored amateur baseball circuit.[cliv]

Prominent and enduring, Whit Ellis' Restaurant, one of the few places in Chandler where black families could obtain a cash line of credit, became Chandler's signature black business. In the mid-1920s and 1930s, these lines of credit totaled no more than fifty dollars.[clv] A widespread system of non-cash remuneration mitigated the need for currency during this period.

After operating Whit Ellis' Restaurant in Guthrie, Whit Ellis and his bride, Maggie, returned to Chandler in 1907 to open a similar venture, also known as Whit Ellis' Restaurant. In the mid-1920s, Whit Ellis' Restaurant reached peak performance in terms of popularity and revenue-generation.

Whit Ellis' lunch and dinner menus included beef, beef stew, pork chops with side dishes, and a variety of desserts. Breakfast fare consisted of bacon, eggs, and grits with biscuits. Whit's much-in-demand chili, the house special, became a gastronomical sensation. An aromatic batch of the signature chili—the perfect blend of chili peppers, kidney beans, tomatoes, and the special ingredient, the *piece de resistance*, corned beef brisket—could always be found simmering in an oversized cast iron pot on Whit's cookstove burner.[clvi] Legions of chili connoisseurs converged from miles around to feast on the zesty dish. Some aficionados even toted their own pots and pans in which to transport some of Whit's one-of-a-kind concoction back to family and friends.[clvii]

Strong sales and an equally strong economic outlook spurred excitement and optimism. The *ka-ching* of the cash register proved music to Whit's ears. Others overheard the sweet sounds of his success and scored a plan to free him of it. Whit's bounty led to an attempt by a group of white Chandler merchants to sabotage his business.

At the time, everyone, both black and white, knew of and respected both Whit Ellis' Restaurant and its proprietor. It was no surprise, then, when the white owner of a nearby car dealership began making daily visits, bantering about the weather, commerce, and the development of Chandler. Maggie and Whit Ellis welcomed the repartee.

After several months, the car dealer inquired about Mr. Ellis' desire to sell the restaurant, suggesting that a significant profit could be made off the sale. Talks about the sale of the restaurant continued, soon dominating the conversations between the suitor and Mr. Ellis.

The car dealer's persistence paid off. Whit Ellis agreed to sell, intending to open a better and larger restaurant somewhere else on Manvel Avenue with the proceeds. Mr. and Mrs. Ellis eagerly anticipated the large profit expected on the transaction.

The prospective purchaser prepared sale papers. The car dealer and his lawyer arrived at Whit Ellis' Restaurant on the day of the closing.

As Mr. Ellis took a last quick look at the final sales papers, he noticed a startling, previously overlooked, clause on the last page of the primary document, a restrictive covenant. This provision, which had neither been discussed nor brought to Mr. Ellis's attention by the prospective purchaser, prohibited Mr. Ellis from operating another business on Manvel Avenue, Chandler's main street, after completion of the sale.

It dawned on Mr. Ellis that what had appeared to be jocular conversations over a period of weeks were in fact initial salvos in an attack on Chandler's black merchants, at least those on Manvel Avenue. He vocalized aloud what he had previously read in stunned silence, haltingly voicing the objectionable paragraph, and then pausing. Mr. Ellis rose from his seat and, still maintaining his composure, declared, "I am no longer interested in selling the business and I would appreciate you leaving my store. Thank you very much." With that, he picked up the papers and tossed them to a handful of white businessmen who had gathered to witness the unsavory sale.

Neither Mr. Ellis nor Chandler's other black business leaders ever forgot that moment.[clviii]

Whit Ellis' Restaurant bounced from location to location to location, with three different addresses, all on Manvel Avenue between 12th and 13th Streets. Mr. Ellis' death, coupled with the nationwide depression, doomed Whit Ellis' Restaurant in 1932.

Other black establishments in Chandler included Dave Reed's Restaurant in the 1300 block of Manvel Avenue. Dave Reed's opened several years after Whit Ellis' Restaurant closed, and survived until the mid-1940s. Brown's Hotel also sported an address in the 1300 block of Manvel Avenue.

Edward Marshall Brown and his partner, Allen "Tootsie" Neal, purchased their hard-to-categorize establishment from Dave Reed, who left Chandler for Chickasha. Locals knew the business as "The First Blue Moon," a combination beer tavern, barbeque joint, and hotel in the Sawner Building between 11th and 12th Streets. Opened around 1947, it also featured a backroom theater with once-a-week movies shown by Mr. Mingo.

Mr. Brown eventually bought out his partner and relocated his multifunctional enterprise to 1302 South Manvel Street around 1949. Mr. Brown's mother, Elizabeth "Lizzie" Gasper Brown, owned the building he moved into and other properties in Chandler, including the present site of a Turner Turnpike toll booth.[clix]

Not to be eclipsed by its predecessor, this next cycle of the business, known as "The Second Blue Moon," welcomed black and white Chandler patrons. Like the town itself, The Second Blue Moon projected an open, everybody-knows-my-name feel.

Mr. Brown's brothers beseeched him to join them in California. He declined. He loved Chandler, and he wanted to make a go of it on the home front, engaging in commerce with fellow Chandlerites. That hometown zeal and community-mindedness extended into Mr. Brown's later years. In the early-to-mid 1960s, he even became a constable under Lincoln County Sheriff L.P. Orr.

Entrepreneurship ran in the family. Mr. Brown's father-in-law, William "Bill" Esters, owned a bustling business known simply as "Bill's" or "Bill Esters'" located on 12th and Allison Streets. As with the Blue Moon establishments, Bill's drew racially mixed patrons.

Given Oklahoma's history of both *de jure* and *de facto* segregation, Chandler's rather loose and fluid racial comingling seems, in retrospect, anomalous. In many ways, it was.

Chandlerites' relative nonchalance on matters of race may be partially attributable to practical considerations about food and drink. African Americans owned and operated many of the barbeque joints in Chandler and elsewhere. Fans of the slow-fired, smoky indulgence had few qualms about crossing racial lines to satiate their cravings. Moreover, Oklahoma remained dry until 1959 when Oklahomans voted to end Prohibition.[clx] A number of enterprising African Americans helped supply liquor to temperance scofflaws. Enterprising black bootleggers sold whiskey out of restaurants and bars, often to spirited white customers.[clxi]

Until the mid-1960s, public accommodations, services, restaurants, public transportation, medical services, and hotel accommodations remained largely segregated. Even in the throes of the Jim Crow era, and despite virulent criticism and, on occasion, personal threats, from their neighbors, some businesses ignored segregation edicts. They defied prevailing law, custom, and practice, choosing instead to serve blacks and Native Americans right along with Chandler's white citizens. A.D. Wright's Drugstore chose the latter course.

A.D. Wright, founder of one of Chandler's first businesses and

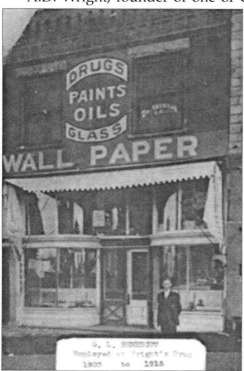

Wright's Drug, early 1900s.[clxiii]

a member of the town's first board of trustees, hailed from the north. His leadership on the issue of race proved pivotal in Chandler's relatively progressive racial climate, particularly in terms of housing. Though housing segregation was commonplace elsewhere, the Sawners owned rental property adjacent to their Chandler home in which white tenants lived.[clxii]

Mr. Wright set up his drugstore in a pitched tent just a few days following the town's founding in 1891. The Wright Pharmacy, 1004 Manvel Avenue, served Chandlerites for more than sixty years. Mr. Wright welcomed all customers in all areas of the establishment. He encouraged black and white patrons alike to sit and eat in the front of his establishment, a breach of prevailing social etiquette. Some African American customers, conditioned for subservience, balked. Even when presented with the opportunity to dine with equal dignity, they opted instead for the familiarity of second-class citizenship. Mr. Wright's acknowledgment of black dignity and display of basic human respect demonstrated the courage of his convictions, despite the social and economic risks attendant to bucking ole Jim Crow.

A.D. Wright and grandchild, *circa* 1923.[clxiv]

A.D. Wright found a kindred spirit in the person of Dr. John Adams, whose medical practice reflected the unusual racial sensitivity and openness extant in early twentieth century Chandler. Dr. Adams made house calls without regard to race.

Another white physician, Dr. J. Paul Smith, also accepted black patients. Dr. Smith assisted with the birth of Chandler historian Melvin Chatman and his brother, Whit Ellis, both born at the Ellis home on 12th Street in the early 1940s.

A life-threatening medical problem untreatable in Chandler complicated Mr. Chatman's birth. He needed care that only a large hospital could provide. That meant rushing to Oklahoma City for care in a hundred-plus-bed facility. Unfortunately for Mr. Chatman, prevailing protocol dictated that only four of those beds could be occupied by "colored" patients.

Tapping into his social network, Dr. Smith made arrangements for Chatman's post-delivery admission to and treatment in the Oklahoma City hospital. Surgeons there performed the critical procedure he needed.[clxvi] The intervention of his white physician saved Mr. Chatman's life.

While ground-level race relations in Chandler remained remarkably civil, even congenial, undercurrents of white supremacy flowed just beneath the surface. Black/white tensions heated up, but never quite reached ebullition. An incident involving a teenaged George Sawner Ellis came just short of bringing slow-simmering racial misgivings to the boiling point.

Mrs. Sawner took special interest in George Sawner Ellis, the son of close friends Maggie and Whit Ellis. He was born on August 28, 1924, just months after the passing of Mrs. Sawner's husband, George W.F. Sawner. The Ellises christened the boy George Sawner Ellis in memory of their friend, George Sawner.

On the occasion of George's first birthday, Mrs. Sawner, the still-grieving widow, decided to invest in the young Ellis boy. She opened a savings account in his name at First National Bank in Chandler. George's beginning balance: five dollars. That investment paid dividends. Like the other Ellis children, George thrived. His future seemed sunny, at least until the storm clouds of race overshadowed the innocence in his world.

George attended Douglass School through the first part of his senior year, 1940 to 1941. Ambling along his usual walking route, he regularly encountered Imogene Houston sauntering along the same path, but headed in the opposite direction. George lived on East 12th Street. He traveled west to get to Douglass. The caramel-colored, athletic, just-under-six-feet-tall whippersnapper came from a prominent, middle class black family.

Imogene lived on West 12th Street. She headed east toward her destination, Chandler High School. Imogene, a comely fifteen-year-old of slightly below-average height with strawberry blond hair, hailed from a wrong-side-of-the-tracks white family.

The mutual infatuation was immediate. The two teens routinely flirted, exchanged smiles and, on occasion, engaged in innocent banter. Besides these street meetings, George and Imogene saw one another only once, and then, only in passing—a fleeting moment at the integrated Lincoln County Fair. This chance-encounter-turned-secret-rendezvous routine continued uninterrupted for weeks. Finally, the star-crossed youngsters exchanged names.

One December evening, this wholesome, reciprocal crush took an unexpected and potentially lethal turn. At about 8:00 p.m. that day, Mrs. Goodberry, a neighborly white woman known to and trusted by a number of black Chandler families, paid an unannounced visit to the Ellis family home. Though not privy to the curt conversation, George sensed trouble brewing. The behind-closed-doors whispers and contorted facial expressions could not be ignored.

After Mrs. Goodberry's hasty departure, Mrs. Ellis began scurrying about the house, gathering George's essential belongings. She moved with robotic efficiency and no small measure of emotional detachment. Her silence masked the din of emotions welling up inside her, fear and love foremost among them. Her Solomonic decision would all too soon become apparent.

Without explanation or excuse, Mrs. Ellis arranged for a relative to drive George out of Chandler, subsistence belongings in tow, to the all-black town of Langston for the remainder of the academic year. Separated from family and friends, and unsure of the reason for his abrupt exile, George settled into his Langston University dormitory room. Like any stranger on foreign soil, he trod circumspectly, navigating this new landscape with an end in mind: rapid repatriation to Chandler. George missed the latter half of his senior year at Douglass School, and instead graduated from Langston High School in May of 1941 at age sixteen.

At some point during George's Langston sojourn, the mystery surrounding his banishment from Chandler began to clear. He learned that a newcomer to Chandler, likely some relative of Imogene, the girl with whom he had playfully engaged, had either seen or learned of the teens' furtive, socially inappropriate dalliances. Determined to muzzle the budding puppy love between them, the unknown man issued the ultimate threat: "We need to teach that Nigger a lesson." When alerted to this threat by Mrs. Goodberry, Mrs. Ellis's motherly instincts took over. Forced to choose between Scylla and Charybdis, she elected to protect George, even if it meant sending him away long enough for the Chandler seas to quiet.

The Chandler waters having stilled, George returned home after his high school graduation. Upon arrival, he marched through town in a demonstrative public announcement of his triumphal return.

After a brief stint back home, George moved from Chandler to Ann Arbor, Michigan. He finally closed the account Mrs. Sawner opened on his behalf what seemed a lifetime ago. The proceeds had by then grown more than eleven-fold—to a whopping fifty-six dollars. By her simple act of kindness, Mrs. Sawner taught George a lifelong lesson in savings and thrift.

George subsequently served in the United States Army. He visited Chandler after his discharge. On that visit, he happened upon a disheveled, pregnant young woman. It was Imogene Houston, the object of his years-old schoolboy fascination—the girl at the heart of his expatriation years earlier.

Imogene, sullen and haggard beyond her twenty-something years, had by this time borne two children. George and Imogene exchanged greetings for the final time, a decidedly subdued ending to what might have been, but for reservations attendant to race, a blossoming relationship.[clxvii]

Despite such periodic episodes, Chandler maintained notably positive race relations. The town's rather enlightened race relations stemmed from the influence of rare individuals like George and Lena Sawner, who passed seamlessly into and out of the two worlds to which race and history had consigned them and thrived in this most unexpected of places. Both of them left permanent imprints in the town of Chandler, in the County of Lincoln, and in the State of Oklahoma. Future generations trod on the bridges they built.

Following is a 1920 map of Chandler.[clxviii] Note that Douglass School is located in area number 5. Chandler High School is located in area number 1. Chandler City Hall is located in area number 3.

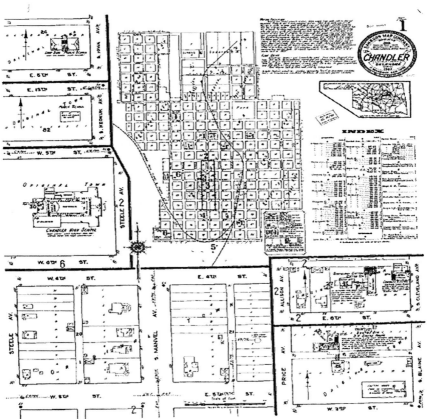

The Index to the foregoing map appears below:

INDEX

* Indicates only one side of Street shown.

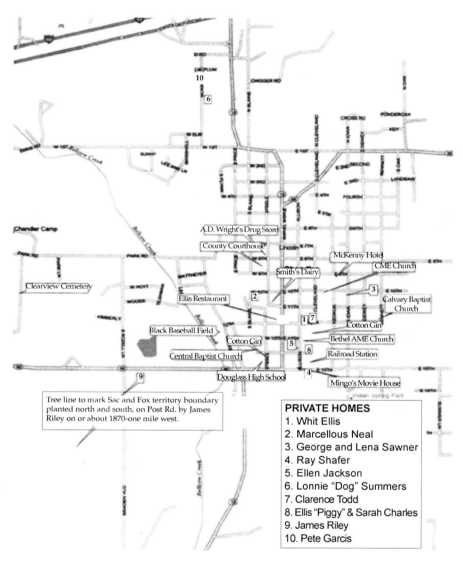

10
6

A.D. Wright's Drug Store
County Courthouse
Lincoln
McKenny Hotel
CME Church
Smith's Dairy
Chandler Camp
Clearview Cemetery
Ellis Restaurant
Calvary Baptist Church
Black Baseball Field
Cotton Gin
Cotton Gin
Bethel AME Church
Central Baptist Church
Railroad Station
Douglass High School
Mingo's Movie House

Tree line to mark Sac and Fox territory boundary
planted north and south, on Post Rd. by James
Riley on or about 1870-one mile west.

PRIVATE HOMES
1. Whit Ellis
2. Marcellous Neal
3. George and Lena Sawner
4. Ray Shafer
5. Ellen Jackson
6. Lonnie "Dog" Summers
7. Clarence Todd
8. Ellis "Piggy" & Sarah Charles
9. James Riley
10. Pete Garcis

Chandler, Oklahoma, *circa* 1920s – 1930s[clxix]

Like these maps, George Sawner's life turned on direction and intersection. Though a self-motivated, self-made man, Mr. Sawner understood the importance of path-crossings—of relationships—not just as a social matter, but also as a business imperative.

Chapter Three: The Gentleman George Sawner

"If you want to lift yourself up, lift up someone else."

— Booker T. Washington

George W.F. Sawner, *circa* 1910 and 1918, respectively.[clxx]

George Sawner seemingly had it all. Handsome, well-educated, and cosmopolitan, he held many of the keys to the kingdom. Add to these assets an unmistakable lightness of being—a serenity and pleasantness—coupled with a facility for trans-racial engagement, and the whole exceeded the sum of its individual parts. A man of limitless leadership potential, Mr. Sawner built upon his blessings, emerging as a trailblazer in Oklahoma politics, commerce, and civic affairs. His ascendancy during the nadir of race relations in America speaks to the uniqueness of person and place.

Birthed into slavery as one of a dozen children on March 10, 1859, George Sawner began life in Mississippi, a state freshly militarized in response to the failed raid of abolitionist John Brown at Harpers Fer-

Lena Sawner (kneeling), George Sawner (standing, holding Mrs. Sawner's hand) and friends, *circa* 1923.[clxxi]

ry, Virginia. Brown's attempt at inciting a slave revolt led to his conviction on treason charges and, ultimately, his martyrdom in death by hanging.[clxxii] The incident at Harpers Ferry galvanized the Mississippi Legislature and, at the urging of Governor William McWillie,[clxxiii] Mississippi solons expanded the state militia.[clxxiv]

Despite the Magnolia State's fortification and subsequent Southern strategies for maintaining the *status quo*, the peculiar institution ultimately collapsed under the weight of the internecine, years-long American Civil War. At the war's end, long-suffering souls who had labored under the yoke of Southern oppression first tasted freedom. A puerile George Sawner, now liberated, wasted no time emancipating his mind.

Academically precocious, Mr. Sawner began teaching school at the age of fifteen. Education, he believed, could unloose the shackled minds of newly freed African Americans.

George Sawner left Mississippi for LaGrange, Texas. There, he tied the knot with Ida Ferrell, daughter of Dave Ferrell and Mollie Reeves,[clxxv] on April 17, 1888.[clxxvi] She bore one child, Juanita.[clxxvii]

Ida Ferrell outlived George Sawner. Born in Texas in 1867, she died of pellagra[clxxviii] on December 19, 1927, and was laid to rest in LaGrange.[clxxix] Juanita (Sawner) Hogget witnessed her mother's death certificate.[clxxx]

The circumstances surrounding George Sawner's separation from Ida (Ferrell) Sawner remain opaque, particularly in light of the fact that Ida (Ferrell) Sawner's death certificate listed her as widowed.[clxxxi] George Sawner, though then deceased (having died in 1924), had long since been remarried. Although not a common practice, the designation "widow" has been applied to the surviving former spouse of a deceased man who had remarried prior to his death.[clxxxii]

This much is clear: George Sawner left Texas for Oklahoma in 1890. A little over a decade later, he took Lena Lowery as his second bride and, together, they led largely transparent public lives.

Mr. Sawner moved to Oklahoma just after the initial opening of Oklahoma Territory in 1889. That momentous occasion drew adventurers from far and wide. By the time of the scheduled start of the run at high noon on April 22, 1889, some 50,000 people had queued up like sprinters angling for a prime position at the starting line of a high-profile race, ready to make a run for a parcel of the available two million acres.[clxxxiii]

Mr. Sawner's mother, native Mississippian Maria Farmer, joined him in Oklahoma, settling in Guthrie in 1892. At the time of her death at age 85 in 1916, only one of her dozen children, George Sawner, survived.[clxxxiv]

Once in Oklahoma, Mr. Sawner joined forces with two other African American counselors to form Oklahoma's first all-black law firm, Sadler, Sawner and Twine (*circa* 1891), located in Guthrie. Friends affectionately referred to the triumvirate as "The Three Musketeers.[clxxxv]

In addition to this famed troika, an impressive array of black lawyers practiced in Oklahoma Territory. Many of these pre-statehood professionals hung their shingles in the capital, Guthrie, which remained the post-statehood hub of government until 1910. Early African American legal eagles in Oklahoma included: B.C. Franklin[clxxxvi] (Ardmore, Rentiesville, and Tulsa), George N. Perkins (Guthrie), Robert Emmett Stewart (Guthrie), G.W.P. Brown (Guthrie), A.L. Ayers (Langston), William H. Harrison (Tulsa and Oklahoma City), and James Coody Johnson (Wewoka).[clxxxvii]

James Coody Johnson
(1864 – 1927)[clxxxviii]

At the turn of the twentieth century, present-day Oklahoma boasted some thirty black lawyers. Indeed, "Guthrie and Logan County became the Mecca for some of the most cultured, best-educated, and progressive Negroes in the United States."[clxxxix] These remarkable men received high praise, not just from their black colleagues, clients, and communities, but from the white press as well.[cxc] This brigade of black barristers formed the Negro Bar Association of the State of Oklahoma.[cxci]

Unlike their white counterparts, black attorneys-at-law concerned themselves with far more than individual cases of a civil or criminal nature. They represented hope for systemic change in America, from the inside out, on matters of race. They often labored in pursuit not just of personal justice, but of social justice, both for their clients and for themselves.

Mr. Sawner championed racial justice throughout his career. He attended a convention of African American men in Langston City on June 2, 1894, at which delegates passed resolutions fairly summarizing his views on race:

> WHEREAS, The negro, by reason of his numbers, intelligence, property and production, has become a factor in Oklahoma; therefore, be it
>
> *Resolved,* That we request that the office of county clerk be conceded to the colored contingent of the republican party, and such other appointive places as our suffrage as a political factor in justice demands; further
>
> *Resolved,* That we believe the republican party is the only party of progress and advancement, and the only safeguard into whose hands the affairs of this government may be safely entrusted; be it further
>
> *Resolved,* That it is the sense of this convention that we denounce 'mob law' in any part of this country with all the vehemency [sic] of our souls; be it further
>
> *Resolved,* That we insist upon and demand for ourselves all rights of American citizens, as are accorded to any other race; and we here recommend and endorse the actions of the Colored Men's convention held in Cincinnati, O., in December, 1893. Be it further
>
> *Resolved,* That whereas the colored people of the south are oppressed and illtreated [sic] in every conceivable manner without any chance of bettering their condition, that we invite and encourage them to emigrate to this, the 'land of the free and the home of the brave.'
>
> *Resolved,* That these resolutions be given to the press of Oklahoma.

G.N. PERKINS,
C.H. TANDY,
G.W.F. SAWNER,
T.D. JACKSON,
T.J. AUSTIN,
W.H. MCCARVER,
    Committee[cxcii]

George Sawner intensified his pursuit of justice on behalf of African Americans from his perch in Chandler. Though the precise date of his arrival there remains unknown, Mr. Sawner taught school in Chandler as early as 1895.[cxciii] He participated in the Lincoln County Colored Teachers' Association that same year.[cxciv]

In 1896, Mr. Sawner spoke before representatives of Chandler's black and white citizens at an emancipation celebration held at the city park. He and other dignitaries, including his colleague, W.H. Twine of Muskogee, offered stirring patriotic speeches while park patrons feasted on an Oklahoma Territory delicacy, mouth-watering barbeque.[cxcv]

In 1897, Mr. Sawner led a group of African American men who hosted a reception in the Chandler courthouse honoring Oklahoma Territory Governor Cassius McDonald Barnes.[cxcvi] That same year, he helped organize The Colored Territorial Convention in Guthrie, "for the purpose of taking steps for the best interest of the party. . . ."[cxcvii]

In 1898, Chandler voters elected George Sawner Justice of the Peace,[cxcviii] a civil public officer with limited power,[cxcix] but a prominent position in local government. An Enid, Oklahoma, newspaper reported the election results in folksy language: "Geo. W. Sawner, a negro, was elected Justice of the Peace of Chandler township, Lincoln [C]ounty. Now . . . white folks bettah look out ober in Linkun county."[cc]

George Sawner's fair skin, relative wealth, and facility with the King's English, afforded him entrée into white society at levels unimaginable for ordinary black folks. Still, he could not soar above the reach of Jim Crow.

He continued to advocate for the full citizenship rights of African Americans as the twentieth century neared, and then dawned. Mr. Sawner served a stint as President of the Negro Protective League of Lincoln County in 1900.[ccii] Governor Thompson Benton Ferguson appointed him to represent Oklahoma Territory at the Southern Negro Congress in Galveston, Texas, held on July 1, 1902.[cciii]

George Sawner and his betrothed, Lena Lowery, married on June 2, 1903, in the central Kansas town of Winfield, a stone's throw from the Walnut River, some 120 miles due north of Chandler. The union, the second for him and the first for her, could scarcely have been more perfect. Together, the Sawners evolved into a formidable social, political, and economic force in Oklahoma. They even met with African American statesman Booker T. Washington in Guthrie in 1905.[cciv]

The descriptors "cultured," "well-educated," and "progressive" suited George W.F. Sawner to a tee. This polymath not only practiced law, but also made his presence felt in the social, political, and economic spheres as a teacher, devout Christian, philanthropist, civil rights advocate, in-demand public speaker, Republican Party stalwart, elected official, property owner, and cotton broker. George Sawner secured a place among "Oklahoma's most prominent and useful pioneers."[ccv]

Dr. W.E.B. Du Bois, among the foremost intellectuals and civil rights advocates of the era, ranked Sawner among the "Talented Tenth," the highest echelon of African American leaders, a sort of black aristocracy. Judged by education, occupation, and income, Dr. Du Bois postulated that the Talented Tenth would deliver the African American masses from their too-often-woeful circumstances attributable, in large part, to an American-made racial conundrum.[ccvi]

Addressing the new twenty-eighth President of the United States, Woodrow Wilson, in a 1913 open letter, W.E.B. Du Bois pointed to the contradictions between black docility and American democracy and hinted that only agitation, not accommodation, could ultimately resolve the conflict.

> Sir: Your inauguration to the Presidency of the United States is to the colored people, to the white South and to the nation a momentous occasion.
>
> . . . .
>
> We believe that the Negro problem is in many respects the greatest problem facing the nation, and we believe that you have the opportunity of beginning a just and righteous solution of this burning human wrong. This opportunity is yours because, while a Southerner in birth and tradition, you have escaped the provincial training of the South and you have not had burned into your soul desperate hatred and despising of your darker fellow men.
>
> . . . .

[Y]ou face no insoluble problem. The only time when the Negro problem is insoluble is when men insist on settling it wrong by asking absolutely contradictory things. You cannot make 10,000,000 people at one and the same time servile and dignified, docile and self-reliant, servants and independent leaders, segregated and yet part of the industrial organism, disfranchised and citizens of a democracy, ignorant and intelligent. This is impossible and the impossibility is not factitious; it is in the very nature of things.[ccvii]

. . . .

The Negro race, like all races, is going to be saved by its exceptional men. The problem of education, then, among Negroes must first of all deal with the Talented Tenth; it is the problem of developing the Best[sic]of this race that they may guide the Mass[sic] away from the contamination and death of the Worst, in their own and other races. Now the training of men is a difficult and intricate task. Its technique is a matter for educational experts, but its object is for the vision of seers. If we make money the object of man-training, we shall develop money-makers but not necessarily men; if we make technical skill the object of education, we may possess artisans but not, in nature, men. Men we shall have only as we make manhood the object of the work of the schools—intelligence, broad sympathy, knowledge of the world that was and is, and of the relation of men to it—this is the curriculum of that Higher Education which must underlie true life. On this foundation we may build bread winning, skill of hand and quickness of brain, with never a fear lest the child and man mistake the means of living for the object of life . . . .[ccviii]

Members of the Talented Tenth, the *crème de la crème* of black society in the United States, would, in Dr. Du Bois's view, challenge both overt racism and "the soft bigotry of low expectations" prevalent even among some allies in the racial justice movement.[ccix] These patricians would internalize a sense of *noblesse oblige*, using their relatively privileged status not just for personal gain, but also for the betterment of the African American *hoi polloi*.

Like other high achieving Tenth-types, George Sawner seized perceived opportunities as they manifested. In the early 1900s, he planted himself squarely within the burgeoning Oklahoma cotton industry. Cotton, though threaded throughout George Sawner's mercantile life, comprised but a part of the larger fabric of this eclectic entrepreneur. At the time of his death in 1924, Mr. Sawner's patchwork of cotton operations included gins in Boley, Muskogee, and Redbird. As Boley's King Cotton, he catapulted the town into the forefront of the cotton commodity trade.

BOLEY, May 3 [1924]—The Farmers and Merchants Bank of this city closed its doors today in memory and honor of G.W. Sawner, whose funeral was held in the city of Chandler. The president of the Farmers and Merchants Bank, together with all the officers and employees of the institution, attended the funeral.

William Edward Burghardt Du Bois (February 23, 1868 – August 27, 1963), scholar, editor, African American activist, first African American to earn a Ph.D. from Harvard (1895), and founding member of the N.A.A.C.P. ccx

Made Cotton Market.

According to a statement made by one of the officials of the institution, Sawner made the cotton market at Boley. He started operations in Boley in 1904, and it was out of his effort that Boley forged to the forefront as a cotton center. Together with M.I. Donaldson, Sawner operated a gin at Childsville, and he owned other property at Clarksville, which was managed by W. H. Twine of Muskogee.ccxi

Other Activities.

Sawner maintained his residence and home in the city of Chandler, but he took an interest in Boley that will make his loss felt for some time to come. He owned several rent houses in Boley, two farms in Lincoln [C]ounty and valuable business property on South Second [S]treet in Muskogee.ccxi

Though perhaps not king, cotton rose to at least princely levels in Chandler, affecting the lives of virtually all of the townsfolk, at least until the mid-1920s. Cotton fields ringed the residential sector of the town. Children as young as six, black and white, labored under harsh conditions to help reap a bountiful harvest of the much-in-demand

Cotton wagons on Chandler's main street, *circa* 1895.[ccxii]

fiber each September and October. Older children sometimes chose truancy, skipping school until mid-November to pluck the fluffy white currency from its prickly brown boll.

George Sawner dealt in another, equally thorny, commodity, too. He traded widely in political capital. Mr. Sawner assumed a leading role in Republican Party politics, delivering stump speeches for the party as early as 1894. *The Daily Oklahoma State Capital* in Guthrie reported that his speeches "elicited numerous bursts of applause."[ccxiii]

Mr. Sawner and E.P. McCabe, the leading black town booster and the founder of Langston, Oklahoma, spoke at a picnic for African Americans of the Cimarron and Iowa townships that same year. An announcement for the event extended an invitation to "[a]ll republicans and candidates, with their families and friends. . . ."[ccxiv]

In 1895, Mr. Sawner appeared among the three "Colored" men reported in the retinue of the legislature: "Mr. Page, Kingfisher [C]ounty, watchman of the council; G.W. F. Sawner, assistant sergeant-at-arms of the hour, and E.P. McCabe, Logan [C]ounty, for assistant chief clerk of the house."[ccxv] Mr. Sawner subsequently served on the Central Committee of the Lincoln County Republican Party[ccxvi] and as a delegate to the Lincoln County Republican Party convention.[ccxii]

Other prominent public roles materialized. Mr. Sawner chaired a memorial service honoring Frederick Douglass, who died on February 20, 1895. The March 1895 gathering offered a heart-felt resolution honoring the larger-than-life American statesman:

> To the greatness of an illustrious character and the evidence
> of American possibilities and to the height [sic] and depth

and breadth of the great man, deceased, as statesman, diplomat and countryman; that his reverence has first place in our hearts and that his memory shall ever be kept green upon the pages of our country.[ccxiii]

Mr. Sawner spoke regularly at Republican Party confabs, earning glowing reviews for his rhetorical virtuosity. In 1896, he served as a Lincoln County delegate to the Republican Territorial Convention in Oklahoma City.[ccxix] An account of a meeting in Choctaw in 1900 detailed his eloquence.

Mr. C.D. Clem of Edmond and Mr. G.W.F. Sawner of Chandler, [sic] held the audience spell-bound for two hours with their logical utterances and forciable [sic] declarations of Republicanism. So attentive was the audience that at times a pin might have been heard if dropped, then again[,] it would burst forth in such cheers that the speakers would have to stop until the enthusiasm subsided. Many have said that it was the most instructive and entertaining political meeting they have attended in years.[ccxx]

In 1904, Mr. Sawner competed for a delegate spot at his party's national convention during the Oklahoma Territorial Republican Party Convention, uniting the Lincoln County delegation around his nomination.

There was no delegation in the convention more harmonious or compact than the Lincoln [C]ounty boys, and there was no delegation that made a harder fight for its candidate for delegate than this county put up for Sawner. There was no disposition to compromise or surrender. Success or licking were the only alternatives, and we got the latter.[ccxxi]

Though ultimately unsuccessful, Mr. Sawner received the endorsement of *The Chandler News*:

In endorsing G.W.F. Sawner for delegate to the national republican convention[,] the republicans of the county showed last Saturday a willingness to give recognition to the colored men of the county. It has never been a question of willingness with the majority of the republicans of the county, however, nor a question of prejudice, but a question of whether it could be done, whether the person who sought recognition as the representative of his race was [s]uitable and worthy, and whether the members of his race stood solidly behind him.[ccxxii]

The Party faithful elected Mr. Sawner as an alternate delegate to the 1905 statehood convention.[ccxxxii] That same year, as a member of the Negro Executive Committee of Oklahoma and Indian Territories, Mr. Sawner issued a call for delegates to attend the Inter-Territorial Statehood Convention in Muskogee. The conclave brought together Negroes in Oklahoma and Indian Territories to air concerns and build relationships in anticipation of Oklahoma statehood.[ccxxiv] The two hundred eighteen delegates assembled passed resolutions supporting single statehood for Oklahoma.[ccxxv]

Mr. Sawner took part in inaugural festivities for the ninth Governor of Oklahoma Territory, Frank Frantz, in 1906.[ccxxvi] In quick succession, he addressed an enthusiastic crowd at the Chandler Republican Convention in that same year,[ccxxvii] and the Lincoln County Republican Convention in 1907,[ccxxvii] the latter gathering drew rave media reviews, including one characterizing it as "one of the most peaceful, harmonious and enthusiastic gatherings of the kind ever held in the county, as well as one of the most largely attended."[ccxxix] Mr. Sawner continued to be active in Republican Party politics throughout his life.[ccxxx]

In his earlier days in Oklahoma, George Sawner represented the Negro Protective League[ccxxxi] and the Afro-American League[ccxxxii] as a delegate from the Twin Territories to Washington, D.C. He continued that advocacy as Oklahoma lurched toward statehood.

Mr. Sawner also continued to advocate for black rights. *The New York Times* reported on February 2, 1907, that delegates to the Oklahoma Constitutional Convention provoked a confrontation with President Theodore Roosevelt over "Jim Crow" laws. These citizens pushed for the rigid separation of "Negroes" and whites in social, economic, and political spheres written into the new state's constitution. President Roosevelt vowed to veto Oklahoma statehood over the issue of constitutionally ensconced racial segregation. George Sawner stood among those who implored the President to stand firm.

> The convention was in a difficult position. The Democrats carried Oklahoma on the race questions, and were expected by the people to lose no time in making good the issue on which they were elected. They hit upon this happy method of getting themselves out of the dilemma and at the same time drawing the President's fire.
>
> . . . .
>
> The anti-negro provisions which are proposed are simply the

'Jim Crow' provisions which are in force in the Southern States, and as these have stood the test in the courts it is argued that the President could not possibly decide them to be unrepublican or unconstitutional if adopted by the new State.[ccxxxiii]

In the end, Constitution Convention delegates succeeded at including a separate schools provision in the Oklahoma Constitution. Their efforts to incorporate across-the-board social segregation measures failed, at least temporarily. Though broad-based, state-sanctioned segregation as a matter of state constitutional law had been defeated, leaders of the new State of Oklahoma would soon flock to Jim Crow, both *de jure* and *de facto*.

Mr. Sawner, together with select other prominent African American leaders from throughout the state, addressed the Constitutional League of Oklahoma in Oklahoma City on November 25, 1913, at Calvary Baptist Church. The meeting focused on a pivotal Oklahoma voting rights case pending before the United States Supreme Court.

> Let every Negro in the state from the pulpit down, every citizen who has the interest of the race at heart, come to this meeting that we may all have an understanding in common as to our future welfare in this state. The 'Jim Crow' case, now in the Supreme Court of the United States[,] will soon be set for hearing at Washington, D.C. We, the Negroes of the state[,] must raise funds to pay the costs and expenses incident to the filing of said cause, etc. We have gone through the Circuit Court at St. Paul, Minn., and we are in the Supreme Court. Come to this meeting and bring whatever you can raise.[ccxxxiv]

When ultimately decided in 1915, the case dealt a significant, though fleeting, blow to Jim Crow in Oklahoma. *Guinn v. United States*[ccxxxv] invalidated the grandfather clause in Oklahoma's Voter Registration Act of 1910 because it violated the Fifteenth Amendment to the United States Constitution. The law mandated a reading test for some citizens as a prerequisite to voting. It exempted all those who were entitled to vote on January 1, 1866, just after the American Civil War ended and before the approval in 1870 of the Fifteenth Amendment, the Constitutional guarantee of voting rights for all male citizens, regardless of race, as well as their descendants. In practical effect, the law afforded those whose "grandfathers" were entitled to vote in 1866 (*i.e.*, white male citizens) the unfettered right to register and vote. It effectively disenfranchised others (*i.e.*, African American male citizens) by sanctioning an onerous, discriminatorily-administered literacy test as a condition precedent to voting.[ccxxxvi]

In response to the adverse *Guinn* decision, the Oklahoma Legislature adopted crafty voter registration requirements that again effectively stripped the state's African American citizens of the franchise. It would be 1939 before these fresh *de jure* impediments to African American voting rights would be lifted by court edict.[ccxxxvii]

In 1914, Mr. Sawner addressed the third annual session of the State Negro Business League at its conference in Tulsa's Greenwood District, the African American entrepreneurial hub that would become known as "Black Wall Street." The meeting, held in the auditorium of the Gem Theatre on Greenwood Avenue, drew some 150 delegates. Mr. Sawner spoke on the need for black businesspersons to take full advantage of the available opportunities in Oklahoma.[ccxxxviii]

Later that year, Booker T. Washington visited Muskogee, Oklahoma, just fifty miles southeast of Tulsa, in his role as chief spokesperson and business ambassador for the National Negro Business League ("N.N.B.L."). Addressing throngs, Washington praised the potential of the region and challenged listeners to become more business friendly.

NATIONAL NEGRO BUSINESS LEAGUE ADDRESS, 1914
B.T. Washington / E.J. Scott
Convention Hall, Muskogee, Oklahoma
August 19, 1914

The National Negro Business League, under whose auspices we are gathered today in the new state of Oklahoma in such large numbers, is simply one of the many agencies employed to promote further progress among us.

The National Negro Business League has a unique history. Organized by a small group of men and women in the city of Boston, Massachusetts, in 1900, it has grown in power and influence till its spirit is felt and is being carried on in the form of local Business leagues, or similar organizations, in nearly every centre of Negro population throughout the United States. Getting its strength and its standing from these Local Leagues, the National Negro Business League at each annual session grows in dignity and influence.

Before beginning the body of my remarks, there are a few simple but fundamental things to which I wish to direct the special attention of each Local League. These things I ask in order that the usefulness of the League may be still further felt among the ten millions of our people.

1. First of all, do not fritter away too much time in your meetings in technicalities known as "parliamentary rules."

2. Let each Local League study the condition and needs of our people in its community, and devote itself to doing that which will promote the commercial, industrial, educational, professional and moral life of our race in that community.

3. Have a regular time of meeting, and always have a meeting at that time.

4. Strive to have a regular place of meeting, one that shall be attractive and convenient.

5. Have for each meeting a carefully arranged program that shall strike at some definite thing. A general program means little.

6. Each Local League should strive to gather into its membership every man and woman who is interested in any kind of honorable business, no matter how humble that business may appear to be.

7. Each League should have for one of its objects the bringing of the White man by whose side we live into friendly and sympathetic contact with the progress of the race. One way to do this is to invite successful White men to visit and speak to the Local League. The White man will help and we will be helped.

8. Try to stimulate competition and up-to-date business methods.

. . . .

As I have stated, in no other part of the United States is there greater opportunity for the Negro than in the six states adjacent to Muskogee: namely, Kansas, Missouri, Arkansas, Louisiana, Texas and Oklahoma.

. . . .

When the 2,000,000 Negroes of the Southwest have made the most of their opportunities and have let down their buckets deep into the earth and brought up the riches contained therein in the forms of cotton, corn, oats, wheat, potatoes, chickens, turkeys, hogs, horses, mules and cattle, they will be able to support in Kansas, Missouri, Arkansas, Louisiana, Texas, and Oklahoma, 1,000 more grocery stores owned by Negroes, 500 additional dry goods stores, 300 more show stores, 200 more restaurants and hotels, 300 additional millinery stores, 200 additional drug stores and 40 more banks.

George Sawner became an early life member of the New York-incorporated N.N.B.L., this black chamber of commerce of the early twentieth century. His undated membership certificate, signed by Booker T. Washington himself, bears the number seventy-seven, in-

No. *77*   *$25⁰⁰*

Life Membership
National Negro Business League

This is to Certify THAT Mr._*G. W. F. Sawner*_

*of the City of*_*Chandler*_   _of the State of_

*Oklahoma* _has complied with the By-Laws of the_

NATIONAL NEGRO BUSINESS LEAGUE, *a membership corporation,*

incorporated under the laws of the State of New York, by paying

the required LIFE MEMBERSHIP *fee of $25.00, and is entitled to*

all of the privileges conferred by that organization, subject to the

by-laws, rules and regulations of said League.

  Witness *the corporate name and seal of the*

  NATIONAL NEGRO BUSINESS LEAGUE

     Booker T. Washington
          PRESIDENT

     Emmett J. Scott
         CORRESPONDING SECRETARY

     Napier
       CHAIRMAN, EXECUTIVE COMMITTEE

dicating Mr. Sawner's ranking among that organization's first members. That Sawner chose a twenty-five-dollar life membership in the N.N.B.L. attests to his financial wherewithal and, more significantly, his commitment to the ideals of economic uplift the N.N.B.L. championed.[ccxl]

The N.N.B.L., with self-help, networking, and racial solidarity among its core principles, represented the aspirations of a nascent black business and entrepreneurial class. The founding of and the inspiration for the N.N.B.L. shed light of the overall condition of black America during the Sawners' early twentieth century experience in Oklahoma.

> Booker T. Washington founded the National Negro Business League in 1900 with the primary purpose of improving the economic condition of African Americans. Washington saw the NNBL as an important aspect of his overall strategy for the improvement of race relations, to build up the African American community from within so that white Americans would think more highly of it, draw on its resources, and eventually grant it equality.

ENTERPRISING BUSINESS MEN
The Executive Committee of the "National Negro Business League." The purpose of this league is to bring the business men together for mutual co-operation and trade advancement.

N.N.B.L. Executive Committee, *circa* 1917
(Booker T. Washington, back row, fourth from the left)[ccxli]

The NNBL was founded during what scholars have called the nadir of race relations in the United States. During those years, blacks were being driven from the ballot box in the South and confronted with the rise of the system of institutional discrimination known as Jim Crow. With the sanction of the Supreme Court's *Plessy v. Ferguson* decision in 1896, African Americans were deprived of virtually all vestiges of Reconstruction-period gains and often reduced to conditions quite similar to those under slavery.

The overwhelming majority of African Americans lived in the South and did agricultural labor . . . African Americans throughout the country suffered from a lack of access to such financial resources as land and capital.

It is in this context that Booker T. Washington embarked upon his strategy for racial advancement through self-help and racial solidarity. A combination of individual and collective responsibility characterized the activities of the NNBL. Based at Tuskegee from 1900 until 1923, the NNBL was an integral part of what became known as the "Tuskegee Machine." Washington drew upon his wide contacts among the white economic elite, such as Robert C. Ogden, John Wanamaker, and Andrew Carnegie, for examples of the success that African American businessmen and business women should strive to emulate.[ccxlii]

Mr. Sawner's affiliation with the N.N.B.L. seemed the perfect match. The organization's philosophical bent toward black advancement through self-help and business endeavors dovetailed beautifully with his personal experience and worldview. Indeed, George Sawner could have been the N.N.B.L. poster child.

Like Booker T. Washington, George Sawner believed in the promise of Oklahoma, and of America. He and his wife, Lena, demonstrated that love of state and country one crisp, fall day in 1917 when they attended a farewell reception at the local courthouse for fifty Lincoln County conscripts bound for service in World War I. African American and white citizens alike came out to boost the spirits of the draftees and remind the soon-to-be combatants of the American ideals at stake in the conflict. The patriotic event, replete with songs and speeches, culminated in a parade headed by "the big touring car of Mr. and Mrs. G. W. F. Sawner . . . decorated with stars and stripes."[ccxliii]

Mr. Sawner balanced his patriotic zeal with civic engagement. J.

Coody Johnson of Wewoka, a prominent Muscogee (Creek) Freedman and president of the Negro Protective League for the State of Oklahoma, selected Mr. Sawner as one of several delegates to the National Colored Congress, held in Washington, D.C., May 29 – June 2, 1918. The gathering focused on "taking action to secure from the Government a guarantee of equality of civil and political rights and abolution [sic] of injustice and discrimination on Color lines as our share of the World Democracy for which our race is legally bound to offer life in the World War." Other prominent delegates, in addition to Messrs. Johnson and Sawner, included: J. M. Marquess, Langston; E. T. Barbour, El Reno; T. H. Traylor, Oklahoma City; T. J. Elliott, Muskogee; A. J. Smitherman, Tulsa; R. Emmett Steward, Muskogee; and W.H. Twine, Muskogee.[ccxliv]

Mr. Sawner also attended a special Inter-Racial Conference in Oklahoma City on October 7, 1920. Speakers took dead aim at ole Jim Crow, mob violence against African Americans, and black disenfranchisement. T.D. Turner, a white, seventy-two-year-old former Confederate soldier, excoriated those who would deny Negroes their fundamental rights. With the fury of a country preacher, voice quivering and body trembling, the general stood in the Senate Chamber and bellowed: "[Negroes] haven't the protection that slaves in the country once had. You have a right to complain and there is only one answer to the question of ADJUSTMENT, and that is to give the Negro all of his rights."[ccxlv]

Judge James R. Keaton of Oklahoma City presided. He charged the assemblage with finding a way for the two races to live together in harmony. Mr. Sawner made it clear that solutions lay squarely on the doorstep on white Americans: "The white race has been great enough to take world leadership, to controll [sic] everything but themselves, and it is up to the white man to put down mob violence and all of the other shameful outrages that it perpetrated against the black man."[ccxlvi]

On June 13, 1921, Oklahoma Governor J.B.A. Robertson officially appointed George Sawner to the Oklahoma Commission on Inter-Racial Co-operation, a body charged with promoting "a better understanding between the races [so that] justice may be more evenly established."[ccxlvii] The commission began to congeal as early as December of 1920, with members being added along the way. Those joining Mr. Sawner on the commission included: *African American members*—W.H. Twine (Muskogee); J.H. Lilly (McAlester); D.J. Turner (Boley); D.J. Wallace (Okmulgee); Roscoe Dunjee (Oklahoma City);

and S.D. Hooker (Tulsa); *White members*—F.M. Deerhake (Oklahoma City); L.L. Bronson (El Reno); Dr. A.R. Lewis (Ryan); Mont Powell (Oklahoma City); and Charles Page (Tulsa).[ccxlviii]

The 1921 Tulsa Race Riot, the worst of the "race riots" in twentieth century American history, added a sense of urgency to the work of the Commission.[ccxlix] The Riot leveled the Greenwood District, and, in the process, laid waste to its nationally renowned black center of commerce and enterprise. It left enduring psychic scars and relational fissures.[ccl]

In addition to business and professional pursuits, Mr. Sawner served as a director of the Farmers and Merchants Bank of Boley,[ccli] America's first black-owned bank. He also served as a director of the Southwestern Realty and Investment Company of Muskogee.

Mr. Sawner also supported the N.A.A.C.P., the national, interracial civil rights organization founded in 1909.[cclii] He made a habit of joining the N.A.A.C.P. branches where he spoke or visited.

Mr. Sawner offered remarks in Boley on the occasion of a visit by N.A.A.C.P. Field Secretary Dean William Pickens in 1920. Mr. Pickens had by this time gained a national reputation for his fiery, truth-telling oratory. He pointed out contradictions between American ideals and American realities, and emphasized the common fate black and white Americans of necessity shared:

> Some day either they will cease to burn men in Texas and Mississippi, or they will burn them in New York. Some day either they will not burn black men or they will burn white men.

> There is not a place in the United States of America where the colored people really are free, and if the freedom of the black man suffers, the freedom of the white man is sure to be degraded.[ccliii]

At an N.A.A.C.P. mass meeting in Oklahoma City in 1921, Mr. Sawner roused the crowd with a wide-ranging talk on education, black business, and citizenship. A newspaper account noted: "On account of his color he has many times fought for his race and converted his hearers who thought he was not a Negro."[ccliv]

Mr. Sawner's light complexion made for more than a few colorful incidents. An encounter on a railcar exposed both the precarious nature of racial classifications and the absurdity of Jim Crow in Oklahoma and elsewhere.

Mr. Sawner and a friend, Ed McDaniel of McAlester, a once-prominent African American railroad conductor, boarded the Jim Crow coach of a train together, bound for a fraternal convention. Though they had just argued, they sat side by side.

When the conductor entered the Jim Crow car, Mr. McDaniel raised a ruckus: "Conductor," he exclaimed, "I want you to make this old white man get on out of this coach; he has come in here and sat down by me and even presumes to try to talk to me; make him get on out of there into his coach before you have trouble." Mr. McDaniel sat stone-faced as Mr. Sawner protested that he belonged in the Jim Crow car and that he knew McDaniel.

The conductor, believing Mr. Sawner to be a white man, collared him, forcibly escorting him to his rightful place on the white coach, where Mr. Sawner remained until he reached his final destination. Mr. McDaniel's ruse played perfectly. He assuaged his anger at George Sawner over their pre-trip argument, and he put one over on ole Jim Crow, too.[cclv]

Even Mr. Sawner's choice of religious affiliation seemed to signal his black pride. The African Methodist Episcopal Church ("A.M.E. Church") became an important part of Mr. Sawner's life. Founded in Philadelphia in 1816, the A.M.E. Church rejected slavery and white supremacy.[cclvi]

The unique focus of the A.M.E. Church on African American uplift no doubt attracted Mr. Sawner. He, after all, defied the inferiority myth. In the face of low expectations and barriers, both overt and covert, he offered living proof of African American industriousness and intellectual capacity. As if touched by an angel, he, a black man in a white man's world, lived what looked from afar like a divinely inspired life.

In addition to his religious ties, Mr. Sawner relished his association with Freemasonry, with its rich history in the African American community. He belonged to several fraternal orders, including the Masonic,[cclvii] Knights of Pythias,[cclviii] and Odd Fellows.[cclix]

The Pythians took bold stances on the issues of the day. For example, the Oklahoma Pythian Grand Lodge passed resolutions in 1918 supporting the World War I effort, but highlighting differential and discriminatory treatment for African Americans on the home front.

> BE IT RESOLVED, That we, the delegates to the Grand Lodge. . .
> do here affirm the right of black men's voice to be heard in the
> definition of Democracy in this crucial hour, when we affirm
> with our lives and blood our unswerving love of home and
> country;

BE IT RESOLVED, That we call upon the President of the United States and Congress to vitalize the spirit of the time through and by the passage of such laws as will blot and eradicate from American life, Mob Violence and its brother with legal status, Jim Crowism;

BE IT FURTHER RESOLVED, That we, hereby proclaim that we cannot feel that our native land should demand for other men, in the adjustment of international affairs, more of privilege, comfort and safety than that accorded our own citizens;

RESOLVED, That we call every member of the race to throw his full support behind the War Program of this nation and her allies with the hope and the belief that as we reach the higher levels for which the world is struggling our racial groups shall be also lifted from the thralldom of restriction and persecution wherein we now find ourselves.

The Black Dispatch newspaper touted Mr. Sawner as the ideal candidate for Grand Master of the Masonic Order in 1920:

Whose name is being prominently mentioned for Grand Master of the Masonic Order[?] Mr. Sawner has been for years an outstanding figure in Negro leadership of the state. He is beloved by all who know him because of his uncompromising fight for the things that are right. He is eminently qualified to step into the shoes of the present Grand Master, who has given notice that he will retire....[T]he Masons of Oklahoma could not find in any of it membership, more sterling worth than in George Sawner, the man who in the last quarter of a century of struggle in this state has made good as a farmer, lawyer, banker and leader of his people.[cclxi]

Mr. Sawner's various pursuits earned him respect and admiration generally, but particularly so among Oklahoma's African American population. *The Tulsa Star*, in an article entitled "Sage of Chandler Visits Tulsa," recounted a 1920 visit to Tulsa by Mr. Sawner:

The Hon. G.W.F. Sawner, the well known cotton buyer and political leader of Chandler, passed thru Tulsa Monday [en route] to Muskogee, and while here spent a few hours visiting some of his old friends. Mr. Sawner talked quite knowingly and interestingly of the great political conflict between Hamon and McGraw for supremacy in republican political affairs.[cclxii]

Despite the odds stacked against African Americans, George Sawner made his way. Determination, integrity, humility, and compassion undergirded his indomitable will to succeed. This jack-of-all-trades thrived as a teacher, lawyer, property owner, cotton dealer, civic leader, elected official, political activist, and philanthropist. At his death of natural causes on May 1, 1924, his disconsolate widow, the City of Chandler, and a considerable portion of an infant state, mourned.

The *Chandler News-Publicist* lucidly expressed the prevailing sentiment:

The Passing of G. W. F. Sawner.

The people of Chandler and the community roundabout, were shocked and saddened at the news of the passing of G. W. F. Sawner, one of the country's earliest and most respected citizens, whose death occurred at the family residence in East Chandler, last Thursday morning at 10 o'clock from a complication of complaints, chiefly of which was kidney and bladder trouble. Mr. Sawner had been in failing health for many months, but he was of such an uncomplaining nature that only his closest friends know of his condition, and for that reason his demise was a distinct shock to the city and community. He was stricken with a severe chill and nervous breakdown last Sunday night, although everything that loving hands could do or medical skill devise was done to avert the inevitable, they were equally of no avail. The great destroyer had placed His signet on his brow and today hundreds who loved and respected him living, mourn him dead.

There is no language at our command by which we can fittingly portray the sincerity of regret which his hundreds of friends express at his passing. He was one of the most unique and influential characters in this section of the state and one of the most trusted and outstanding men of his race in Oklahoma.

Funeral arrangements have been made as follows: Services at the home in East Chandler, Saturday afternoon at 3 o'clock. Interment in family plot at Newkirk, Oklahoma, Sunday morning at 11 o'clock.

The great sympathetic heart of Chandler goes out to Mrs. Sawner in the great loss she has sustained and to all the sorrowing ones sincere condolence.—*Chandler News-Publicist*[cdlxiii]

The Black Dispatch[cclxiv] also covered the Sawner funeral in an article entitled, *Entire State Mourns Death of Pioneer Citizen: Men and Women of Both Races Honor Fallen Leader; Body Enterred [sic] at Newkirk; Masons Have Charge of Funeral:*

CHANDLER, May 3 [1924]—Citizens, regardless of color, turned out in masse today to do honor to the late Hon. G.W.F. Sawner, who passed away in his home Thursday evening, as a result of kidney trouble that had affected him for some time. Early morning trains began to drop off delegations of race men from all sections of the state, and before the funeral services, which were held from the home, fully a hundred prominent Masons, Odd Fellows and Pythians, together with his immediate friends, had entered the city to join with his fellow townsmen in performing the last sad rites at the bier of one of Oklahoma's most prominent and useful pioneers.

Wife Prostrated.

Mrs. L. Lena Sawner, principal of the Chandler schools and wife of the deceased, was prostrated in the home and it was with difficulty that she was able to sustain herself during the funeral services that were conducted under the auspices of the Masonic order. Grand Master Webber was in charge, but delegated Attorney D.J. Wallace of Okmulgee as master of ceremonies. Wallace and Sawner had been close friends for more than thirty years. Wallace himself was almost in a state of hysteria during the services.

. . . .

Ship to Newkirk.

The remains were taken immediately from the home [and] shipped to Newkirk, [Oklahoma]. Both white and colored friends filled the long procession on its way to the depot through the principal street of the little village. Those chosen by the family to act as pallbearers were W.H. Twine, Muskogee; Roscoe Dunjee, Oklahoma City; S.F. Jordan, Guthrie; Dr. H.W. Conrad, Guthrie; D.J. Turner, Boley; E.I. Saddler, Tulsa. Mrs. Sawner, together with her immediate friends, [boarded] the 5 o'clock Frisco for Oklahoma City, where she remained thru Saturday night. The remains are to be interred in the family burial plot at Newkirk, the home of Mrs. Sawner's parents. cclxv

. . . .

As noted, pallbearers for George Sawner's Mason-supervised services included illustrious Oklahoma men of color: W.H. Twine (Muskogee); Roscoe Dunjee (Oklahoma City); S. Jordan (Guthrie); Dr. H.W. Conrad (Guthrie); D.J. Turner (Boley); and E.I. Saddler (Tulsa). Throngs of mourners, white and black, lined the streets as the funeral cortege moved from the Sawner family home, through Chandler, and onto a train for George's final ride north to Newkirk for burial.

Tributes to the fallen black hero comforted a grieving Mrs. Sawner. Whit and Maggie Ellis expressed their sorrow and well wishes, as did Langston President Inman E. Page. The Business League of Tulsa sent flowers, and the Muskogee Business League sent a resolution of condolence. Extension Secretary J.R.E. Lee noted: "We all regarded Mr. Sawner as one of the most important factors in Negro business." J.M. Marquess of Philadelphia, Pennsylvania, summed up the prevailing sentiments well: "Mr. Sawner was representative. He was the type the race so sorely needed to make the proper impression. He was capable, courageous, efficient, broadminded, farsighted and 'distinctive.' He was the rare exception both in society and in business."[cclxvi]

Correspondence from fellow men of the bar in Okmulgee and I.W. Lane[cclxvii] in Red Bird, respectively, both extolled George Sawner's virtues and captured the magnitude of the loss occasioned by his death.

Okmulgee, Okla., May 2, 1924.

Mme. G. W. F. Sawner,
Chandler, Oklahoma.

The striking down of your splendid husband in the prime of life and career, by the ever vigilant sentinel, death, was quite a blow to his race and friends, as well as to his family and surviving relatives. And with solemn reservation, the undersigned members of the Okmulgee bar, beg the acceptance of this wreath, and with it, our condolences, as a leading and most sacred tribute to his sterling qualities as a citizen, a lawyer, a business man, a husband and a race leader.

D.J. Wallace,
J.H. Stephens,
R.S. Gamble,
A.L.J. Merriweather

809 So. 18th Street,[cclxviii]

Red Bird, Okla., May 11, 1924.

Mrs. G.W.F. Sawner, Chandler, Oklahoma

Dear Mrs. Sawner:

This is to extend to you my heartfelt sympathy in your bereavement. Though I am not personally acquainted with you, only through your dear husband, I regret very much to hear of the death of Mr. Sawner. He was indeed a very great man and was much needed in this community. His worth in the business world among our people is untold, but we must all bow to the will of the Almighty   God who doeth all things well. All the good people of Red Bird join me in this word of consolation in your bereavement. May [his] will be done on earth as it is in heaven.

Yours in His name,
I.W. Lane.[cclxix]

The loss of her soulmate devastated Mrs. Sawner.[cclxx] George Sawner's funeral program closed with fitting solemnity and resolve in the form of a poem by Alfred, Lord Tennyson (1809 – 1892), a Poet Laureate of the United Kingdom, and a special note from Mrs. Sawner:

Crossing the Bar

Sunset and evening star,
    And one clear call for me;
And may there be no moaning of the bar
    When I put out to sea.

But such a time as moving seems asleep,
    Too full for sound and foam,
When that which drew from out the boundless deep
    Turns again home.

Twilight and evening bell,
    And after that the dark;
And may there be no sadness of farewell
    When I embark.

For, though from out our bourne of time and place,
    The flood may bear me afar,
I hope to see my pilot face to face
    When I have crossed the bar.

--Tennyson

In loving remembrance of my darling husband,
L. LENA SAWNER. [cclxxi]

For years after the death of George Sawner, Mrs. Sawner paid tribute to him in *The Black Dispatch* during the month of his death. She placed his photo, accompanied by a poem, in the paper. This was her way of reminding readers of her deep and undying love for her late husband. [cclxxii]

In 1931, Lena Sawner contributed the following poem, together with a picture of her late husband, to *The Black Dispatch*:

IN MEMORIAM
MAY 1

1924   1931

He still seems near
Constant as one of nature's laws
So that I seem to hear him breathe, as here I pause!
And do the dead we love go far away
And never make return? Can it be true
They never come again? No; truth to say
They come again to us and oft renew—
Unseen, unheard,—the vanished moments few.
And thus it is with us. My solitude
Is oft disturbed, and he in life I knew
Sits with me in the hours I watch and brood
Groping in silence after life's eternal good.

T. Thomas Fortune.

A TRIBUTE OF LOVE TO THE MEMORY OF A BELOVED HUSBAND.

L. LENA SAWNER. [cclxxiii]

George Sawner, being a prudent lawyer and business magnate, prepared for his death with a carefully crafted will, pursuant to which Mrs. Sawner served as executrix. The estate closed on March 26, 1927.

Mr. Sawner left the lion's share of his holdings to Mrs. Sawner, including property in Lincoln, Okfuskee, Wagoner, and Oklahoma counties. The Wagoner County property included a one-half interest in a cotton gin in Red Bird. He also bequeathed Mrs. Sawner numerous shares of stock in various businesses, including a realty company, the Farmers Co-operative Gin Company, Farmers & Merchant's Bank in Boley, a mining company, and various oil and gas companies. She inherited his accounts receivable—the dozen-or-so debts owed by various individuals (including W.H. Twine), as well as a damage claim in the amount of $9,815 against the Missouri-Kansas-Texas Railroad, known as MKT or, simply, the "Katy."

Mr. Sawner left $500 to Juanita Sawner, his daughter from his

George W.F. Sawner and Lena Sawner,
circa 1923

marriage to Ida Ferrell. He bequeathed $100 to Bessie Allen, another daughter from a different, as yet undocumented, relationship.[cclxxiv]

Thanks in part to George Sawner's astute estate planning, Mrs. Sawner remained on firm financial footing well after his passing. She felt no economic urgency to remarry. Independent in mind and means, she could afford to wait, and she did just that.[cclxxv]

Despite the deep emotional wound occasioned by her husband's passing, Mrs. Sawner found solace among friends and family. Virtually everyone associated with Douglass School, her pride and joy, could be considered both.

Chapter Four: The Lady Lena Sawner

The paradox of education is precisely this—that as one begins to become conscious one begins to examine the society in which he is being educated. — James A. Baldwin

Lena Lowery Sawner, *circa* 1925

An olive-skinned lady of African extraction strikes a majestic pose, resplendent in a flowing, purple frock. A plumed, wide-brimmed hat crowns this picture of refinement. Head cocked back, eyes fixed forward, she exudes self-assurance. She radiates "hattitude"—a kind of headwear-inspired confidence and panache common among church-going black women.[cclxxvi]

Polished and poised, she looks like misplaced royalty—a woman from and of another place and time. She epitomizes the idealized queen; magnanimous, the undisputed ruler of her realm. This empress, she of impeccable pedigree and refinement, is Lena Sawner, a master educator and children's champion; an effortless ambassador for positive black/white race relations; a woman of style and substance.

Lena Sawner, with her unmistakable bearing and inescapable charm, gave blackness a new face in Oklahoma. Her physical appearance afforded her unusual entrée into the white world. Mrs. Sawner's ability to sustain a presence in that rarefied universe and to leverage her special connections so as to benefit the black community depended upon something more than skin deep. Her personal attributes—her character—counted.

She connected. She spoke perfect English perfectly, nary a shade of Southern accent or a hint of black dialect.[cclxxvii] Her medium-pitched, pleasant voice catered to context, flowing fluidly from conversational to commanding.[cclxxviii] When this ace elocutionist spoke, people listened.

She engaged. She moved with circumspection, exuding a sophisticated innocence. Wherever she went, Mrs. Sawner lit up the room. She captured the hearts, minds, and imaginations of her charges, convincing them that all things were indeed possible. Under her guidance and tutelage, they took flight and soared. Unforgettable: that is what she was.

She nurtured. Mrs. Sawner's love of children knew no bounds.[cclxxix] She dedicated her professional and personal life to shaping future generations. She invested wisely in the most precious of resources.

Mrs. Sawner's standards of excellence extended to all facets of her life. Conventional wisdom holds that one never gets a second chance to make a good first impression. Mrs. Sawner seldom, if ever, required a do-over.

This woman of substance maintained a reputation for style. The epitome of elegance and class, she donned cosmopolitan clothes, dabbed on Parisian perfumes,[cclxxx] and sported glamorous jewelry. Artifacts maintained by the LCHS Museum of Pioneer History confirm Mrs. Sawner's penchant for *haute couture* and other trappings of wealth: velvet gowns, elaborate daywear, ornate jewelry, expensive furs, lace-trimmed silk lingerie, and silver monogrammed bathroom accessories.[cclxxxi]

A woman of her stature required an appropriate, crowning brim to be fully and properly dressed. Mrs. Sawner's hats—masterpieces that they were—favored form over function. Her beautiful chapeaus, often the *pièce de résistance* and fit for a sovereign, radiated determination, daring, and, sometimes, just a wee bit of devilishness.

Mrs. Sawner's head coverings added a whimsical flourish that capped off her colorful fashion sense. Some of her trademark hats boasted ostrich plumes valued at as much as $30—over $350 dollars in today's money.[cclxxxii]

Her creative crowns revealed a side of her personality and, more broadly, a dimension of black women, often unrecognized amidst the blindness of racial stereotyping. Regularly relegated to marginalized roles as mammies and maids in the public consciousness of the time, black women could also be objects of beauty and desire.[cclxxxiii]

Ladies like Mrs. Sawner sported hats during all seasons, a proper topper for all moods and all functions: the church lady, the mourner, the stroller, the mother, the temptress, the socialite, the laborer, and the housewife. Treasured headpieces became family heirlooms, diadems of the dispossessed, proudly passed from one generation to the next.

Mrs. Sawner's upscale tastes did not end with voguish clothing and stylish jewelry. Fiercely independent and a woman of particular preferences, her relative wealth accommodated all manner of peccadillos and indulgences. Her stylish automobile could be counted

Lena Lowery Sawner (1874 – 1949)[cclxxxv]

among such personal privileges. At a time when relatively few in Chandler drove cars (and, with respect to women, fewer still), Mrs. Sawner took the wheel of one of the finest automobiles in town.[cclxxxiv]

As was the case with so many well-heeled women of her era, Mrs. Sawner's rich community life included participation in a host of charitable endeavors and social and civic clubs. In the mid-1930s, she joined an exclusive local women's club that implemented and maintained a strict dress code. On pain of a five-dollar fine, the club's fashion protocol required members to dress in black apparel at all meetings. All but one club member complied with the club's narrow, limiting strictures on appropriate dress for meetings. Lena Sawner, the lone dissenter, chose a mild form of civil disobedience.

Mrs. Sawner preferred brightly colored clothing. Though always dressed to the nines, she refused to wear black, and most especially upon command. She appeared at regular club meetings in her reds and yellows and greens and blues and, primary among them, her prized purple, standing out against the sea of black like coffee on a freshly pressed white shirt.

At each gathering, Mrs. Sawner, this prismatic non-conformer, placed her five-dollar fine on the table in full view of her suddenly silent sisters, and then proceeded directly to her seat. The dress code remained intact. So, too, did Mrs. Sawner's principles and preferences. She managed to hold on to her independence while simultaneously surrendering to the prescribed order.[cclxxxvi]

Mrs. Sawner's leanings toward luxury could easily have been taken as a sign of arrogance and elitism. Those closest to her made no such miscalculation. The woman they knew wore grace and humility as though they, too, were fashion-forward accessories.[cclxxxix]

Two examples demonstrated the exceptional compassion and humanity Mrs. Sawner effortlessly exemplified. One instance involved the family of a Douglass student, Booker Smith, whose family fell upon hard times. Young Booker showed up for school several consecutive days sporting the same tattered, dingy shirt, likely the only one he owned. Mrs. Sawner, concerned about Booker's welfare, took the self-conscious child aside for a private conversation. The two chatted briefly before Mrs. Sawner hammered home her critical take-away.

"You may just have one shirt, Booker, but it must always be clean; your clothes may be old, but they must never be dirty," she gently, but firmly, instructed. "Yes, Ma'am, Mrs. Sawner," a sheepish Booker replied. Like a mother in the moment, she immediately diffused the uncomfortable encounter by providing Booker with another shirt. She asked the boy to change into the new top and leave his old shirt with her. She washed and returned it. Young Booker learned that poverty should never be used as an excuse for a lack of personal pride.

In yet another show of magnanimity, Mrs. Sawner offered selections from her book collection to individuals in Chandler who indicated a particular interest in a career-related subject matter. Those who took advantage of her generosity did so without a *quid pro quo* or the expectation that the books be returned. Mrs. Sawner found fulfillment in the knowledge that she had helped the recipient advance him/herself.[ccxc]

Lena Sawner, pictured without one of her trademark, ubiquitous "crowns."[cclxxxvii]

Lena Sawner and dear friend, "adopted daughter," Nellie ("Nell") Beridon (Turner), *circa* 1924.[cclxxxviii]

Just as Mrs. Sawner's epicurean tastes coexisted with genuine human compassion, her attachment to elegance in no way diminished her intellectual gravitas. Rather, her gentility, including her embrace life's luxuries, enhanced her professional stature and personal standing, providing an opportunity for more people to notice her brilliance.

A February 18, 1909, letter of recommendation from James Brooks Ayers Robertson, a Chandler lawyer with the law firm Hoffman & Robertson, to the Honorable E.D. Cameron, State Superintendent in Guthrie, praised Mrs. Sawner's sagacity:

> The bearer of this letter, Mrs. Lena Sawner, is Principal of our colored schools and has occupied this position for several years, (and, coincidentally, she will likely continue in her present position so long as she desires.) She is a very successful teacher and has the love and respect and exercises the most perfect control of her pupils. She is an exceptionally well educated woman and her reputation for morality and high ideals, good citizenship, etc., is of the very best. She is capable of holding a chair in any of the higher institutions of learning. She is entitled to the most favorable consideration of your honorable board, to whom, I am informed, she is making application for a life certificate. Any favors shown her will be

duly appreciated and I am sure no one will ever have cause to regret any aid they may render to this deserving teacher. With best wishes, I beg to remain, Yours Obediently. J.B.A. Robertson.[ccxci]

J.B.A. Robertson became the fourth governor of the State of Oklahoma (1919-1923), presiding over the state during the calamitous 1921 Tulsa Race Riot.[ccxcii] Others joined Governor Robertson in singing Mrs. Sawner's praises.

J.H. Bayes, Superintendent of Schools, Chandler (February 8, 1909), and H.G. Stettmund, Oklahoma State Representative, Chandler, Lincoln County (February 8, 1909) offered similarly glowing tributes.[ccxiv] Additional honors followed.

Mrs. Sawner earned a reputation as an educational

Oklahoma Governor James B.A. Robertson[ccxciv] guru, a master teacher and school administrator. She even instructed other Oklahoma educators at the Langston "Summer Normal."[ccxcv] On July 27, 1911, attorney and banker Lee Cruce, in his capacity as the second Governor of the State of Oklahoma, appointed Mrs. Sawner as a delegate to the National Negro Educational Congress, held in Denver, Colorado, August 12–15, 1911.[ccxcvi]

Lena Sawner, bold, black, and beautiful, rose to these heights in a most antipathetic environment for African Americans. Indeed, she emerged as a true wonder of the West: an educator extraordinaire in an all-black school in white-dominated, small-town Oklahoma; a one-of-a-kind community ambassador on matters of race.

In a 2015 retrospective on her life, *The Lincoln County News* lauded Mrs. Sawner as an "educator and socialite" who "[led] the effort to transfer the negative energy of segregation and racism into a positive force for improving performance in the black community."[ccxcvii]

Lena Sawner, like the trains on the railroad tracks that racially bisected so many American towns, moved between the black and white communities, ready, willing, and able to reach out and touch people on either side. Her near-transcendence in racially antagonistic times set her apart. Her provenance helps explain her suitability for the role of race ambassador.

Lena Lowery Sawner, the daughter of Priscilla and Julius Lowery, [ccxcviii] rose from humble beginnings. Her mother, Priscilla Crane, born in Richmond, Indiana, on May 22, 1856, married Julius Lowery on October 17, 1873, in Dover, Indiana. Priscilla was seventeen. Julius Lowery, born into slavery on March 10, 1846, near Greensboro, North Carolina, served in a non-combat role with the Union Army during the Civil War.

Lena Lowery came of age in the wake of the Civil War. Born in 1874 in Richmond, Indiana, [ccxcix] her formative years coincided with the wane of the golden age of Reconstruction (1865–1877), an era marked by the rebuilding and re-ordering of the decimated American South. The nation undertook affirmative measures (arguably, *half-measures*) to weave African Americans into the social, political, and economic tapestry of the South. The vanquished South, whose fortunes rested upon the flawed foundation of chattel slavery and its accompanying white supremacist ideology, had long resisted efforts to assimilate African Americans. [ccc] For African Americans, Reconstruction opened a brief window of promise and possibility. [ccci]

Reconstruction officially ended with the withdrawal of all federal troops from the South in 1877. As white dominance reemerged, African Americans surrendered many of their cherished civil and political rights. Economic marginalization accelerated.

Still, kernels of racial equality had become embedded in the American soil. Lena Lowery and others African Americans like her cultivated the generations-old cash crop that had just begun to flower: a true and enduring sense of black humanity that blossomed in direct proportion to recognition of full American citizenship.

"Colored," "mulatto," "Negro," or "black" in a world marked by white hegemony, Lena Sawner deftly gravitated between the white and black spheres, not without occasional objection, but always with a modicum of success. Hers was not the life of the classic "tragic mulatto" [cccii] —the self-doubting, self-loathing mixed-breed aching for acceptance. She bore little in common with the women derided in a *New York Times* article published in 1874, the year of her birth.

No close observer who visits Huntsville [Alabama] on 'nigger day' can fail to appreciate the significance of the term 'colored women...' I saw one or two young women whose cream-like complexion would have justly excited the envy of many a New York belle. The condition of the women of the latter class is most deplorable. Beautiful almost beyond description, many of them educated and refined, with the best white blood of the South in their veins, it is perhaps only natural that they should refuse to mate themselves with coarse and ignorant black men. Socially they are not recognized by the whites; they are often without money enough to buy the barest necessities of life; honorably they can never procure sufficient means to gratify their luxurious tastes; their mothers have taught them how to sin; fathers they never know; debauched white men are ready to take advantage of their destitution, and after living a short life of shame and dishonor they sink into early and unhallowed graves. Living they were despised by whites and blacks alike, dead they are mourned by none.[ccciii]

Others shared the writer's conception of how black women of "cream-like complexion" lived, moved, and had their being. The lives this editorialist and others of his ilk[ccciv] imagined for black women with "the best white blood of the South in their veins," lives filled with debauchery, dishonor, and disrespect, scarcely reflected the life Lena Sawner led. She fully embraced her blackness, but refused to be limited or defined by it.

Lena Sawner's parents, the Lowerys, lived in Dover, Indiana, until 1888, at which time they purchased a farm near Arkansas City, Kansas. Julius Lowery took part in the September 16, 1893, opening of the eastern Cherokee Outlet, the largest land run in the United States.[cccv] The Lowerys secured a homestead some six miles west of Newkirk on which they operated a successful farm.

In addition to farming, Mr. Lowery dove into local politics. The *Newkirk Demo-*

Beatrice Williams, left, and Lena Lowery (Sawner), right, *circa* 1910.[cccviii]

crat reported on an October 26, 1894, meeting of Kay County African American voters at which participants elected Julius Lowery of Vernon Township chairman of "the wide awake colored political club."[cccvi]

Lena Lowrey accompanied her parents to Newkirk in the early 1890s. She graduated from high school in the southwestern Kansas town of Arkansas City, and, according to a newspaper account, went on to attain her A.B. degree from the University of Chicago.[cccvii] She lived a charmed life.

Mr. Lowery proved to be a proficient provider. The fact that his daughter posed for studio portraits, a signal of relative privilege, attests to Mr. Lowery's success and standing. Indeed, one of Oklahoma's best-known frontier photographers, William S. Prettyman, captured an image of a nubile, creamy-complexioned beauty named Lena Lowery in 1895. Prettyman owned a photography studio in Arkansas City, Kansas, and gained fame for his pictures of cowboys along the Cherokee Strip and various Native American tribes in Indian Territory.[cccx]

Mr. Prettyman's 1895 studio portrait is but one of several studio photographs and snapshots taken of Lena Lowery Sawner during her lifetime. Mrs. Sawner and her family prized the ability to preserve images for posterity through the relatively new medium of photography and possessed the financial wherewithal to purchase professional portraits and newfangled cameras, the latter doubling as both as luxury items and cutting-edge technological devices.[cccxi]

The America in which Mrs. Sawner began her professional life in turn-of-the-century Chandler seemed but a distant relative to the America of her birth—the America of her parents. Race mattered mightily, but opportunity loomed amidst the tumult of the times.

At the dawn of the twen-

Lena Lowery, 1895[cccix]

tieth century, political upheaval, economic uncertainty, and technological innovation dominated the national spotlight. America grap-
pled with existential questions.

An assassin's bullet felled President William McKinley on September 14, 1901. Theodore Roosevelt and William Howard Taft followed as Commanders-in-Chief. Civil rights and human rights questions loomed on the home front as Jim Crow laws and race-based
violence plagued the nation. Materialism and consumerism took
hold as mass production pushed prices down to all-time lows. Congress enacted food safety and environmental laws.

Job openings for secretarial services proliferated. The St. Louis World's Fair opened in 1904. Americans ranked the Bible as the
most-read book. The Sears, Roebuck & Company and Montgomery
Ward catalogs, respectively, followed in popularity. "Teddy" became
a bear—and a runaway national fad.

Technology shrank the world: Henry Leland founded Cadillac in
1902. The Wright Brothers took flight in 1903. Radio communication
mushroomed.[cccxiii]

As Lena Sawner began her teaching career in the first decade
of the twentieth century, yet another revolutionary development
had begun: the progressive education movement.[cccxiv] John Dewey
founded a laboratory school at the University of Chicago that took
a student-centric approach to learning, less regimented and more
democratic. Italian educator and physician, Maria Montessori, pio-
neered her trademark "Montessori method," an approach to learning
characterized by emphasis on independence, freedom within limits,
and respect for a child's natural psychological, physical, and social
development.[cccxv]

High schools, begun some twenty years prior, continued to expand
across the country. Junior high schools followed. A flood of immigrants
posed new challenges. Teacher education improved.[cccxvi] Annual
teacher pay during for the decade hovered around $325.[cccxvii] Testing
became the norm. The Association of American Universities formed
in 1900 to promote high standards among colleges.[cccxviii]

Philanthropists Julius Rosenwald, John D. Rockefeller, Sr., and
Anson Phelps Stokes called for improvements in African American
education as a system of separate-and-unequal racial segregation
enveloped the country.[cccxix] Mary McLeod Bethune, educator, civil
rights leader, and advisor to President Franklin Delano Roosevelt,
opened the first school for African American girls in Daytona Beach,
Florida. That school evolved into Bethune-Cookman University.[cccxx]

Prior to statehood, Oklahoma's leading white citizens tele-graphed their intentions to make the new state a bastion of segrega-tion. The initial Oklahoma Territorial Legislature, convened in 1890, banned race-mixing in public schools. Laws prohibited blacks and whites from attending the same school and forbade anyone teaching pupils of the "opposite race." Counties levied property taxes used for a County Separate School Fund. The fund paid for any separate facilities and teachers deemed necessary in each county. In Oklahoma Territory, the first separate schools—schools designated for African Americans only—opened in Oklahoma City and Guthrie in 1891 and in Kingfisher in 1892.

Townsfolk in Chandler initially opted for integrated schools at-tended by whites, blacks, and Indians. Later, in about 1896, town leaders established a separate school for "Colored" children. This school apparently became Douglass School sometime just after the turn of the century.[cccxxi]

Variations on the theme of the one-room schoolhouse[cccxxii] dotted the segregated landscape of rural Oklahoma in the early part of the twentieth century. These educational citadels, prominent throughout the United States in its early history, evoke bucolic reminiscences of simpler times.[cccxxiii] Philosophically, the one-room schoolhouse pre-saged the modern "community school,"[cccxxiv] taking more holistic view of education.

Like Douglass School, many one-room schoolhouses arose to sat-isfy separate school laws that denied African Americans access to bet-ter-funded white public school district facilities. Though underfund-ed and marginalized, these ragtag institutions regularly churned out capable and confident black students.

When Lena Lowery accepted a teaching position at Douglass School in Chandler in 1902, Douglass ranked as one of only six "Col-ored" schools in Oklahoma Territory. At the time of her arrival, a scant six students attended Douglass School, initially convened at a local church.

At first, Douglass welcomed only first through eighth-graders. According to a newspaper account, the original dry pine structure burned in an apparent arson fire in 1908, and a "new and more com-modious building" followed.[cccxxv] In 1911, the school added grades nine through twelve. In 1912, builders added another two rooms to the one-story, two-room facility. The first graduating class in 1915 in-cluded four students.[cccxxvi] In 1922, a larger brick building replaced the old structure, and workmen added a gymnasium to the school in

1927.

Throughout Douglass's early years, Oklahoma officials crowed about the wonders of segregated schools. In a September 15, 1902, report, the governor of Oklahoma Territory, Thompson Benton Ferguson, gloated: "Throughout Oklahoma a system of separate schools is now maintained with perfect satisfaction to the races. The advantages offered are identical and the system is generally popular." The next year, Governor Ferguson proclaimed: "The separate school law is working very satisfactorily. Last year there was some misunderstanding of its provisions. It takes some time for a law to become effective."[cccxvii]

Lena Lowery wed George Sawner in 1903. Her profile only grew. The couple soon joined the power elite in Oklahoma, as defined by wealth, power, influence, and reputation.

Despite the blind and irrational adherence to color-coded customs in the South and in Chandler, the Sawners broke new ground. Mrs. Sawner earned universal respect as a leading Chandler educator. George Sawner rose to prominence as a property owner with real estate on Chandler's main thoroughfare, Manvel Avenue,[cccxviii] and as a multi-talented business leader and public servant.

The Chandler News reported that the twosome concealed their betrothal and nuptials for months:

> It has recently become known that G. W. F. Sawner and Miss Lena Lowery have been married for several months but have succeeded until the close of the school here in keeping the fact a secret from their friends. Miss Lowery has for two years past been the teacher in the colored school here and there is probably not a more successful school in the teritory [sic] than hers. Mr. Sawner is one of the most intelligent and progressive colored men in the territory. He is a practicing attorney and a successful business man and is prominent in political affairs. The friends of the couple extend hearty congratulations.[cccxxix]

After the marriage, Mrs. Sawner created an enduring mystery when she, Lena Lowery Sawner, inexplicably began signing her name "L. Lena Sawner." No matter how she signed her new name or why she signed it as she did, Lena Sawner, by virtue of the marriage, emerged an even more formidable force in Chandler and beyond.

During the first years of the twentieth century, an increasing number of black teachers entered the Oklahoma marketplace, in large measure due to the emergence of present-day Langston University and the fact that some counties had begun permitting Negroes to attend the annual, four-week County Normal Institute held in each county.

Despite this influx of new Negro teachers, the education market never fully opened. Oklahoma Territory leaders continued to salute school segregation. In a 1905 report to Governor Ferguson, Territorial Superintendent L.W. Baxter touted the success of segregation in Oklahoma Territory:

> Probably no other State or Territory has built as strong a barrier against mixed schools . . . . If there should be one Negro child in a district, provision must be made for its common school education by the establishment of a school, the employment of a tutor, sending the child at district's expense to an adjoining district where a school is established or sending the child to the Territorial school at Langston.[cccxxx]

Activists formed associations for Negro teachers in both Indian and Oklahoma Territory to address the needs of these separate and unequal schools. At statehood in 1907, the Oklahoma Constitution carried forward the concept of race advanced in pre-statehood Oklahoma Territory. As defined, race became a binary construct: "The term 'colored children'. . . shall be construed to mean children of African descent. The term 'white children' shall mean all other children.[cccxxxi] This one-drop rule in effect labeled as toxic and subject to educational sequestration any person "infected" with African blood.

In 1907, Mrs. Sawner and several dozen black teachers came together at what is now Langston University to create a statewide advocacy group devoted to raising the standards of education for black children. While some black schools succeeded against the long odds, segregated black schools routinely lagged behind their white counterparts in enrollment, funding, facilities, materials and supplies, teacher training, and student retention in the higher grades, all the while operating under externally imposed limitations on curriculum.[cccxxxii]

Inman E. Page, then in his ninth year as president of the host institution, convened the meeting that gave birth to the Oklahoma Association of Negro Teachers ("O.A.N.T."). O.A.N.T. led the charge to improve educational outcomes for black children and youth with a focus on pedagogy and increased funding for separate schools. It raised questions of parity and fairness, even at the risk of adverse political, social, and economic consequences.[cccxxxiii] Mrs. Sawner served on the O.A.N.T. executive committee alongside heavyweights like

Inman Edward Page (1853 – 1935), the inaugural President of Langston University.[cccxxxv]

Sign for "White" and "Colored" drinking fountains.[cccxxxvi]

E.W. Woods, principal of Tulsa's Booker T. Washington High School.[cccxxxiv]

Mrs. Sawner's leadership on the educational front helped rouse Chandler from its slumber on race matters, a sleepy hamlet turned vibrant village. Chandler became an oasis of tolerance amidst a desert of unrelenting racial stratification; a unified, albeit imperfect, community. Elsewhere in state and nation, racial separation and, arguably, a racial caste structure, prevailed.

As the surge toward Oklahoma statehood intensified, so, too, did the push for racial segregation in the public square. At statehood, Jim Crow measures proliferated, many enacted into law, others understood as a matter of custom and enforced, if need be, through extra-legal means.[cccxxxvii]

Though positive interracial interactions and relationships seemed to be the norm in Chandler, the town, like so many other places in America, abided a sort of formal social apartheid that prevailed beyond the segregated schools. Chandler establishments sported signs designating separate areas and facilities for its "Colored" citizens. Townsfolk for a time even maintained separate water dippers, one marked "Colored," the other marked "White," for a common bucket of water.

Like their brothers and sisters in the Deep South, black citizens in Oklahoma Territory accepted the "separate but equal" regime, sometimes grudgingly and under protest—a scheme markedly unequal until its bitter end. Pernicious racial discrimination in all facets of life prevailed in a large swath of the country. So, too, did gender inequality.

Women faced overt discrimination and the denial of basic civil rights. Black women like Lena Sawner thus faced a double whammy,[cccxxxviii] as both race and gender severely constricted their social, political, and economic possibilities. Despite external constraints in an era oblivious to diversity and inclusion, Mrs. Sawner fashioned a life festooned with success and acclaim.

Polite society considered teaching to be an honorable profession for women.[cccxxxix] For African American women, teaching took on a noble, munificent quality given the realities of race, including, but not limited to, educational apartheid.[cccxl]

> By the turn of the 20th century, nearly 75 percent of America's teachers were women. But women made up a far smaller percentage of administrators, and their power decreased with each higher level of authority. Their deportment had always been closely watched; increasingly their work in the schoolroom was not only scrutinized, but rigidly controlled. Teacher autonomy was on the decline, and teachers resented it.
>
> . . . .
>
> African-American teachers especially suffered from inadequate materials and funding. Though their communities were eager for schooling, teachers found that money was rarely abundant. Well into the 20th century, black school systems relied on hand-me-down textbooks and used equipment, discarded by their white counterparts. African American teachers were usually paid significantly less than their white peers and their civil rights were often compromised.[cccxli]

Despite challenges on the accessibility and equity fronts, many African Americans still viewed education, an engine of social progress to which they had regularly and routinely been denied the keys, as the essential driving force behind racial uplift.

> Individuals are generally educated for their intended roles in society. Education, called one of the 'essential amenities of human progress,' has historically been withheld from African Americans as a means to keep them under control. Concurrently, blacks have waged a long-standing battle to attain equal education and full socioeconomic mobility.[cccxlii]

Scholar and social activist W.E.B. Du Bois echoed this view, with emphasis on the subversive power of an educated mind: "[Th]e South believed an educated Negro to be a dangerous Negro. And the South was not wholly wrong; for education among all kinds of men always had, and always will have, an element of danger and revolution, of dissatisfaction and discontent."[cccxliii]

The Sawners melded the oft-contrasted approaches to black up-lift attributed to Booker T. Washington and Dr. W.E.B. Du Bois, a difference in views that forged a still-raging, souls-deep schism among black intelligentsia. The former voiced a subtle, nuanced approach to social change with an emphasis of self-help, education, and training, sometimes derided as accommodation and gradualism. Dr. Du Bois focused on the immediate need for political agitation, a kind of full-court press toward black civil rights and full American citizenship; a shot across the bow at engrained institutional barriers to black progress.[cccxliv] Though the Washingtonian, bottom-up, strategy for racial uplift struck some as being at odds with the top-down, Du Boisian model (*e.g.*, Talent Tenth), both men set out to disprove the ultimate lie: the white supremacist notion of black inferiority and pathogenicity. That falsehood underlay educational segregation, a system that shortchanged black children.

Positionally, Lena Sawner seemed a quintessential Tenth-type. Her consummate professionalism challenged the status quo. She possessed the social and psychological grounding necessary to counter the prevailing black inferiority myth and its accompanying physical privations. She impressed the powerful and privileged, and simultaneously inspired fellow African Americans. Her students came to believe themselves similarly capable of defying the odds and deflating their detractors. Moreover, she and George Sawner kept their eyes on the prize. They never stopped agitating and advocating for black civil rights.

Philosophically, though, Mrs. Sawner closely aligned with Booker T. Washington. She believed in self-help, and she saw education and economic empowerment as central to the evolution of African Americans.

Mrs. Sawner earned her Teacher's City Certificate from Chandler Public Schools in 1905 and additional credentials shortly thereafter. She expected as much from herself as she did from her students and, not surprisingly, attained high marks on all of her certification examinations. Teaching certificates from June 6, 1905, October 31, 1909, and January 25, 1917, attest to Mrs. Sawner's qualification for and mastery of her craft.[cccxlv]

The State of Oklahoma subjected its teachers to robust testing, stiffening certification requirements over the years so as to require encyclopedic knowledge of its would-be pedagogues. For example, the certification examination administered on April 26 - 28, 1928, covered a stunning breadth of disciplines: Oklahoma history and

No. 212

Instructor's Normal Institute Certificate

Expires Oct 31 1911

These Presents Declare, That _Lena Sawner_

having furnished satisfactory evidence of good moral character, and having shown superior ability and success as an educator is by order of the STATE BOARD OF EDUCATION granted this

Instructor's Normal Institute Certificate

which shall be valid in any County in the State of Oklahoma for a period of _two years_ from the date hereof unless revoked.

It is hereby certified that the holder has the following grades on each of the subjects named below:

American Literature	90	Psychology	98
English Literature	90	Rhetoric and Composition	89
History of Education	90	Theory and Practice	80

GIVEN UNDER OUR HANDS at Guthrie, Oklahoma, this 31st

day of October 1909

SECRETARY STATE BOARD OF EDUCATION

PRESIDENT

No. 737

State Board of Education

STATE OF OKLAHOMA

Conductor's Normal Institute Certificate

IS GRANTED THIS

Certificate

and is hereby authorized to teach in any Normal Institute in the State of Oklahoma subject to the conditions prescribed by the State Board of Education

This Certificate Issued the 25 day of Jan 1914 Expires the 1 day of Dec 1917

Douglass School, constructed *circa* 1910.

government; agriculture; domestic science; geography; grammar, penmanship; reading; United States history; arithmetic; physiology; music; composition; orthography; theory and practice; civil government; elementary psychology; American literature; general history; algebra; and physics.[cccxlvi]

The rigor of the certification process no doubt kept Mrs. Sawner and her Douglass teaching staff on their toes. So, too, did Mrs. Sawner's high personal standards and love for the children under her tutelage.

For much of her tenure at Douglass, Lincoln County powerbrokers afforded Mrs. Sawner virtual free reign. She and she alone captained the educational ship. This latitude and the nod of confidence it implied fostered creativity, vision, and impressive results.

Douglass School with second story addition, 1918.

Douglass School, 1922

Douglass School faculty, friends, and students; Lena Sawner, far left, front; George Sawner, in hat, second row, second from left, *circa* 1922.[cccxlvii]

Top teachers at Douglass School, from left to right, Francis Harold, George Alexander, Roberta Ellis, Unidentified, Maedella Summers, Nell Beridon, and Mrs. Sawner. 1924.[cccxlviii]

Douglass High School Senior Class of 1933: Back row, left-right—Jesse Armstead, _____ Hargrave, Abbey Henderson, Floyd Brown, and Leslie Austin; Front row, left-right—Unknown, Dillard Allen, Ora Ellis, Martha Franklin, and Charleslo Williams.

Douglass School Girls Basketball Team, 1925: (left-right) Ion Gates, Anna Merrill Sneed, Zelma Henderson, Olive Sneed, Mae Brown, Winnie Taylor, Alberta Flowers (holding basketball), Thelma Gordon, and Coach George Alexander.

Douglass School Boys Basketball Team, 1925: (left-right) John Benford, Steve Martin, Lee Long, Lewis Glover, Ovid Brown, and Adolph Sneed, Douglas High School, Chandler Oklahoma: *Photos courtesy the Ellis Family.*[cccxlix]

"The foundation of the State is the education of its youth." These words appear high above the front (east) entrance of the former Chandler High School (1942 – 1994), located at 515 Steele in the northwest section of Chandler. Black teens attended Chandler High School after the closing of Douglass in 1955 in the wake of nationwide, court-mandated school desegregation.

The building, constructed as an initiative of the Work Projects Administration (the "WPA," formerly, the Works Progress Administration) in 1941, became part of the National Register of Historic Places in 1996. An additional etched quotation appears above the south entrance: "Wisdom is the principal thing; therefore, get wisdom and with all thy getting, get understanding."[cccl]

First-rate all-black schools owed their successes, in large measure, to the art of individual leadership. Competence, confidence, and charisma characterized these exceptional chieftains. Mrs. Sawner possessed the kind of dynamic personal power that impressed and inspired.

Under the superintendence of Mrs. Sawner, Douglass grew from a tiny country schoolhouse with six students in 1902 to well-managed, fully accredited school in a brick building serving grades one through twelve. In fact, this little-school-that-could became one of the first black schools to gain accreditation from the State of Oklahoma after the vetting process began in 1916.

As previously noted, Mrs. Sawner, who served Douglass School for more than thirty years, stepped aside in 1934 as she began to lose her vision. She who, with near clairvoyance, saw the promise and possibility ahead for the black children of Chandler, would soon thereafter be blind.

Former Chandler High School, now Memorial School (1942 - 1994)

Mrs. Sawner recognized the stultifying contradictions she and her charges faced. The freedom, justice, and equality they studied in school existed for others, but not fully for them. These abstractions flew in the face of the tyranny of racism that mired their day-to-day lives. Still, she refused to allow the racist sentiments surrounding her to diminish her dignity or savage the self-worth of her students. She never lost hope.

Despite glaring race-based disparities in education, or, more likely, because of them, Mrs. Sawner went the extra mile for Chandler's African American kids. She epitomized the lofty standards she set for her pupils. She modeled the kind of walk-the-talk integrity she preached and, in the process, forever changed countless lives.

Teachers from other all-black schools in Lincoln County and in Oklahoma generally also benefitted from Mrs. Sawner's laser-like focus on pedagogy and substantive content. She recruited, trained, and mentored scores of them, including teachers from the nearby Dunbar School north of Wellston, Lincoln County's only Rosenwald School.[ccli]

During her three-plus decades as Douglass School principal, Lena Sawner shaped the lives of some two hundred children, the vast majority of whom emerged from the experience well educated and prepared for life. According to the Ellis family, one of the many families whose brood grew up under Mrs. Sawner, in excess of ninety percent of the Douglass School students who reached the ninth grade graduated from high school.[cclii] By way of comparison, the high school graduation rate in the United States in 1920 was 16.8 percent; in 1940, 50.8 percent.[ccliii] Mrs. Sawner's phenomenal success at grooming and graduating students dwarfed those of her contemporaries.

All ten Ellis children, the offspring of Whit and Maggie Ellis highlighted previously, benefited from Mrs. Sawner's teaching prowess. She commanded their respect. She demanded that they live up to their full potential. She encouraged pride in their black heritage. Mrs. Sawner's influence, coupled with a home life filled with motivation, support, and encouragement, led the Ellis offspring to remarkable heights and accomplishments in their adult lives.[cccliv]

For the many Chandler kids who lacked such a foundation, Mrs. Sawner became a bright and singular guiding light. By the time the Douglass School closed, she had left an indelible mark.[ccclv] Like the ripples of a rock skipped across the water, the multiplier effect of her life's work spanned generations.[ccclvi]

Mrs. Sawner's engagement with Chandler students and their families steeled her in difficult times. Those emotional valleys included the death of her husband, George, in 1924, and, later, the passing of her parents.

In 1927, her parents, Julius and Priscilla Lowery, by now in declining health, moved to Chandler to be with their daughter. On October 31, 1928, Julius Lowery died. Priscilla Lowery died a few years later, on October 21, 1931.[ccclvii] Lena Sawner soldiered on as a Chandler civic leader and philanthropist, believing, unflinchingly, in the transformative capacity of education and, possessed, critically, with the courage of her convictions. She leaned heavily upon her Christian faith to see her through trying times.

Priscilla Lowery's 1931 obituary in *The Chandler News-Publicist* chronicled her "beautiful Christian life," praised her as an inspiration to all whom she encountered. The obituary included a poem bearing the hallmark of Lena Sawner that extolled the virtues of "Mother":

Mother is not gone she is just away.
With a cheery, smile, and a wave of the hand,
She has wandered into an unknown land.
And left us dreaming how very fair
It needs must be since she lingers there.
So we think of her faring on as dear
In the love of There, as the love of Here.
So we think of her still as the same and say
Mother is not gone—she is just away.[ccclviii]

Despite life-altering deaths of those most dear to her, Mrs. Sawner continued to live her life in service to others: her Douglass School students, their families, and her community. Mrs. Sawner's dedication to education and community service[ccclix] inspired the people of Chandler.[ccclx]

During her tenure at Douglass School, Chandler grew. Word spread of the refined, exacting school headmistress who gave respect and demanded it. As the Douglass School student body expanded, Mrs. Sawner homed in on academic excellence

The home of George and Lena Sawner, Iowa Street, Chandler, Oklahoma, *circa* 1930s.[ccclxi]

while simultaneously stressing the need for social skills.

Douglass School continued to prosper after Mrs. Sawner's departure. In addition to its academic concentrations, the school offered a wide range of vocational options for students. Future school leaders internalized Mrs. Sawner's emphasis on academic excellence and, perhaps as a necessary consequence, suffered through athletic mediocrity.

George Sawner Ellis recalled his three-year membership on the hapless Douglass High School football team. This was no Hollywood, "Remember The Titans"-esque story of a charismatic coach who inspired an unlikely group of misfits and miscreants, who united a band of brothers in triumph on the gridiron. During Mr. Ellis's entire stint with the team, Douglass's motley crew managed no victories and only one goal crossing with the pigskin. That solitary touchdown came not from a well-executed play, but on a fumble recovery—a mistake on the other side. At Douglass, only one field of play really mattered: the classroom.

In the broad sweep of history, Douglass School spanned United States presidencies from Theodore Roosevelt (1901-1909) to Dwight D. Eisenhower (1953-1961), and, in Oklahoma, the tenures of the governors of Oklahoma Territory, Thompson Benton Ferguson (1901-1906) and Frank Frantz (1906-1907), through the term of the fifteenth governor of the State of Oklahoma, Raymond D. Gary (1955-1959). The school flourished during World War I, the Roaring Twenties, the Great Depression, the Dust Bowl, World War II, and other momentous events.

Lena Sawner influenced generations. She shared her infectious belief that education held the key to progress and prosperity. Her charm, charisma, and compassion enabled her to fuel her pupils with a set of fundamental values and ignite in them a passion for life and living. That is what made her so special.

Chapter Five: Mrs. Sawner's Laws

Education, then, beyond all other devices of human origin, is the great equalizer of the conditions of man. — Horace Mann

These photographs of Lena Sawner, *circa* 1920, illustrate her remarkable style and panache.[ccclxvi]

The Teacher

Lord, who am I to teach the way
To little children day by day,
So prone myself to go astray?

I teach them KNOWLEDGE, but I know
How faint they flicker and how low
The candles of my knowledge glow.

I teach them POWER to will and do,
But only now to learn anew
My own great weakness through and through.

I teach them LOVE for all mankind
And all God's creatures, but I find
My love comes lagging far behind.

Lord, if their guide I still must be,
Oh, let the little children see
The teacher leaning hard on Thee.[ccclxvii]

These undated photos of Lena Sawner appeared in *The Lincoln County News* on May 9, 1985, in connection with an article entitled, "Principal of first black high school 'exacting'." On the left, Mrs. Sawner is pictured with Nellie ("Nell") Beridon Turner from California, described as "like a daughter." On the right (a slightly different version of the picture that appears at the beginning of the chapter), in a photo courtesy of Mr. and Mrs. M.D. McCormick, Mrs. Sawner sports a satin dress, fur-collared coat, and plumed hat.[ccclxviii]

The Teacher captures the competence, confidence, and humility that defined Lena Sawner. She strove for perfection, yet realized the impossibility of its achievement. She began with an end in mind, but understood that critical life lessons would be gleaned from the journey itself. She recognized her gifts, but credited them to a higher power.

Black faith in the leveling capacity of education dates back to the African experience with American slavery. Slave-masters generally withheld access to education from those over whom they lorded, though they sometimes relented as a matter of self-interest. Some bondsmen pursued education surreptitiously. First-person accounts collected in the 1930s as part of the WPA Federal Writers' Project are illustrative.

> I learned to read, write and figger [*i.e.,* "figure"] at an early age. Master Brown's boy and I were the same age you see (14 years old) and he would send me to school to protect his kids, and I would have to sit up there until school was out. So while sitting there I listened to what the white teacher was telling the kids, and caught on how to read, write and figger—but I never let on.
>
> *Hal Hutson, Oklahoma City, Oklahoma.* [ccclxix]

> My father, he belonged to a doctor and the doctor, he was a kind of a wait man to him. And the doctor learnt [*i.e.,* "taught"] him how to read and write. Right after the War, he was a teacher. He was ready to be a teacher before most other people because he learnt to read and write in slavery. There were so many folks that came to see the doctor and wanted to leave numbers and addresses that he had to have someone to 'tend to that and he taught my father to read and write so that he could do it.
>
> *J.H. Curry, Washington, Arkansas* [ccclxx]

Once discovered, enslaved Africans who dared seek literacy often faced the brutality and barbarity of self-appointed masters. Sympathizers who aided and abetted these knowledge-seeking rebels did so at their own risk. [ccclxxi]

Carolyn A. Dorsey, writing for *The African American Experience,* noted: "Individuals are generally educated for their intended roles in society. Education, called one of the 'essential amenities of human progress,' has historically been withheld from African Americans as a means to keep them under control. Concurrently, blacks have waged a long-standing battle to attain equal education and full socioeconomic mobility." [ccclxxii]

The seeming herculean efforts to secure educational opportunities for African Americans could not be fully restrained. For generations of Americans, the surname Douglass captured the essence of the African American quest for equal dignity and humanity, in large measure through education. Douglass School's namesake, Frederick Douglass, exhorted his once-enslaved brothers and sisters to cast off the shackles of the mind through education.

In the 1880s, Jennie Dean, a Christian evangelist born in slavery in Prince William County, Virginia, joined other black citizens in lobbying for expanded higher education and vocational training for black youth. Wealthy white philanthropists supported the effort, but success required more than mere financial heft. Black families contributed money, labor, and goods in a show of grassroots community support.[ccclxxiii] It took a village.

On September 3, 1894, Frederick Douglass addressed a rapt audience at the dedication of the Manassas Industrial School:

Frederick Douglass[ccclxxiv]

To found an educational institution for any people is worthy of note; but to found a school in which to instruct, improve and develop all that is noblest and best in the souls of a deeply wronged and long neglected people, is especially noteworthy. This spot, once the scene of fratricidal war, and the witness of its innumerable and [indescribable] horrors, is, we hope to be hereafter the scene of brotherly kindness, charity and peace. We are to witness here a display of the best elements of advanced civilization and good citizenship. It is to be the place where the children of a once enslaved people may realize the blessings of liberty and education, and learn how to make for themselves and for all others the best of both worlds.[ccclxxv]

Educators like Lena Sawner became crucial agents of black social, economic, and political mobility in American society. Between the end of the Civil War in 1865 and the turn of the twentieth century, some 30,000 African Americans earned teaching credentials. These educators shepherded the black masses into the realm of formal learning. More than one-half of the African American population achieved literacy by 1900.[ccclxxvi]

Mrs. Sawner and her cohorts, pedagogues to the powerless, revolutionized the socioeconomic strata of the country. These champions of and catalysts for educational opportunities within the African American community undergirded the twentieth century civil rights movement.

Women like Mrs. Sawner entered teaching for myriad reasons, most prominently, the relative independence the profession offered.

> Despite the socially accepted middle-class stereotype of submissiveness, American women have persisted in seeking outlets for their individuality. For many white and black women, the teaching profession has served as a significant avenue for personal expression and independence outside the roles of wife and mother. Certainly this was true of Oklahoma female teachers during the first half of the twentieth century.[ccclxxvii]

Like Frederick Douglass, Mrs. Sawner believed in individual empowerment. She refused to allow her students to wallow in self-pity despite a long history of subjugation and maltreatment. She knew her Douglass students could, and on her watch would, excel, despite the gulf between their resources and those of their privileged white counterparts. Like a top-flight quartermaster, Mrs. Sawner took it upon herself to provide them with the armaments of confidence and skill needed to shield them from a too-often-bellicose world.

Mrs. Sawner believed in the power of education to mold and metamorphose malleable minds. She backed that fundamental belief with both her performance and her purse. She invested in Douglass School and the community it served.

Mrs. Sawner purchased books and materials for her students. She prepared Thanksgiving and Christmas dinners for children and families who might otherwise go without. Like a fairy godmother, she granted children's holiday wishes, chaperoning them on Christmastime shopping excursions to Oklahoma City. If only momentarily, such out-of-town trips to the big city for toys, trinkets, and treats transported these children to worlds beyond their everyday reach. Lena Sawner, a veritable saint by popular acclamation, went above and beyond, giving the most of herself to the least among others.[ccclxxviii]

Mrs. Sawner swore by early childhood education. Children, she thought, should start school when mature enough to learn: at age four, five, or six, depending upon the child. As a general rule, though, children started school at six or seven years of age and earned academic promotion through satisfactory performance. Underachieving students repeated grades.

Mrs. Sawner eliminated the eleventh grade for stellar students, allowing them to skip from grade ten to grade twelve.[ccclxxix] As a result of this accelerated learning policy and her innovative early education initiative, a number of Douglass students graduated by age sixteen.

Educators of her ilk and era prized literacy and formal education as means to an end: hoisting the destitute and denied from the depths of socioeconomic despair. Like Mrs. Sawner, many such educators employed a values-based pedagogy.

Mrs. Sawner harbored the near-heretical belief that all black children could achieve and excel. First, though, they needed to be free of the psychological chains of self-doubt linked to enslavement and its vestiges. Perhaps Carter G. Woodson, historian and author, said it best:

> If you can control a man's thinking, you don't have to worry about his actions. If you can determine what a man thinks you do not have worry about what he will do. If you can make a man believe that he is inferior, you don't have to compel him to seek an inferior status, he will do so without being told and if you can make a man believe that he is justly an outcast, you don't have to order him to the back door, he will go to the back door on his own and if there is no back door, the very nature of the man will demand that you build one.[ccclxxx]

Mrs. Sawner encouraged her Chandler children to think beyond the confines of their rural environs; to dream big. Indeed, at each weekly school assembly, she recounted her mantra: "In all thy getting, get understanding." That "understanding" included both an understanding of self and an understanding of the world each person must navigate.

There would be no back doors for Chandler's African American boys and girls. Mrs. Sawner would have none of that. What she preached—self-respect, self-love, and self-help—proved antithetical to the racialized psychosis of the shackled mind against which Dr. Woodson railed.

Mrs. Sawner coupled lessons on "how to do" with guidance on "how to be." The expansive list of how the Douglass kids *should* behave got the students' attention.

She led by example. Her students *should* keep themselves neat and clean. She did. Her students *should* aspire to something beyond that within their immediate grasp. She did. Her students *should* "walk circumspect"—carry themselves in a proud and dignified manner. She did. Her students *should* speak properly. She did.

Mrs. Sawner embraced a set of core beliefs, tacitly translating them into unwritten, informal mandates she applied to her teaching and school leadership. Like the ancient Code of Hammurabi[ccclxxxii] and other legal codes, these tacit canons of education helped shape relationships, promote order, and provide stability, all within the context of American-style educational apartheid.

Press reports offer a barometer of the efficacy of Mrs. Sawner's teaching methods and administrative prowess. Local media heaped mounds of praise on her Midas touch with black children. In 1905, *The Chandler Publicist* crowed:

> The [Douglass School] commencement exercises were unusually well arranged and presented. The credit of this is due to Mrs. Sawner. She has been a teacher of this school for three years....When one remembers that this colored school has been organized since the beginning of the town, and it is only within the past years while she has been here that there has been such development in this school, it can readily be seen that the credit is hers. Her influence is plain to be seen upon the children in their deportment in every respect.[ccclxxxiii]

The near-universal accolades showered on Mrs. Sawner invariably highlighted the performances of Douglass students. At annual commencement exercises, members of the small class of graduating Douglass seniors took to the stage. The brilliance of their performances only further cemented Mrs. Sawners stature as principal *par excellence.*

Just one year prior, in 1904, the Egbert Opera House, the largest available public facility in Chandler at the time,[ccclxxxiv] hosted the commencement ceremonies for both Chandler High School, the "white" school, and Douglass School, the "black" school. Local newspapers raved about the Douglass School services: "The Egbert opera house was packed to the doors last Saturday night by our citizens who came to witness the commencement exercises of the Chandler colored schools. It was the biggest crowd that has ever assembled in the new opera house."[ccclxxxv]

Douglass School held subsequent graduation rites in other prominent public accommodations in Chandler. For example, the Lincoln County Courthouse hosted the 1921 services in its district courtroom. ccclxxxvi Such welcome access to the town's prized edifices was, in an era of rampant and rigid segregation, exceedingly rare. Chandler opened her doors even as other communities closed the gates on those whom they deemed unworthy of full equality.

Mrs. Sawner made the best of Chandler's warmth. She never rested on her laurels. Year in, year out, brilliant student performances punctuated carefully crafted graduation exercises. Valedictory and salutatory addresses, interspersed with song selections and various drills, thrilled audiences. A local paper described the featured addresses in 1919 as "splendid examples of youthful oratory, showing careful and judicious training." That same news outlet lauded Mrs. Sawner, noting that she had "given most general satisfaction at the head of the Douglass High School and her merit has been recognized by other cities of the state, as one of the foremost educators of her race."ccclxxxviii

While the Chandler press poured plaudits on Mrs. Sawner, some early voices among the chorus of praise singers flatly revealed notes of racial condescension.

> All in all, these exercises were unusually well arranged and presented, and too much credit cannot be given to the teacher, Miss Lena Lowery, whose untiring labor brought the term to such a successful climax. She has been in charge of the school the past two years, and surely it is in good hands. If all colored schools could be blessed with teachers like her the 'race problem' would soon solve itself.ccclxxxix

Mrs. Sawner insisted that her students outperform white students who attended better-resourced schools and who faced fewer outside obstacles to academic achievement. They obliged, and kudos for Mrs. Sawner crescendoed.

> As a whole the program was unusually well planned and carried out. It is conceded here that Mrs. Sawner who is principal [f]ar excels the white schools in the class of work given the pupils, and as for her programs they far excel those given by the whites and this they concede. Mrs. Sawner has been the principal here for several years and so well has she done the work, and with so much esteem is she held by both races, that it would be impossible for [anyone] to super[s]

ede her. The summer school at Langston and Mus[k]ogee are both asking for her services this summer, showing that all over the state she is recognized for her intelligence and leadership in school work.[cccxc]

Douglass School patrons presented Lena Sawner with this loving cup inscribed: "Presented to Mrs. L. Lena Sawner by patrons of Douglass School in loving remembrance for service and self-sacrifice, 1902 – 1922."[cccxi]

Mrs. Sawner's general educational philosophy,[cccxcii] distilled in a few key principles, set the stage for academic performance, without exception or excuse. Six plain truths from Mrs. Sawner's reserve retain remarkable currency more than one hundred years removed from their articulation:

1. If they apply themselves, all children can learn.
2. Worthwhile education must be holistic. It includes learning about both the academic and the practical. For example, studying mathematics and science is academic. Honing social skills is practical.
3. Black children need to be provided with role models and imbued with a sense of pride in order to achieve educationally.
4. A school is a part of a community. The school must support the community and the community must support the school. Teachers must be able to relate not just to their students, but to the families of those students as well.
5. Teachers must be motivated and highly qualified.
6. Students need to understand the role of competition in society and know how to compete.[cccxciii]

These precepts guided Mrs. Sawner's teaching and learning paradigm and grounded her charges. One central character trait, discipline, undergirded each of the tenets: discipline on the part of educators; discipline on the part of students; and discipline on the part of the community.

1. If they apply themselves, all children can learn.

Mrs. Sawner believed in preparation and application—that all students, under proper tutelage and through self-discipline, possessed the capacity to excel. She displayed little tolerance for inept teachers or wayward students, and held both teachers and students accountable for academic results.

Barring a specific reason like marriage, illness, or full-time employment, Mrs. Sawner expected every Douglass student to graduate. Graduation required preparation, and the nexus between preparation and regular attendance was crystal clear. Mrs. Sawner took truancy personally, and there would be no mollycoddling. A student absent without explanation or excuse could expect a home visit, not from just anyone, but from Mrs. Sawner herself.

2. Worthwhile education must be holistic. It includes learning about both the academic and the practical. For example, studying mathematics and science is academic. Honing social stills is practical.

The learning experience should focus on academic rigor, but provide guidance on social and life skills as well. Mrs. Sawner exposed Douglass students to a positive instructional environment using the highest quality educational resources at her disposal. Her methods prepared graduating students for the life outside the educational chrysalis—the grown-up world in which they would soon spread their wings, take flight, and, ideally, ascend. She encouraged introspection, and fostered the determination and confidence necessary to gain advantage in a racialized, competitive world.

School at Douglass began sharply at 8:45 a.m. every morning with a school-wide assembly. Recitation of the Pledge of Allegiance and readings from the Bible became standard fare. Mrs. Sawner and her teachers canvassed the day's highlights.

Beyond assemblies and daily rituals, Douglass School dances and other social events offered intermittent escape from the intensity of academics. However, these, too, offered teachable moments, including opportunities to explore social and gender roles.

Douglass offered separate sessions for boys and girls on sensitive personal matters such as health and hygiene. These sometimes controversial forums, together with gender-mixing at school social events, riled some black parents, so much so that in 1927, a small group of disillusioned parents started their own, short-lived school. Following a rocky, year-long experiment, the critics, newly familiar with the daunting task of running a thriving educational institution, returned their children to the welcoming embrace of Mrs. Sawner.

In addition to traditional academics and health/wellness offerings, Mrs. Sawner supported vocational education through 4-H, and Douglass School often hosted Lincoln County 4-H meetings. 4-H remains a leading youth leadership and development organization sponsored by the United States Department of Agriculture that focuses on four key areas: head, heart, hands, and health.[cccxcv]

3. Black children need to be provided with role models and imbued with a sense of pride in order to achieve educationally.

Mrs. Sawner wore pride and passion equally well. A religious woman, she saw every child, first and foremost, as a child of God. She encouraged Douglass students to attend church services and insisted that her teachers engage actively with a congregation.[cccxcvi]

Mrs. Sawner saw her students' divine connection as a central reason for both pride and hope. She believed self-esteem and faith to be the twin towers bolstering her children's success. Her persistent positivity resonated with her acolytes who, outside the walls of Douglass, faced a barrage of stifling signals suggesting their inherent inferiority. Though by no means impervious to the vicissitudes of early twentieth century African American life, Douglass students emerged ready for the challenge; steeled for the fight.

Mrs. Sawner believed in the power of positive black role models. During Douglass's early years, teachers boarded with members of the community. That closeness, that physical proximity, strengthened the bonds between school and community. It elevated Douglass teachers to role model status among Douglass students and the members of Chandler's black community.

Contact with positive images motivated Douglass students to reach beyond their immediate grasp. Photographs of black leaders and their inspirational quotations adorned the walls of Douglass classrooms. Copies of *The Crisis,* the official magazine of the N.A.A.C.P., and *The Black Dispatch*, Roscoe Dunjee's popular Oklahoma City-based newspaper, could always be found, thanks in part to the fact that the Ellis boys, the sons of Whit and Maggie Ellis and students of Mrs. Sawner, worked as paperboys for the publication.[cccxcviiii]

The Black Dispatch served for decades as the major source of information about the African American experience in Oklahoma. The newspaper highlighted the role of the eight Ellis "agents" in its February 29, 1936, issue, featuring a group photo of the lads on the front page. The article celebrated the Ellis octet as distributors of *The Black Dispatch*, but also praised the boys who, in its estimation, were "developing into fine, outstanding leaders among the younger generation of the state."[cccxcix]

1928 photo of the sons of Whit and Maggie Ellis, on front page of the February 19, 1936, issue of *The Black Dispatch*.[cd]

The Douglass library housed other affirming publications, too, including *The National Negro Yearbook* and Booker T. Washington's *Up From Slavery*. Douglass students routinely found themselves—or, perhaps more accurately, their future selves—reflected in print. Self-esteem flourished.

Like Booker T. Washington, Mrs. Sawner viewed self-esteem as necessary, but not sufficient, for success. She ignited the passions of her students. She pushed them toward greatness. She saw blackness as a state of being, not as an inalterable deficit; not as an excuse for poor performance. She believed that self-esteem, coupled with high academic standards, competitiveness, and determination—attitude plus effort—could challenge, if not wholly overcome, the individual and structural racism that otherwise ordered lives and determined destinies.

Mrs. Sawner recognized the power of connections—of establishing a network of friends and allies able to provide personal and professional support. As a woman of means, she traveled throughout the United States, mixing and mingling with influential black leaders.[cdi] Her powers of personality and persuasion brought a veritable hit parade of black role models and dignitaries to Douglass: Oscar De Priest, the first twentieth century African American elected to the United States House of Representatives and a leading politician; Roscoe Dunjee, civil rights activist and editor of *The Black Dispatch*; and Thurgood Marshall, general counsel for the N.A.A.C.P.[cdii] These luminaries embodied the possibilities Douglass students believed to be within their reach.

Mrs. Sawner also used her home as a venue for the cultural enrichment of Douglass students and others. She hosted musical concerts and other community events. In the true spirit of community, these gatherings drew guests from both sides of the racial divide during a profoundly segregated era in Oklahoma.

4. A school is a part of a community. The school must support the community and the community must support the school. Teachers must be able to relate not just to their students, but to the families of those students as well.

Mrs. Sawner and all Douglass teachers maintained close contact with the local black community creating, in effect, an educational village. As previously noted, most teachers, single black women from distant areas, found housing with local black families, arrangements that facilitated community bonding.

Douglass teachers closely monitored student progress, both academically and socially. After one semester of teaching, Douglass faculty members visited the homes of each of their students. This whole-family philosophy, now key to the modern community schools movement, strengthened the relationships between and among the school, the teachers, the students, and the families. It also helped forge a sense of accountability for the welfare of Douglass children that extended well beyond the walls of the schoolhouse.

Issues in the greater community of Chandler periodically affected the Douglass experience. As already noted, Chandler largely escaped the gross acts of racial violence that plagued the nation, including Oklahoma. It did not, however, remain wholly untouched by acts of overt racism.

On occasion, a few white Chandlerites harassed Douglass students as they walked home from school, spewing racial epithets and violent threats. The unnerved, and sometimes frightened, children turned to Mrs. Sawner for guidance and protection.

Mrs. Sawner did not suffer fools gladly. She thought little of the venomous verbiage, and even less of those who uttered it. She devised a plan to make her feelings known and, simultaneously, telegraph a clear message to all of Chandler.

When notified of potential acts of incivility and intimidation, Mrs. Sawner sprang into action. At the end of the school day, the unflappable headmistress called an emergency all-school assembly. She lined the children up single file, and then positioned herself at the head of this serpentine formation. Out the school door they went, snaking through all-too-familiar grounds.

This drum major for justice paraded her band of beige-to-black-hued children down the town's main thoroughfare to be seen by the townsfolk-turned-spectators fortuitously stationed along the route. As though surrounded by an impenetrable force field, the intrepid marchers deflected any volleys hurled their way, ricocheting them back to their origins.

Quizzical looks and faint murmurings acknowledged the fleeting interruption of an otherwise ordinary day. Word of the extraordinary encounters spread like wildfire through a tallgrass prairie.

As circumstances demanded, Mrs. Sawner and the Douglass kids reprised this dignified and silent procession. These choreographed drills trumpeted thundering notes of confidence and defiance in the face of harassment and intimidation. Townspeople took notice of this seeming superwoman and her daring disciples.

In addition to her public displays of intestinal fortitude, Mrs. Sawner burnished her standing through community service. She engaged directly in community-building/betterment activities, and she encouraged gratitude, compassion, and charity among Douglass students. For example, a segment in Benny Kent's "Early Days" Oklahoma newsreel entitled "Douglas[s] School Picks Cotton for Red Cross 1916" contains rare moving footage of gleeful Douglass students deftly separating cotton from boll as part of a fundraiser for the Red Cross. Lena Sawner, clad in a print dress and sweater, hatless with her hair fashionably bobbed, not only chaperoned the group, but helped pick cotton, too. Looking every bit the every woman, she lights up the shot with a radiant smile and a friendly wave of the hand. At the end of the minutes-long clip, effervescent children gather for a spirited jitterbug performance as adults clap and cheer them on.[cdiv]

Despite their lack of material resources, the Douglass children understood their relative bounty. Mrs. Sawner taught them to share what they had; that when one gives, one gains.

5. Teachers must be motivated and highly qualified.

Mrs. Sawner handpicked her teachers, searching not just for competency in various subject matter areas, but for dedication and leadership skills, too. She cultivated close relationships with black colleges in Oklahoma and neighboring states, a strategy that proved instrumental in hiring of exceptional recruits. She gained a reputation for luring the crème de la crème—the "brightest of the bright" black female graduating college seniors—to Douglass.

In addition to hiring exceptionally qualified teachers, Mrs. Sawner's choices included many physically attractive candidates. This bevy of educated beauties—youthful, single, and often fair-skinned—on the Douglass faculty likely enticed some of the many famous male visitors who eagerly visited there year after year.

6. Students need to understand the role of competition in society and know how to compete.

Douglass held annual academic and athletic competitions for grades six through twelve. Organizers awarded prizes, including the L.L. Sawner Loving Cup, a special trophy going to the winning team, to be retained by any school that won three successive years.[cdv]

These weekend contests, open to all black children attending Lincoln County schools, motivated students to perform at their optimum and lavished high performers with rewards. Typically, more than two hundred children competed for grade-level prizes in categories as diverse as athletics, mathematics, civics, science, geography, Oklahoma and United States history, penmanship, English, and similar academic studies.

Douglass students yearned to perform. Some petitioned for a school band. In 1927, Mrs. Sawner organized another cotton-picking event to raise money to buy musical instruments. Students and teachers took three days off from school to pick cotton, using their earnings to purchase the instruments. No barriers. No excuses. So it was with Lena Sawner.[cdvi]

Mrs. Sawner's educational concepts worked. As previously noted, more than ninety percent of Douglass students who entered the ninth grade earned diplomas.[cdvii] Douglass graduates left equipped with an unsurpassed education and emboldened with the self-esteem, substantive knowledge, and social skills necessary to survive, and often, thrive, in a harsh, segregated world.

Douglass benefitted not just the students who attended the school, but the community as a whole. Among many other contributions, Mrs. Sawner established the first free evening adult literacy classes in Lincoln County.

As indicated, Mrs. Sawner adorned the walls of Douglass with images and quotations of black strivers, famous historical figures who had or were succeeding against the odds posed by racism. Imagine the wisdom:

Sojourner Truth

Evangelist, Abolitionist, Social Reformer: 1797 - 1883

- *"The Spirit calls me, and I must go."*

- *"Truth is powerful and it prevails."*

- *"It is the mind that makes the body."*

- *"Religion without humanity is very poor human stuff."*

- *"That man over there says that women need to be helped into carriages, and lifted over ditches, and to have the best place everywhere. Nobody ever helps me into carriages, or over mud-puddles, or gives me any best place! And ain't I a woman? Look at me! Look at my arm! I have ploughed and planted, and gathered into barns, and no man could head me! And ain't I a woman? I could work as much and eat as much as a man - when I could get it - and bear the lash as well! And ain't I a woman? I have borne thirteen children, and seen most all sold off to slavery, and when I cried out with my mother's grief, none but Jesus heard me! And ain't I a woman?"*

Frederick Douglass

Abolitionist, Women's Suffragist, Editor, Orator, Author, Statesman, Minister, and Reformer: *circa* **1818 – 1895**

- *"Without a struggle, there can be no progress."*
- *"The soul that is within me no man can degrade."*
- *"It is not light that we need, but fire; it is not the gentle shower, but thunder. We need the storm, the whirlwind, and the earthquake."*
- *"People might not get all they work for in this world, but they must certainly work for all they get."*
- *"A little learning, indeed, may be a dangerous thing, but the want of learning is a calamity to any people."*

Booker T. Washington

Educator, Statesman, and Author: 1856 – 1915

- *"Character, not circumstances, makes the man."*
- *"You can't hold a man down without staying down with him."*
- *"Property, brains and character will settle the question of civil rights."*

- "*There is no power on earth that can neutralize the influence of a high, simple and useful life.*"

- "*There are two ways of exerting one's strength: one is pushing down, the other is pulling up.*"

Mrs. Sawner embodied the quotations and affirmations she embraced and shared with her Douglass students. Effervescence and professionalism defined her decades-long career as an educator. Her spirit lives on through those whom she touched.

At an Alumni Days exhibit at the LCHS Museum of Pioneer History in the spring of 1985, patrons showed their appreciation for one half of the power couple who made life in Chandler and beyond just a bit better. They attested to the might and majesty of educator extraordinaire, Lena Sawner:

'[Mrs. Sawner] taught her boys and girls how to present themselves.'

'[Mrs. Sawner] reminded them of proper behavior wherever they were.'

'[Mrs. Sawner] was considered one, if not the, best-dressed woman in town.'

'[Mrs. Sawner] ruled the school with an iron hand.'

'[Mrs. Sawner's] favorite color was purple.'

'[Mrs. Sawner] taught Ancient History, and could translate and teach Latin so well that I could learn it from one of her students since I couldn't afford to go to school.'

'I will always remember [Mrs. Sawner] every afternoon marching up Manvel Avenue in her high heels with the children, steering them North through the business section toward their homes to make sure there was no trouble.'[cdviii]

Such reminiscences speak to the ability of one special woman to make a world of difference and a difference in her world. She recognized both the crisis and opportunity attendant to being a Negro woman in America in the first half of the twentieth century. She seized the moment, making the union a tad more perfect than she found it.

Toward the end of her journey, Mrs. Sawner, this woman of insight and vision, had been blind for some sixteen years. Her failing eyesight led her to resign as principal of Douglass after thirty-three years. She suffered a paralytic stroke months prior to her death. Mr.

and Mrs. M. D. McCormick shared Mrs. Sawner's home for the last few years of her life. Mrs. McCormick became a fixture—a constant companion and confidante.[cdix]

Despite these and other challenges, Mrs. Sawner's majesty diminished only ever so slightly. She required the assistance of a companion, the functional equivalent of a lady-in-waiting, who guarded the palace gates. She still held court, but did so from the secure confines of her boudoir. The canopied bed in her sleeping chamber became her throne. Sitting up, resplendent and regal, she stayed fully engaged, reigning supreme until the end.[cdx]

Even in her last and final days, Mrs. Sawner dressed like royalty. In full makeup and with salon-perfect hair, she awaited visits from admirers and well-wishers. "Mrs. Sawner will see you now," became a frequent refrain from Mrs. Sawner's courtier. Like subjects of the realm, guests rose up and filed in upon command, grateful for the chance to appear before their queen.

Family and friends bid farewell to Mrs. Sawner at a morning funeral service held March 5, 1949, at Bethel A.M.E. Church in Chandler, after which they laid her to rest. The homegoing service for Mrs. Sawner reflected the depth of the human connections she made. Songs like *Abide With Me* and *Sweet Bye and Bye* reminded mourners that Lena Sawner lingered—she left a legacy—though she was gone in an earthly, physical sense. So, too, did the poem "Away":

Away
(Unknown)

I cannot say, and I will not say
That she is dead. She is just away.
With a cheery smile and a wave of the hand,
She has wandered into an unknown land,
And left us dreaming how very fair
It needs must be since she lingers there.
And you, O you, who the wildest yearn
For the old-time step and the glad return,
Think of her faring on, as dear
In the love of there as the love of here.
Think of her still as the same, I say,
She is not dead, she is just away![cdxi]

Conclusion

George Sawner died in 1924. Lena Sawner succumbed twenty-five years later, in 1949. They rest together for all eternity in a well-manicured family plot in Newkirk, Oklahoma, purchased by Mrs. Sawner's parents, the Lowerys.

That the Sawners chose as their final resting place a site other than Chandler should not be read as a slight to their beloved hometown, a love they no doubt carried with them to the crypt. Rather, the Sawners' interment in a Newkirk cemetery attests to Lena Sawner's close ties to her parents, for whom she served as caregiver in their later lives.

Those who knew them, the multitudes whom they touched, never forgot them. In death, both of the Sawners received an outpouring of sympathy and gratitude: sympathy for what Oklahomans had lost; gratitude for what each Sawner had given.

All business in Boley closed for a day on the occasion of George Sawner's death. *The Black Dispatch* newspaper printed nearly a full page of tributes to his life and legacy. Decades later, Mrs. Sawner's death likewise generated a geyser of heartfelt reflections.

George and Lena Sawner knew of Dred Scott[cdxii] and Homer Plessy,[cdxiii] both of whom sparked distressing decisions about the role and relative worth of African Americans in society. Before her death, Mrs. Sawner witnessed a couple of remarkable *de jure* advancements in race relations: the desegregation of the military and the outlawing of restrictive covenants that kept housing segregated.[cdxv]

George and Lena Sawner never knew of Linda Brown.[cdxvi] They did not live to see Rosa Parks rise up against discrimination in Montgomery, Alabama, public transit by sitting down and staying put, sparking the Montgomery Bus Boycott. They escaped the pain that radiated through the black community upon learning of the vicious murder of fourteen-year-old Chicagoan Emmett Till, slaughtered for allegedly flirting with a white woman while visiting family in Money, Mississippi. They missed the federal showdown over school desegregation in Arkansas sparked by the enrollment of the Little Rock Nine at Central High School. Death deprived them of the chance to accompany Dr. Martin Luther King, Jr., on that March on Washington in

1963. They knew nothing of the mobs and mayhem that marred the Freedom Rides and Freedom Summer. They did not bear witness to the tragic assassinations—of Kennedy, of Malcolm X, of King, and of yet another Kennedy—that defined a decade, or the Watts and Newark and Detroit riots that burned black oppression into the nation's collective consciousness. They were not here with us when, at long last, a man of color ascended to the highest office in the land.

The Sawners were present for a different set of battles that shaped the many skirmishes and successes that would follow in succeeding decades. They set the standard for black Oklahomans. Bold without being brash; sophisticated without being snobbish; and exacting without being exclusive—they epitomized the triumph of character.

Nelson Henderson said, "The true meaning of life is to plant trees, under whose shade you do not expect to sit."[cdxvii] The Sawners did just that. Their unique and varied contributions still resonate. They and those of their ilk, the African Americans who worked tirelessly to create better lives for themselves and those around them, set the stage for future movements and advancements they would not live, physically, to see.

Though gone before many of the seminal moments of the American civil rights movement, the Sawners and their fellow trailblazers no doubt bore spiritual witness. The Sawners and other largely invisible pioneers like them gave birth to the generations of civil rights advocates and notables who emerged in the mid-to-late twentieth century, not just in Oklahoma, but across the nation. Their examples, individually and collectively, became part of the underpinnings upon which our unprecedented, if imperfect, civil rights rest.

Mr. Sawner's business acumen and national civil rights advocacy earned him respect, not just among fellow African Americans, but across the color chasm. Active and engaged, he used his twenty-plus years in Chandler to boost his brand and build his stature throughout Oklahoma, though he never gained broad national recognition.

Mrs. Sawner's three-decade journey as educator *par excellence* at Douglass School garnered statewide notice. Her subtle, significant, and sustained role in fostering positive race relations in small-town Oklahoma during a racially hostile era in America likewise drew attention, primarily at the local level. National fame escaped her, too.

The generation-spanning, culture-shaping work of the Sawners buttressed the lives of untold individuals. One of the legions who leveraged the Sawners legacy became an undeniable Chandler legend in his own right. Luther-born Berton Zephaniah "Lee Lee" Lewis

(September 19, 1923 – May 19, 2015) built upon the solid foundation laid by the Sawners, constructing lifelong relationships across racial fissures. Lewis left behind a reservoir of trust and goodwill that will no doubt inspire others to break barriers and build bridges in matters of race.[cdxviii] Lewis's saga began with a critical decision about military service.[cdxix]

Lee Lee Lewis enlisted in the Oklahoma Army National Guard ("Guard") as its first African American member. A beloved, lifelong Chandlerite, Lewis served in a battalion supply role, ferrying needed resources to field artillery batteries. A Guard-booster, he recruited sixteen other African American soldiers and ended his decades-long Guard service at the rank of Sergeant First Class.[cdxx]

Prior to joining the Guard, Lewis served in World War II with the all-black 92nd Infantry Division, a regiment deployed to Europe and Africa. He also worked in Africa, Sicily, and Italy with the 416th Trucking Company, hauling supplies to General George Patton's troops on the front lines. John Coffey recruited Lewis for the Guard when progressive Oklahoma Governor Raymond Gary ordered its desegregation.[cdxxi]

After retiring from the Guard, Lewis, also a pastor, worked for the Federal Reserve Bank. Following yet another retirement, he signed on as a security guard and door greeter at the Chandler Wal-Mart, a role he relished even as an octogenarian. Active in the community, Lewis served a stint on the Chandler School Board,[cdxxii] a noteworthy ascendancy for a man who once worked as a custodian at Chandler High School.[cdxxiii]

With Sawner-like dignity and grace, Lee Lee Lewis no doubt smoothed the way for others in the Guard, known and as yet unknown, and for many others whose paths he illuminated. He did for others what pioneers like the Sawners had done for him. He paved a road along which they and future generations might travel just a bit more comfortably.

The long slog toward full citizenship for African Americans, the centuries-old, sometimes-Sisyphean push for social, economic, and political rights—remains central to an understanding of America herself. Race continues to shape, and in some ways, contort, both perception and reality.[cdxxiv]

America may not soon transcend race, but the lives of the Sawners offer guidance on movement in that direction. George and Lena Sawner invested all whom they met with an undeniable humanity and found in them the potential for self-actualization. They nurtured a sense of community that tapped into that promise. In so doing, they made Chandler—and Oklahoma—and America—better. The Sawners' lives illustrate the works that, of necessity, must accompany the faith embodied in the black national anthem.[cdxxv]

Lift Every Voice and Sing

Lift every voice and sing, till earth and Heaven ring,
Ring with the harmonies of liberty;
Let our rejoicing rise, high as the listening skies,
Let it resound loud as the rolling sea.
Sing a song full of the faith that the dark past has taught us,
Sing a song full of the hope that the present has brought us;
Facing the rising sun of our new day begun,
Let us march on till victory is won.

Stony the road we trod, bitter the chastening rod,
Felt in the days when hope unborn had died;
Yet with a steady beat, have not our weary feet,
Come to the place for which our fathers sighed?
We have come over a way that with tears has been watered,
We have come, treading our path through the blood of the slaughtered;
Out from the gloomy past, till now we stand at last
Where the white gleam of our bright star is cast.

God of our weary years, God of our silent tears,
Thou Who hast brought us thus far on the way;
Thou Who hast by Thy might, led us into the light,
Keep us forever in the path, we pray.
Lest our feet stray from the places, our God, where we met Thee.
Lest our hearts, drunk with the wine of the world, we forget Thee.
Shadowed beneath Thy hand, may we forever stand,
True to our God, true to our native land.[cdxxvi]

Pilgrims. Pioneers. Pathfinders. These three nouns capture the essence of the Sawners, near-perfect partners who knew who they were, loved where they lived, and gave of what they had. The Sawners' inspired lives helped transfigure America, incrementally, into what many believe to be the most perfect of imperfect democracies on the planet.

On the meaning of life, theoretical physicist Michio Kaku said: "Beyond work and love, I would add two other ingredients that give meaning to life. First, to fulfill whatever talents we are born with. . . Second, we should try to leave the world a better place than when we entered it."[cdxxvii] By these measures, too, the Sawners' lives were well lived; imbued with meaning. Both found work they loved: He, a businessman; she a teacher. They found love in each other and for their community, Chandler. Each fulfilled his/her talents, honing them along the way. Together, they left the world a better place than they found it.

We—all of us—owe a great debt of gratitude to the Sawners and others like them who laid the cornerstone upon which our still-evolving senses of being and belonging rest. George and Lena Sawner, prodigious professionals with servants' hearts, deserve a place among the pantheon of American cultural luminaries. Their decades-long contributions to business, civil rights, education, and race relations in Oklahoma enriched countless lives in ways great and small. For that, they should be recognized, resurrected, and remembered.

Sit-in at Katz Drug Store downtown Oklahoma City, Oklahoma, *circa* 1958.[cdxxviii]

Rev. Dr. Martin Luther King, Jr. salutes the crowd at the March on Washington for Jobs and Freedom, August 28, 1963.^{cdxxix}

Rev. Dr. Martin Luther King, Jr. National Memorial, Washington, D.C., 2013.^{cdxxx}

Final resting places for and Lena L. Sawner (June 20, 1874 – March 1, 1949) and George W.F. Sawner (February 10, 1860 – May 1, 1924), in the Newkirk, Oklahoma, Cemetery.[cdxxxi]

Appendix A

Oklahoma Abbreviated
*A Timeline**

- 1500s: Spanish explorers, including *Hernando de Soto* and *Francisco Vasquez de Coronado*, passed through Oklahoma.

- 1682: French explorer *Rene'-Robert Cavelier, Sieur de la Salle,* claimed Oklahoma for France.

- 1803: The United States acquired most of Oklahoma from France in the Louisiana Purchase.

- 1830s - 1840s: The United States government, led by President Andrew Jackson, forced the Cherokee, Chickasaw, Choctaw, Muscogee (Creek), and Seminole tribes (the "Five Civilized Tribes") to relocate from their native lands to Oklahoma, what was then denominated "Indian Territory." Thousands of Native Americans lost their lives on the bloody marches to Oklahoma.

- 1842: The remaining Seminole Indians from Florida moved to Oklahoma.

- 1860s: After the Civil War, because the Five Civilized Tribes officially sided with the Confederacy, they faced ruin and forfeiture of their lands. All Five Tribes executed post-Civil War treaties with the federal government.

- 1870s: The federal government moved an additional twenty-five tribes to Oklahoma to reside on federal lands.

- 1872: The railroad crossed Oklahoma. Routes of commerce began to open.

- 1875: At the Battle of Washita, George Custer defeated remaining Indian forces. For all intents and purposes, this defeat ended the Indian Wars.

- 1889: The United States government opened all unassigned Oklahoma lands for settlement. Thousands of settlers crossed the border to stake claims.

- 1890: Oklahoma Territory was created. This new Territory coexisted with Indian Territory in what is today Oklahoma.

- 1907: Oklahoma joined the Union as the forty-sixth state.

- 1930s: A severe drought and the national economic depression ruined most of Oklahoma's farmers.

- 1959: Alcohol prohibition was repealed in Oklahoma.

- 1971: The McClellan-Kerr Arkansas River Navigation System opened, connecting Tulsa (and Oklahoma) to the Mississippi River.

- 1990: Oklahoma became the first state to limit the terms of legislators.

- 1995: Domestic terrorist Timothy McVeigh and accomplices blew up the Murrah Federal Building in downtown Oklahoma City, killing 168 people, injuring hundreds more, and damaging adjacent property.

Adapted from: Worldatlas.com, http://www.worldatlas.com/webimage/countrys/ namerica/usstates/oktimeln.htm, last viewed June 21, 2010.

Appendix B

Milestones in African American Education

1837   Institute for Colored Youth founded by Richard Humphreys; later became Cheyney University.

1854   Ashmun Institute, the first school of higher learning for young black men, founded by John Miller Dickey and his wife, Sarah Emlen Cresson; later (1866) renamed Lincoln University (Pennsylvania) after President Abraham Lincoln.

1856   Wilberforce University, the first black school of higher learning owned and operated by African Americans, founded by the African Methodist Episcopal Church. Its president, Daniel A. Payne, became the first African American University president in the country.

1869   Howard University's law school becomes the country's first black law school.

1876   Meharry Medical College, the first black medical school in the U.S., founded by the Freedman's Aid Society of the Methodist Episcopal Church.

1881   Spelman College, the first college for black women in the U.S., founded by Sophia B. Packard and Harriet E. Giles.

1881   Booker T. Washington founds the Tuskegee Normal and Industrial Institute in Alabama. The school became one of the leading schools of higher learning for African Americans, and stressed the practical application of knowledge. In 1896, George Washington Carver began teaching there as director of the department of agricultural research, gaining an international reputation for his agricultural advances.

1922   William Leo Hansberry teaches the first course in African civilization at an American college, Howard University.

1944   Frederick Douglass Patterson establishes the United Negro College Fund to help support black colleges and black students.

1954   In the landmark case *Brown v. Board of Education*, the Supreme Court rules unanimously that segregation in public schools in unconstitutional.

1957 President Dwight D. Eisenhower sends federal troops to ensure integration of the all-white Central High School in Little Rock, Arkansas. The Little Rock Nine were the first black students to attend the school.

1960 Black and white students form the Student Nonviolent Coordinating Committee (SNCC), dedicated to working against segregation and discrimination.

1962 James Meredith is the first black student to enroll at the University of Mississippi; on the day he enters the university, he is escorted by U.S. marshals.

1963 Despite Governor George Wallace physically blocking their way, Vivian Malone and James Hood register for classes at the University of Alabama.

1968 San Francisco State University becomes the first four-year college to establish a black studies department.

1969 The Ford Foundation gives $1 million to Morgan State University, Howard University, and Yale University to help prepare faculty members to teach courses in African American studies.

2003 In *Grutter v. Bollinger,* the Supreme Court (5-4) upheld the University of Michigan Law School's affirmative action policy, ruling that race can be one of many factors considered by colleges when selecting students because it furthers "a compelling interest in obtaining the educational benefits that flow from a diverse student body."

2007 *The Journal of Blacks in Higher Education* surveyed the nation's highest-ranked research universities, the most selective liberal arts colleges, and the 50 flagship state universities to determine their levels of black faculty. Mount Holyoke College had the highest percentage of black faculty of any of the 100 colleges and universities surveyed, with 9.7 percent. According to the U.S. Deptartment of Education, the 2007 national average was 5.4 percent.

2008 The percentage of all 18-to-24-year-old African Americans enrolled in higher education increases to 32.6 percent from 21.2 percent in 1988.

Source:http://www.infoplease.com/ipa/A0872844.html (last visited July 18, 2013).

African American Civil Rights in the United States A Timeline*

1500

- The African slave trade included the infamous "Middle Passage," a reference to the forcible movement of African people from Africa to the New World that was part and parcel the Atlantic slave trade. The term "Middle Passage" refers specifically to that middle leg of the transatlantic trade triangle. Slave-traders imprisoned, enslaved, and removed millions of Africans from their homelands.

- Ships, loaded with commercial goods, departed Europe for African markets. Traders exchanged those goods for kidnapped Africans, who were then transported across the Atlantic as slaves. Flesh merchants sold or traded the enslaved Africans as commodities for raw materials to be used in the European market, completing the "triangular trade."

- Traders from the Americas and Caribbean received enslaved Africans. Various European, North American, and South American countries took part in the slave trade. Some 15 percent of the Africans captured for the slave trade died at sea. Mortality rates were considerably higher in Africa itself, as the process of capturing and transporting indigenous peoples to slave ships proved deadly. Some two million African deaths were directly attributable to the Middle Passage voyages. Between 1500 and 1900, some four million Africans lost their lives as a direct consequence of the institution of slavery.

- The Middle Passage inalterably influenced the cultural and demographic landscapes of Africa and those countries who participated in the slave trade. Some also view the Middle Passage as a marker of the origin of a distinct African, or "black," social identity.

1619

- The first African slaves arrived in Jamestown, Virginia, on this day in 1619. They were indentured to work for tobacco plantation owners for seven years. Single women from England were also brought over to help. The institution of hereditary lifetime servitude for persons of African ancestry soon developed.

1660s

- The practice of slavery became a legally recognized institution in British America. Colonial assemblies began to enact laws known as slave codes, which restricted the liberty of slaves and protected the institution of slavery.

1776

- The Declaration of Independence declared that "All men are created equal." In spite of that, slavery remained a legal institution in all thirteen of the newly established states.

1777

- Vermont amended its constitution to ban slavery. Over the next 25 years, other Northern states emancipated their slaves and banned the institution: Pennsylvania, 1780; Massachusetts and New Hampshire, 1783; Connecticut and Rhode Island, 1784; New York, 1799; and New Jersey, 1804. Some of the state laws stipulated gradual emancipation.

1787

- The Northwest Ordinance banned slavery in the Northwest Territory (what became the states of Ohio, Indiana, Illinois, Michigan, and Wisconsin). The ordinance, together with state emancipation laws, created a free North.

1787- 1788

- Drafted in 1787 and ratified in 1788, the United States Constitution did not expressly mention the institution of slavery, but it addressed it indirectly in three places: (1) It granted Congress the authority to prohibit the importation of slaves after twenty years; (2) The "three-fifths" clause in Article I settled the debate over whether or not to count slaves for determining taxation and representation. [For those purposes, all free persons in the districts, including indentured servants, were to be counted. To that total was to be added the number of "three fifths of all other persons"—*i.e.*, slaves.]; and (3) Article IV, Section 2 required that a "person held to service or labor" in one state, who escaped to another state, "shall be delivered up on claim of the party to whom such service or labor shall be due." No enforcement mechanism was specified.

1793

- To enforce Article IV, Section 2, the U.S. Congress enacted the Fugitive Slave Law. It allowed slave-owners to cross state lines to recapture their slaves, but required them to subsequently prove ownership in a court of law. In reaction, some Northern states passed personal liberty laws, granting the alleged fugitive slaves the rights to habeas corpus, jury trials, and testimony on their own behalf. These Northern state legislatures also passed anti-kidnapping laws to punish slave-catchers who kidnapped free blacks, instead of fugitive slaves.

1808

- In 1807 Congress banned the importation of slaves, effective January 1, 1808, the earliest date allowed by the Constitution. The internal slave trade continued in states where the institution remained legal.

1820 - 1821

- In the Missouri Compromise, Congress admitted the slave state of Missouri and the free state of Maine into the Union, and banned slavery north of the 36° 30' line of latitude in the Louisiana Territory.

1831

- In Boston, William Lloyd Garrison founded the abolitionist newspaper, *The Liberator*, signaling a dramatic shift in the anti-slavery movement. In the previous decades, it had centered in the South and favored a combination of compensated emancipation and colonization of freed slaves back to Africa. In the 1830s, the abolitionist movement became the dominant voice among anti-slavery advocates. Abolitionists demanded an immediate end to slavery, which they considered a moral evil, without compensation to slave-owners. In 1833, Garrison joined Arthur and Lewis Tappan in the establishment of the American Anti-Slavery Society, an abolitionist organization.

- Nat Turner, a literate slave who believed himself chosen as the Moses of his people, instigated a slave revolt in Virginia. He and his followers killed fifty-seven whites, but the revolt was ultimately unsuccessful. Some two hundred enslaved Africans were killed. After an intense debate, the Virginia legislature narrowly rejected a bill to emancipate Virginia's slaves. The widespread fear of slave revolts, compounded by the rise of abolitionism, led legislatures across the South to increase the harshness of their slave codes. State and private censorship resulted in the suppression of expressions of anti-slavery sentiment throughout the South.

1842

- In *Prigg v. Pennsylvania*, the U.S. Supreme Court upheld the Fugitive Slave Law of 1793, acknowledging a right on the part of slave-owners to retrieve their "property." In so doing, the court ruled Pennsylvania's anti-kidnapping law unconstitutional. At the same time, the Supreme Court declared that enforcement of the Fugitive Slave Law fell upon federal authorities. States therefore could not be compelled to participate. Between 1842 and 1850, nine Northern states passed new personal liberty laws, which forbade state officials from cooperating in the return of alleged fugitive slaves and barred the use of state facilities for that purpose.

1850

- Henry Clay introduced The Compromise of 1850 in Congress as an omnibus bill designed to settle disputes arising from the conclusion of the Mexican War. It passed after Stephen Douglas divided the bill into several parts: California entered the Union as a free state; the slave trade (but not slavery) was abolished in Washington D.C.; the fugitive slave law was strengthened; and the Utah and New Mexico Territories were opened to slavery on the basis of popular sovereignty (allowing territorial voters to decide the issue without federal interference).

1852

- *Uncle Tom's Cabin*, by Harriet Beecher Stowe, debuted. The novel depicted slavery as a horrible evil, but treated white Southerners sympathetically. The villain of the piece, cruel slave-overseer Simon Legree, was a transplanted New Englander. The South banned the book. The North made the book a bestseller.

1854

- The U.S. ministers to Britain, France, and Spain met in Ostend, Belgium. They drafted a policy recommendation to President Franklin Pierce urging him to attempt again to purchase Cuba from Spain and, if Spain refused, to take the island by force. The leak to the press of the secret proposal—the "Ostend Manifesto"—created an uproar since Cuba would likely become another slave state.

- In an attempt to spur population growth in the Western territories in advance of a transcontinental railroad, Stephen Douglas introduced a bill to establish the territories of Kansas and Nebraska. In order to gain Southern support, the bill stipulated that slavery in the territories was to be decided by popular sovereignty. Thus, the Kansas-Nebraska Act repealed the Missouri Compromise ban on slavery north of 36° 30' in the lands of the Louisiana Purchase.

1855 – 1856

- A miniature civil war—known as *Bleeding Kansas*—erupted in the Kansas Territory over the issue of slavery. In May 1856, a proslavery group attacked the free-soil town of Lawrence, destroying and stealing property. In response to the "sack of Lawrence," radical abolitionist John Brown and his followers attacked a proslavery settlement at Pottawatomie Creek, killing five men. By the end of 1856, nearly two hundred Kansans have been killed and property worth $2 million has been damaged or destroyed.

1856

- Senator Charles Sumner delivered a stinging speech in the U.S. Senate, "The Crime against Kansas," in which he attacked both slavery and the South. Senator Sumner singled out his Senate colleague, Andrew Butler of South Carolina, for special criticism. In retaliation, Butler's nephew, Congressman Preston Brooks of South Carolina, attacked Sumner with a cane while the Massachusetts senator was seated at his desk on the floor of the Senate, inflicting injuries that caused Sumner to be absent from the Senate for four years.

1857

- The U.S. Supreme Court decided the Dred Scott case [*Dred Scott v. Sandford*, 60 U.S. (19 How.) 393 (1857)]. In the majority opinion, Chief Justice Roger Taney ruled Scott a slave with no standing to sue. He pronounced that black Americans, slave or free, non-citizens, with no civil rights protected by the U.S. Constitution. Finally, Chief Justice Taney concluded that neither the territorial governments nor the federal government could ban slavery in the territories, and thus the Northwest Ordinance and Missouri Compromise bans on slavery were unconstitutional.

1857 – 1858

- The rivalry in the Kansas Territory between pro- and anti-slavery factions resulted in the establishment of two territorial legislatures, each claiming legitimacy. The pro-slavery legislature at Lecompton drafted a constitution making Kansas a slave state. Anti-slavery forces boycotted the popular referendum on the constitution, which passed and was sent to Congress. Senator Stephen Douglas considered the Lecompton Constitution a perversion of popular sovereignty, but President James Buchanan endorsed it. Congress sent the Lecompton Constitution back to Kansas for another referendum. This time, it was defeated overwhelmingly.

1858

- Illinois Republicans nominated Abraham Lincoln for the U.S. Senate. As part of his acceptance, Lincoln delivered his "House Divided" speech, in which he asserted that the nation cannot endure permanently half-slave and half-free. Incumbent Senator Stephen Douglas agreed to an unprecedented series of debates held in towns across the state. Although the Democrats won control of the state legislature and re-elected Douglas, Lincoln gained notoriety and became a contender for the 1860 presidential nomination.

1859

- John Brown, the radical abolitionist and veteran of *Bleeding Kansas*, failed in his attempt to capture the federal arsenal at Harpers Ferry, Virginia (now, West Virginia) and to use the weapons to foment a slave rebellion. Brown and his co-conspirators were hanged, becoming martyrs to the anti-slavery cause in the eyes of some abolitionists.

1865

- Congress ratified the 13th Amendment, officially ending slavery in America.
  Amendment XIII (Ratified December 6, 1865): 1. Neither slavery nor involuntary servitude, except as a punishment for crime whereof the party shall have been duly convicted, shall exist within the United States, or any place subject to their jurisdiction. 2. Congress shall have power to enforce this article by appropriate legislation.

- "Reconstruction" began. African Americans worked to create an economic base, independent towns, and educational institutions. "Reconstruction" is the term given the period from 1865 to 1877 during which the United States underwent a period of readjustment following the Civil War. The American South, vanquished in the Civil War, lay in ruin. Invading Union forces wrought immense physical destruction. The demise of the South meant the collapse of the old social and economic order founded upon slavery. The eleven Confederate states needed to be restored to their positions in the Union and provided with loyal governments. The role of the emancipated slaves in Southern society begged for redefinition. Reconstruction ended as the political winds shifted and the federal government withdrew all federal troops from the South. White rule reemerged. African Americans lost many civil and political rights. Their economic position remained depressed. Hope for a post-slavery Southern reordering on social and economic fronts seemed doomed. The rise of the one-party solid South cloaked in white supremacist garb had begun.

1868

- Congress ratified the 14th Amendment, granting citizenship to all persons born or naturalized in the United States.
  Amendment XIV (Ratified July 9, 1868): Section 1--All persons born or naturalized in the United States, and subject to the jurisdiction thereof, are citizens of the United States and of the State wherein they reside. No State shall make or enforce any law which shall abridge the privileges or immunities of citizens of the United States; nor shall any State deprive any person of life, liberty, or property, without due process of law; nor deny to any person within its jurisdiction the equal protection of the laws. Section 2 — Representatives shall be apportioned among the several States according to their respective numbers counting the whole number of persons in each State, excluding Indians not taxed. But when the right to vote at any election for the choice of electors for President and Vice-President of the United States, Representatives in Congress, the Executive and Judicial officers of a State, or the members of the Legislature thereof, is denied to any of the male inhabitants of such State, being twenty-one years of age, and citizens of the United States, or in any way abridged, except for participation in rebellion, or other crime, the basis of representation therein shall be reduced in the proportion which the number of such male citizens shall bear to the whole number of male citizens twenty-one years of age in such State. Section 3 — No person shall be a Senator or Representative in Congress, or elector of President and Vice-President, or hold any office, civil or

military, under the United States, or under any State, who, having previously taken an oath, as a member of Congress, or as an officer of the United States, or as a member of any State legislature, or as an executive or judicial officer of any State, to support the Constitution of the United States, shall have engaged in insurrection or rebellion against the same, or given aid or comfort to the enemies thereof. But Congress may by a vote of two-thirds of each House, remove such disability. Section 4 — The validity of the public debt of the United States, authorized by law, including debts incurred for payment of pensions and bounties for services in suppressing insurrection or rebellion, shall not be questioned. But neither the United States nor any State shall assume or pay any debt or obligation incurred in aid of insurrection or rebellion against the United States, or any claim for the loss or emancipation of any slave. But all such debts, obligations and claims shall be held illegal and void. Section 5 — The Congress shall have power to enforce, by appropriate legislation, the provisions of this article.

1870

- Congress ratified the 15th Amendment, granting, theoretically, all citizens the right to vote.

Amendment XV (Ratified February 3, 1870): Section 1 — The right of citizens of the United States to vote shall not be denied or abridged by the United States or by any State on account of race, color, or previous condition of servitude. Section 2--The Congress shall have power to enforce this article by appropriate legislation.

1877

- In the Compromise of 1877, Union troops exited from the South. Federal soldiers had enforced new antislavery laws during Reconstruction. The withdrawal of federal troops doomed Reconstruction.

1881

- Educator and statesman Booker T. Washington founded Tuskegee Institute in Alabama, a vocational school for African Americans. Washington, a staunch advocate of self-reliance, urged African Americans to concentrate on economic uplift rather than agitate for civil rights. The embrace of gradualism put Washington at odds with civil rights advocate and scholar Dr. W.E.B. Du Bois, who urged immediate demands for political and civil rights.

1895

- African American statesman and educator Booker T. Washington delivered The Atlanta Cotton States and International Exposition Speech on September 11, 1895. The talk dealt with American race relations. Washington's philosophical rival, Harvard-educated Dr. W.E.B. Du Bois, labeled the lecture the "Atlanta Compromise." Dr. Du Bois viewed Washington's remarks as embracing an enduring second-class citizenship for African Americans. Thus began the long intellectual rivalry between the politics of accommodation and those of agitation. Washington favored gradualism and a focus on economic uplift. Dr. Du Bois wanted, indeed, demanded, immediate social and political equality for African Americans.

1896

- In *Plessy v. Ferguson*, 163 U.S. 537 (1896), the United States Supreme Court upheld the concept of "separate but equal" public accommodations. The case involved railroad transport, but its implications were much broader. The decision endorsed state-mandated discrimination in public transportation under the "separate but equal" doctrine, which prevailed until its repudiation in the landmark *Brown v. Board of Education* decision [*Brown v. Board of Education*, 347 U.S. 483 (1954)].

1903

- Formed in 1903 on site of Abigail Barnett McCormick's Freedmen's allotment, townsfolk incorporated Boley in 1905. The town sits in central Oklahoma, in Okfuskee County on Highway 62, 68 miles southwest of Tulsa. Booker T. Washington, visiting Boley in 1904, called it "[t]he most enterprising, and in many ways the most interesting of the Negro towns in the U.S." Boley represents a host of all-black communities formed largely between 1890 and 1910. Oklahoma led the nation in terms of spawning these islands of freedom and opportunity for oppressed African Americans. African Americans formed more black towns in Oklahoma than in any other state.

1905

- Intellectual W.E.B. Du Bois and *Boston Guardian* co-founder Monroe Trotter, both Harvard University graduates, founded "The Niagara Movement," a forerunner of the National Association for the Advancement of Colored People ("NAACP"). Activists birthed the latter organization in 1909. The men presented a manifesto calling for "universal manhood suffrage" and the elimination of racial segregation at a meeting attended by civil rights activists. The moniker "The Niagara

Movement" represented the "mighty current" of change the group wanted to effect and the natural landmark, Niagara Falls, located near where the first meeting took place in July of 1905. The Niagara Movement opposed racial segregation and disenfranchisement, as well as the accommodation and conciliation policies outlined in Booker T. Washington's "Atlanta Compromise" speech of 1895.

1909

- Founded February 12, 1909, the National Association for the Advancement of Colored People is the nation's oldest, largest and most widely recognized grassroots–based civil rights organization. Early on, the NAACP focused on challenging the Jim Crow laws prevalent throughout the South, succeeding only in a few early cases. A case in point is the NAACP's victory over Oklahoma's "grandfather clause," which exempted most white voters from stringent literacy requirements that effectively disenfranchised African Americans.

1910

- The National Urban League emerged to assist Southern black emigrants seeking better fortunes in the North. The National Urban League remains vibrant today as a voluntary nonpartisan community service agency. The Nation Urban League seeks to help end racial segregation and discrimination in the United States, especially toward African Americans, and to help economically and socially disadvantaged groups share equally in every aspect of American life.

1915

- In *Guinn v. United States* [*Guinn v. United States*, 238 U.S. 347 (1915)], the United States Supreme Court ruled against "grandfather clauses" used to deny persons of African ancestry the right to vote. Typical grandfather clauses provided an exemption from state property and literacy requirements to citizens, or descendants of citizens, who had the right to vote prior to 1866 or 1867. By design, these clauses, enacted in several southern states around 1890, disenfranchised persons of African ancestry who, by virtue of chattel slavery, did not meet their stipulations.

- *The Birth of a Nation* (a.k.a. *The Clansman*), director D.W. Griffith's silent film lionizing the Ku Klux Klan, became a Hollywood blockbuster. Considered innovative in both technical and narrative senses, the film set off a firestorm because of its sympathetic treatment of white supremacy.

1919

- James Weldon Johnson of the NAACP coined the term "Red Summer" to describe the summer and fall of 1919. Some 26 major "race riots" occurred throughout the United States. These attacks on African American communities, precipitated primarily by racism, were often influenced by economic uncertainty and political instability. Bloody racial conflagrations erupted in several cities in both the American North and South, including Chicago, Illinois; Longview, Texas; Washington, D.C.; Omaha, Nebraska; and Elaine, Arkansas.

1921

- The worst of the so-called "race riots" in twentieth century American history occurred in Tulsa, Oklahoma. The 1921 Tulsa Race Riot destroyed the nationally renowned African American entrepreneurial community known locally as the "Greenwood District," and dubbed "Black Wall Street" by many. Authorities believe that up to 300 people were killed. Hundreds more injured. Thousands were left homeless and destitute. Property damage ran into the millions of dollars. African American Tulsans rebuilt the Greenwood District and, by 1942, the community boasted well over 200 black-owned and black-operated business establishments. The 1921 Tulsa Race Riot became yet another example of the widespread hostility toward African American engagement and achievement that characterized this period in American history. More importantly, it became an example of African American resilience and determination in the face of seemingly insurmountable odds.

1922

- Proposed by Representative L.C. Dyer of Missouri, the Dyer Anti-Lynching Bill would have made lynching a federal crime. The Dyer Bill was an attempt to reduce or eliminate the onslaught of lynchings in the United States in the aftermath of World War I. Lynching, a form of domestic terrorism and vigilantism, targeted persons for a supposed crime or social slight, often based on scant evidence and always without judicial process. A tool of white supremacy, lynching most often targeted African Americans. White mobs meted out summary "justice" with the intent of not only punishing the target, but also sending a message to the group to which the target belonged: Know your place and stay in it. President Warren G. Harding supported the Dyer Bill. The Bill passed the House of Representatives, but was defeated in the Senate on a fili-buster.

1925

- Asa Philip Randolph organized the Brotherhood of Sleeping Car Porters. Randolph (April 15, 1889 – May 16, 1979) became a prominent twentieth-century African American civil rights leader and founded the Brotherhood of Sleeping Car Porters, a landmark organization for labor, and particularly for African American labor organizing.

1929

- The Reverend Dr. Martin Luther King, Jr. (January 15, 1929 – April 4, 1968) was born. King became an American clergyman, activist, and the preeminent leader of the African American civil rights movement; the preeminent icon for the movement. A Nobel Laureate, Dr. King remains a world-renowned human rights symbol.

1935

- Martin Luther King, Sr., father of Dr. Martin Luther King, Jr., led a protest against segregated elevators at the Fulton County, Georgia, Courthouse.

- Martin Luther King, Sr. and the Atlanta branch of the NAACP led a voter registration drive in anticipation of local school bond referendum.

1940

- Thurgood Marshall and others founded The NAACP Legal Defense and Educational Fund, Inc. ("LDF"). Marshall went on to become a famed civil rights attorney, the first African American to serve as United States Solicitor General, and the first African American to sit on the United States Supreme Court. Although LDF's primary purpose was to provide legal assistance to poor African Americans, its work over the years has brought greater justice to all Americans.

1941

- A. Philip Randolph called for a march on Washington to protest employment discrimination in the armed forces and war industry.

- On June 24, 1941, President Franklin D. Roosevelt issued Executive Order 8802 forbidding racial discrimination in defense industries and in government services, which provided, in part:

NOW, THEREFORE, by virtue of the authority vested in me by the Constitution and the statutes, and as a prerequisite to the successful conduct of our national defense production effort, I do hereby reaffirm the policy of the United States that there shall be no discrimination in the employment of workers in defense industries or government because of race, creed, color, or national origin, and I do hereby declare that it is the duty of employers and of labor organizations, in furtherance of said policy and of this order, to provide for the full and equitable participation of all workers in defense industries, without discrimination because of race, creed, color, or national origin[.]

- Executive Order 8802 established The President's Committee on Fair Employment Practices.

1942

- James Farmer founded The Congress for Racial Equality ("CORE") in Chicago. CORE, a civil rights organization dedicated to the use of nonviolent direct action, sought to promote better race relations and end racial discrimination in the United States. It initially focused on activities directed toward the desegregation of public accommodations in Chicago. Later, CORE expanded its program of nonviolent sit-ins to the South. CORE gained national recognition by sponsoring the Freedom Rides in 1961, a series of confrontational bus rides throughout the South by interracial groups of CORE members and supporters. Racist mobs verbally abused and physically assaulted the so-called "Freedom Riders" on numerous occasions. Ultimately, CORE succeeded in ending segregation on interstate bus routes. CORE joined a host of other organizations as a sponsor of the 1963 "March on Washington," at which Dr. Martin Luther King, Jr. delivered his signature "I Have A Dream" speech. After 1966, when James Farmer resigned from CORE, the organization concentrated more on black voter registration in the South and on community problems. More recent CORE leaders have focused on African American political and economic empowerment.

1944

- On April 25, 1944, Frederick D. Patterson, then president of what is now Tuskegee University, Mary McLeod Bethune, and others incorporated The United Negro College Fund ("UNCF"). UNCF is a philanthropic organization that raises funds for college tuition on behalf of African American students and general scholarship funds for thirty-nine private, historically black colleges and universities (referred to as "HBCUs") in the United States.

1946

- African American women formed the Women's Political Council ("WPC") in Montgomery, Alabama. A civic organization for African American professional women in Montgomery, WPC claimed as members numerous educators at Alabama State College or in the public schools of Montgomery. Some forty members attended the first organizational meeting. Mary Fair Burks, head of Alabama State's English department, served as the group's first president. For its first undertaking, WPC registered voters, a daunting task given the prevalence of literacy tests as barriers to African American voting. All the WPC members eventually passed the tests. They then opened schools to help other African Americans complete registration forms and pass literacy tests. Later, WPC initiated the Montgomery Bus Boycott, a watershed event in the civil rights movement.

- Primus King's legal challenge against the State of Georgia [*Chapman v. King*, 154 F.2d 460 (5th Cir. 1946), cert. denied, 327 U.S. 800 (1946)] removed legal barriers to black voting. The Fifth Circuit Court of Appeals struck down Georgia's all-white Democratic primary, declaring the "white primary" unconstitutional. White primaries—primary elections in the South in which non-White voters were prohibited from participating—existed in many Southern states after about 1890 and through the mid-1960s.

- In *Irene Morgan v. Commonwealth of Virginia*, [*Irene Morgan v. Commonwealth of Virginia*, 328 U.S. 373 (1946)], the United States Supreme Court banned segregation in interstate bus travel.

1947

- CORE and the Fellowship of Reconciliation sent the first "Freedom Riders" through the South to test compliance with *Morgan v. Commonwealth* ruling. The "Fellowship of Reconciliation" consisted of a number of religious nonviolent organizations, particularly in English-speaking countries, linked together by affiliation to the International Fellowship of Reconciliation.

1948

- In 1948, the United States Supreme Court ruled in *Sipuel v. Board of Regents of the University of Oklahoma* [*Sipuel v. Board of Regents of the University of Oklahoma*, 332 U.S. 631 (1948)] that the State of Oklahoma must provide instruction for African Americans equal to that of whites. The case involved the desegregation of the University of Oklahoma Law School. Thurgood Marshall, in a forerunner to the *Brown v. Board of Education* [*Brown v. Board of Education*, 347 U.S. 483 (1954)], acted as the lead NAACP counsel on the case. Tulsa, Oklahoma attorney and NAACP Tulsa branch president Amos T. Hall served as co-counsel.

1950

- In *Sweatt v. Painter* [*Sweatt v. Painter*, 339 U.S. 629 (1950)], the United States Supreme Court ordered the University of Texas Law School to admit African American students.

- *McLaurin v. Oklahoma* [*McLaurin v. Oklahoma*, 339 US 637 (1950)] abolished segregation in school classrooms, libraries, and cafeterias.

- *Henderson v. United States* [*Henderson v. United States*, 339 U.S. 816 (1950)] prohibited dining car segregation on trains.

1953

- CORE began sit-ins in Baltimore, Maryland.

- The Baton Rouge, Louisiana, bus boycott began.

1954

- In *Brown v. Board of Education of Topeka, Kansas* [*Brown v. Board of Education*, 347 U.S. 483 (1954)], the United States Supreme Court declared racial segregation in public schools unconstitutional.

1955

- In August 1955, a fourteen-year-old African American boy went to visit relatives near Money, Mississippi. The boy, Emmett Till, knew about racism and segregation. He experienced segregation in his hometown of Chicago. Unaccustomed to the extreme forms of racism that he encountered in Mississippi, Emmett allegedly breached social mores by flirting with a white woman, Carolyn Bryant, in a local store. A few days later, two men barged into the cabin of Mose Wright, Emmett's uncle, in the middle of the night. Roy Bryant, the owner of the store and Carolyn's husband, and J.W. Milam, his brother-in-law, drove off with Emmett. Three days later, Emmett's lifeless, mutilated body turned up in the Tallahatchie River. Emmett's virtually unrecognizable corpse bore all manner of injuries: a gouged out eye; a crushed skull; a bullet-ridden torso. Emmett's mother, Mamie, held an open casket funeral in Chicago. The gruesomeness of Emmett's remains shocked the conscience of many Americans, but not the all-white jury that acquitted Roy Bryant and J.W. Milam of Emmett's murder. Bryant and Milam later confessed. The case galvanized the civil rights movement.

- Authorities arrested seamstress Rosa Parks for refusing to give up her seat on a Montgomery, Alabama bus. So began the Montgomery Bus Boycott, a political and social protest campaign that opposed the city's policy of racial segregation on its public transit system. Dr. Martin Luther King, Jr. helped lead the boycott. Because African Americans constituted a large percentage of people who used public transportation, the Montgomery public transit system lost substantial revenue during the boycott, which lasted from December 1, 1955, to December 20, 1956. In the end, the United States Supreme Court ruled that Alabama and Montgomery laws requiring segregated buses were unconstitutional.

1956

- Montgomery, Alabama, authorities desegregated the local bus system.

1957

- The "Little Rock Nine" entered Central High School in Little Rock, Arkansas, escorted by 1,000 paratroopers under orders from President Dwight Eisenhower. This school desegregation showdown garnered international attention.

1958

- Clara Luper, educator and advisor for the Oklahoma City, Oklahoma, NAACP Youth Council, initiated the first known sit-in. On Tuesday afternoon, August 19, 1958, Luper and her Youth Council members entered the segregated Katz Drugstore in downtown Oklahoma City, Oklahoma. They took seats and asked to be served. Two days later, Katz corporate management in Kansas City desegregated its lunch counters in three states. The Oklahoma City sit-in preceded the February 1, 1960, Greensboro, North Carolina, sit-in often credited with initiating the movement.

1960

- A February sit-in at the Woolworth's lunch counter in Greensboro, North Carolina, drew national attention to the "sit-in" as a tool of civil disobedience aimed at desegregating public eateries.

1961

- The "Freedom Rides" began. Busloads of volunteers of all of races, traveled across the country and through the Deep South in an effort to integrate bus terminals. [See 1942—discussion of CORE, above.]

1962

- On October 1, 1962, James Meredith became the first black student at the University of Mississippi. He had been barred from entering on September 20, 1962. His enrollment, virulently opposed by segregationist Governor Ross Barnett, sparked riots on the Oxford, Mississippi campus. President John F. Kennedy dispatched federal troops and United States Marshals to the University of Mississippi. At the end of the chaos, two people lay dead.

1963

- Martin Luther King, Jr. wrote his "Letter from a Birmingham Jail." King had spent three days in solitary confinement after being arrested for participating in a protest march. That jail stint became his muse for the acclaimed writing.

- Ku Klux Klan ("KKK") bombs killed four little girls at the Sixteenth Street Baptist Church in Birmingham, Alabama. Founded by veterans of the Confederate Army in 1865, the KKK consists of several past and present secret domestic militant organizations in the United States. The KKK originated in the Southern states, but eventually gained national scope. KKK members, known principally for advocating white supremacy and acting as a domestic terrorist organization, often hid their identities behind conical hats, masks and white robes. The KKK created a long record of terrorism, violence, mayhem, and lynching to intimidate, murder, and oppress African Americans, Jews, and, occasionally, other minorities (*e.g.*, Roman Catholics; labor union members).

- More than 30,000 people of all races gathered on the Mall in Washington on August 28th to protest civil inequities and hear Dr. Martin Luther King's famous "I Have a Dream" speech.

- Lee Harvey Oswald assassinated President John Fitzgerald Kennedy on November 22nd.

1964

- Malcolm X (May 19, 1925 – February 21, 1965) delivered his speech, "The Ballot or the Bullet," at the Cory Methodist Church in Cleveland, Ohio. Malcolm X, born Malcolm Little, and also known as El-Hajj Malik El-Shabazz, was an African American Muslim minister, orator, and human rights activist. His admirers saw him as a courageous advocate for the rights of African Americans, a man who indicted white America in the harshest terms for its crimes against African Americans. His detractors accused him of preaching racial violence. Some regard Malcolm X as one of the greatest and most influential African Americans in history.

- Congress passed the Civil Rights Act of 1964, guaranteeing African Americans equal access to public accommodations.

1965

- On February 21, 1965, members of the Nation of Islam assassinated Malcolm X, a prominent black nationalist leader and spokesperson, in Manhattan's Audubon Ballroom. Just a year prior, in 1964, Malcolm X left the Nation of Islam after more than a decade of allegiance to become a Sunni Muslim.

- State troopers attacked civil rights protestors in Selma, Alabama, on "Bloody Sunday," spraying tear gas and wielding batons. Law enforcement officers assailed residents not participating in the demonstration, too. One person died.

- President Lyndon B. Johnson signed the Voting Rights Act of 1965 into law on August 5, 1965.

- The Watts Riots, lasting six days, left at least thirty-four people dead, 1,032 injured, and 3,952 arrested in the Watts neighborhood of Los Angeles, California. The riots began on August 11, 1965, when Lee Minikus, a California Highway Patrol motorcycle officer, pulled over Marquette Frye. Officer Minikus observed Frye driving erratically, and believed him to be intoxicated. Frye failed basic sobriety tests (*e.g.*, walking in a straight line and touching his nose). Minikus arrested him. The officer refused to let Frye's brother, Ronald, drive the car home. He radioed a call to have Frye's vehicle impounded. As events escalated, a crowd of onlookers steadily grew from dozens to hundreds. The mob became violent, throwing rocks and other objects while shouting at the police officers. A struggle ensued, resulting in the arrest of Marquette Frye, Ronald Frye, and their mother. This incident inflamed preexisting racial tensions, triggering the Watts implosion.

1967

- On June 13, 1967, President Lyndon Baines Johnson appointed Thurgood Marshall to the United States Supreme Court following the retirement of Justice Tom C. Clark. President Johnson realized the momentous nature of the appointment, noting that it was "the right thing to do, the right time to do it, the right man and the right place." A 69-11 United States Senate vote confirmed Justice Marshall as Associate Justice of the United States Supreme Court on August 31, 1967.

1968

- James Earl Ray assassinated the Reverend Dr. Martin Luther King, Jr. as King stood on the balcony of the Loraine Motel in Memphis, Tennessee. Authorities captured and arrested the triggerman, who was subsequently convicted of the murder and sentenced to 99 years in jail. Ray died in 1998.

- Sirhan Bishara Sirhan, the son of a Palestinian Christian family, assassinated presidential candidate and United States Senator Robert F. Kennedy at the Ambassador Hotel in Los Angeles, California, on June 5th.

1992

- The Los Angeles riots of 1992 erupted when a jury acquitted four police officers accused in the videotaped beating of black motorist Rodney King following a high-speed pursuit. Thousands of people in the Los Angeles area took part in the massive disturbance aver a six-day period following the verdict. Widespread looting, assault, arson, and murder occurred. Property damage totaled some one billion dollars. Many of the crimes were racially motivated. When the dust settled, 53 people lay dead.

2005

- On June 13, 2005, in an unprecedented resolution, the United States Senate formally apologized for its failure to enact the Dyer Anti-Lynching Bill in 1922 and other anti-lynching bills.

2008

- In November, Americans elected Barack Obama, an African American, as the 44th President of the United States of America. He was subsequently elected to a second term

2009

- The United States Senate, on February 2, 2009, confirmed Eric Holder as the first African American United States Attorney General.

Adapted in part from: Amaela Wiley, Timeline of the American Civil Rights Movement — Looking Back 50 Years After the Montgomery Bus Boycott (AOL Research & Learn, 2006), http://reference.aol.com/nowyouknow/article?id=20050920113009990001; Borgna Brunner, African American History Timeline — A chronology of black history from the early slave trade through Affirmative Action, http://www.infoplease.com/spot/bhmtimeline.html; Toward Racial Equality: Harper's Weekly Reports on Black America, 1857 – 1874, http://blackhistory.harpweek.com/2SlaveryTimeline,.htm.

Appendix D
Ellis Family Education and Accomplishments
(Double asterisk indicates a first for African Americans)

ROBERTA ELLIS (June 7, 1901 - December 5, 1974)
Education
- Master's Degree, University of Michigan, 1948
- Bachelor's Degree, Langston University, 1932

Accomplishments
- Organizer of University of Michigan Delta Psi Omega Graduate Chapter, Alpha Kappa Alpha Sorority, 1948
- Counselor for black women students at the University of Michigan, 1944-52
- 25-year teaching career in Oklahoma and Michigan public school systems
- **President of Washtenaw County, Michigan Teachers Association

WHITT ELLIS JR. (June 17, 1905 - October 30, 1930)
Education
- Bachelor's Degree, Langston University, 1927

CLIFF ELLIS (July 2, 1907 - July 23, 1983)
Education
- Bachelor's Degree, Langston University, 1939

Accomplishments
- Agriculture teacher and consultant with Bristow, Oklahoma, Board of Education
- Coordinator for retiree organic food growing program, Sacramento, California, 1970s
- Agricultural advisor to the Nation of Islam, 1960s-70s
- Well-known organic farmer and beekeeper

WADE ELLIS SR. (June 9, 1909 - November 20, 1989)
Education
- Ph.D., University of Michigan, 1944
- **Master's Degree, University of New Mexico, 1938

- Bachelor's Degree, Wilberforce University, 1928

Accomplishments

- **President of Mary Grove College in Detroit, Michigan, 1979-80
- **Vice chancellor of Academic Affairs at University of Maryland-Eastern Shore, 1977-79
- **Chairman of Michigan Council of Graduate Deans, 1975-77
- **Professor of Mathematics and Associate Dean of Horace H. Rackham School of Graduate Studies, University of Michigan, 1967-77
- **Lecturer and consultant to the higher mathematics communities in Greece, Peru, East Africa and India, 1960-1967
- **Professor of Mathematics, Oberlin College, 1948-67
- **Best doctoral dissertation at University of Michigan Graduate School Math Department, 1944
- **Staff member of MIT Radiation Laboratory, 1943-46
- **Recipient of highest civilian award from government of Peru for establishing national mathematics curriculum
- Highly respected member of the national and international mathematics education communities

JAMES RILEY ELLIS (June 25, 1911 - May 30, 2003)

Education

- **Ph.D., Tulsa University, 1962
- Master's Degree, University of New Mexico, 1939
- Bachelor's Degree, Langston University, 1933

Accomplishments

- Professor of Mathematics and Director of Cooperative Education, Langston University, 1968-76
- Educational consultant, University of Texas, 1967 and University of Colorado, 1964
- Principal of George Washington Carver High School, Tulsa, Oklahoma, 1960-68
- Assistant Principal of Booker T. Washington High School, Tulsa, Oklahoma, 1953-1960
- Teacher at Booker T. Washington High School, Tulsa, Oklahoma, 1940-60
- Teacher in Colbert, Clearview and Tulsa, Oklahoma, 1933-40

HASKO VINTREZ ELLIS (May 13, 1913 - May 22, 1967)

Education
- Master's Degree, Prairie View University, 1950
- Bachelor's Degree, Langston University, 1937

Accomplishments
- Director of Vocational Agriculture, Langston University, 1947-48
- WWII veteran serving Africa, Italy, France and the South Pacific, 1943-46
- Long time agriculture teacher in Athens, Texas, and Shawnee, Oklahoma, 1937-43

ORA HERBERT ELLIS Sr. (March 23, 1916 -)

Education
- Master's Degree in Public Heath, University of Michigan, 1949
- Master's Degree in Education, University of Michigan, 1948
- Bachelor's Degree, Langston University, 1940

Accomplishments
- President of Washtenaw County, Michigan Senior Citizens Guild, 1973
- Teacher of the Year, Ann Arbor, Michigan Public School System, 1960
- Commissioner, Washtenaw County, Michigan, 1958-80; (Chairman of Commissioners, 1967)
- **Teacher, Ann Arbor High School, Ann Arbor, Michigan, 1956-80
- Chairman of Washtenaw County, Michigan Interagency Committee, 1954
- **Vice president of the Michigan Health Council, 1953-56
- Chairman of Washtenaw County, Michigan Tuberculosis Association, 1953

FRANCIS EDWIN ELLIS (August 18, 1918 - January 28, 2004)

Education
- Master's Degree, University of Michigan, 1942
- Bachelor's Degree, Langston University, 1939

Accomplishments
- District Court Magistrate, 15th District Court, Ann Arbor, Michigan, 1983-85
- **Optimist Club Governor for State of Michigan, 1976-77
- **District Court Bailiff, Washtenaw County Michigan, 1972-85

- Counselor, Veterans Administration, 1948-1950
- WWII veteran, infantry officer — served in the South Pacific (wounded in combat), 1943-1946
- Schoolteacher, Wynnewood, Oklahoma, 1939-40
- Longtime businessman in southern Michigan

MARGRETT ANN ELLIS (June 13, 1920 - November 26, 1976)
Education

Education
- Master's Degree, Wayne State University, 1964
- Bachelor's Degree, Langston University, 1948

Accomplishments
- Special Education teacher, Los Angeles, California, Public School System, 1970-1976
- Special Education teacher, Detroit public schools, 1957-70
- **Dietitian and manager of University of Michigan Hospital Cafeteria, 1950-57
- **Teacher, Ann Arbor public schools, 1948-1950

GEORGE SAWNER ELLIS (August 28, 1924 - ____)
Education
- Master's Degree, University of Michigan, 1966
- Bachelor's Degree, University of Michigan, 1952

Accomplishments
- ** Manager for U.S. Air Force projects in Belgium and Tunisia, 1977-87
- Member of Dayton Area Chamber of Commerce (Chairman of World Trade Committee, 1975-77)
- Board of Directors of Dakota Community Center in Dayton, Ohio, 1968-
- **Chrysler Corporation, Executive Manager (including Amplex Division and Airtemp International operations), 1964-76
- **Field advisor and internal auditor for Michigan Employment Security Commission, 1954-64
- World War II veteran – served United States Army in Europe (earned four campaign ribbons), 1943-1946

Appendix E
Chandler: The Ellis Family Story

The following individuals contributed to *Chandler: The Ellis Family Story*. Mel Chatman, Chandler historian, led that effort, researching various documents and records, conducting interviews, compiling photographs, and much more.

Many thanks.

Baker, Bobby
Baker, Connie
Baker, Gwendolyn Calvert
Ballard, Currie
Barnett, William
Beaird, Rita
Beaty, Harold
Beltz, Danny
Bo, Lonnie
Bo, Peggy Riley-Grayson
Booker, Helen
Boone, Maedella Summers
Bostic, Frank "Stump"
Brewer, Agnes
Bridge, Thomas and Blanche
Bridges, Winnie Brooks
Brown, Helen
Brown, Mae
Brown, Victor
Bryant, Hattie
Burchette, Frankie
Burgess, Houston
Caldwell, Bernice Davis
Caldwell, Mae Ora
Cameron, Verner Rean Moore
Campbell, Lydia Lawson
Celestine, Matthew "Toad"
Chatman, Margrett Ann Ellis

Chatman, Whit
Clay, Joyetta
Coleman, Louise Stevens
Dandridge, Patricia Summers
Davis, Eulila Ranger
Douglas, Elnora Cooper
Dye, Karen
Echols, Grace
Elliot, Gerry Greenfield
Ellis, William Whit "Bill"
Ellis, Frank
Ellis, George
Ellis, Herb
Ellis, Herb Jr.
Ellis, James Riley
Ellis, James Riley Jr.
Ellis, Robert
Ellis, Sylvia
Ellis, Wade Jr.
Epstein, Larry
Esters, Hereece
Ferrill, Don and Sally
Fields, Andersen Jr.
Franks, Julius
Galbraith, Donna Sue Shafer
Garcia, Alvin "Buster"
Garcia, Gloria
Godwin, Jack

Good, Betsy
Grayson, Mark
Grayson, Mike
Green, Urban
Greenfield, Georgiann
Grigsby, Margaret
Haley, Jeanette
Harris, Leroy
Harris, Veloria
Harsen, Jim and Vada
Higgs, Lucy
Hix, Danny
Hornbeak, George
Hutton, Velma Echols
Jewett, Coleman
Johnson, Magerina Long
Knapp, Ida Battles
Lawson, Charlene Humphreys
Lawson, La Quinnia
Leonard, Mildred Dupree
Lewis, Burton "Lee"
Long, Barbara Neal
Long, Joe
Lucas, Audrey
Martenia, Vivian Humphrey
Mascho, Bill
Mascho, Robert
McRae, Benny J. Jr.
McCormick, Esther
McCormick, Von Dosta
Milas, Metalis Isaac "Snip"
Miner, Gordon
Mukes, Gwen
Mukes, Mable
Neal, Harold "Chick"
Neal, Ulysses "Spike"
Parker, Patsy Celestine

Parsons, Ann and Gardner
Parsons, Ralph and Barbara
Parsons, Sheila
Patterson, Willis
Pitts, Dorothy
Ragsdale, James
Randolph, Imogene Rankins
Reid, Jack
Riser, Illa B. Ranger
Ritchie, Eleanor Davis
Shinault, Patsy
Smalley, Aleta Baker
Smalley, Aleta Walker
Smith, Dorothy and Nate
Smith, Mattie
Snyder, Charlie
Sporleder, Donald E.
Starr, Tomisa
Stiefenmiller, Helen
Summers, Dorthy
Talley, Lois
Talley, Sharon
Taylor, Beatrice Garcia
Thomas, Geneva Booker
Threat, Edmond
Threat, Elizabeth Hilton
Vassar, Jan
Vassar, Paul
Vaughn, Virginia
Walker, Bobby
Wiley, Lessie
Williams, Leroy
Willis, Rutha Mae
Willis, Wilson
Wilson, Ethel Grey
Wilson, Jesse Mae
Young, Judith

Appendix F
Informal Black Communities in Lincoln County, Oklahoma

Special thanks to Mel Chatman and Jan Vassar for their research and writing on the informal black communities in Lincoln County. The following thumbnail sketches of those communities are derived from their work.

Black Alley

Black Alley was once home to the largest concentration of black people living in Lincoln County. Several miles of roads that crisscrossed within a six-mile radius constituted the community.

Several black families settled in the area in the late 1800s, including the Bookers, possible founders of Black Alley. In 1892, John Booker, his wife, Mary Lewis Holmes Booker, and their seven children moved from Texas to Mulhall, Oklahoma, in Logan County, about fourteen miles from the Oklahoma Territorial capital of Guthrie. Around 1897, the Booker family moved to Black Alley, seven miles east of Chandler and four miles south of Davenport.

Mr. Booker and his sons bought 320 acres of farmland and parlayed those holdings into a money-making operation. The six children of John and Mary produced thirty-five grandchildren. Many Booker offspring still reside in Lincoln County. John Booker donated a parcel of land that became Booker's Cemetery, the final resting place for family members and other persons living in the area.

Black Alley grew naturally as relatives and friends of the original settlers flocked to the community to work the productive land. In these pre-statehood times, Jim Crow had yet to take a chokehold on the area.

The origin of the name "Black Alley" remains a mystery. Newspapers from the period use the name, with one referring to the community's baseball team "the Black Alleys."

For many years, Black Alley bustled. Teachers, barbers, store owners, farmers, cooks, blacksmiths, midwives, preachers, carpenters, electricians, musicians, and others with special talents lived, socialized, and worked together. Several parks dotted the community, including one on the Manning property with a Masonic Hall, a cafe', a dance hall, and the Little Zion Church. On weekends, scores of residents and visitors flocked to the parks to enjoy music, dance, and play croquet and other outdoor games.

Lincoln School District #72, a separate school known as McCall's School, a reference to the family who owned the land on which it sat, served the students of Black Alley.

Prominent Black Alley surnames included: Bryant, Caldwell, Coffee, Daniels, Flowers, Garrett, Hines, Lucas, Polmar, Ragsdale, Sawner, Stewart, Walker, and Woodard.

Black Alley's fortunes soured during the Great Depression years and during and after World War II. Many of its residents left for California in search of better jobs and education. Lincoln County property records confirm that much Black Alley real estate remains in the hands of the original settlers' descendants.[cdxxxii]

DeGraffenreid

For $1,750, Henry DeGraffenreid purchased 160 acres sitting on both sides of the east-west section road beginning at the south end of the Sac and Fox Reservation[cdxxxiii] after it crosses Route 377, about five miles south of Stroud. He reportedly acquired the land in a September 1891 land run. A September 10, 1906, Lincoln County warranty deed in his name documents ownership.

The Pete Scott farm, located just before the section road crosses the Deep Fork River, formed the eastern DeGraffenreid boundary. The section road continued about two miles west, finally arriving at the Herman Cooper farm on the western boundary of the community. For a one-mile distance on both the south and north sides of the section road, DeGraffenreid farms dominated the landscape.

DeGraffenreid, located in a hilly portion of Lincoln County, is subject to flooding. After heavy rains, roads become impassible and home sites isolated. Flooding often causes heavy damage to native local crops, which include cotton, pecans, and a wide range of vegetables and fruits.

Because of its location less than a mile west of the Sac and Fox Reservation, community residents typically maintain more contact with Native Americans (*e.g.*, attendance at events such as stomp dances) than other Lincoln County residents.

Twin Hills, the intersection of two roads at the bottom of a large hill located two miles west of the Sac and Fox Reservation on the section road running through the community, remains *the* DeGraffenreid landmark. From Twin Hills, both roads continue up large hills. For many years, Twin Hills housed the mailboxes for the entire community.

While places help define communities, a community cannot exist without people—people like J.E. Moore, a successful, well-connected farmer, who worked with the government to help regulate the types and amounts of crops produced by area farmers during the Great Depression. As evidence of his success, Moore owned the only automobile in DeGraffenreid for many years.

Elenora Douglass grew up in DeGraffenreid as part of the Herman Cooper family. Poor, but never hungry, the Cooper family grew produce and raised livestock, even throughout the course of the Great Depression.

Mrs. Douglass recalled the presence of visible pools of crude oil that dotted parts of the area, but has no similar recollection of any oil wells whatsoever. Presumably, oilers tapped the precious commodity from another location proximate to the community.

Community also implies intergenerational connections—connections that schools and church often help foster. In DeGraffenreid, children in grades 1-8 attended the School District Number 111 School and worshipped at the adjacent St. Peter's Missionary Baptist Church.

At its peak in the 1930s, some thirty to forty families called DeGraffenreid home. By the end of World War II, most had struck out in search of economic opportunities.

Dudley

Dudley was located in the northwest section of Lincoln County, two-and-one-half miles due west of Carney, on a one-mile strip of sandy land running north from the section road. The community's residents lived close to this road, and a few white residents lived a mile or so away. A never-paved, dusty road ran through the community.

Dudley may be the only Lincoln County informal black community inhabited exclusively by African Americans. Some believe white families first settled in Dudley, with black residents settling, at least initially, just outside the area. Dudley Cemetery (*a.k.a.,* Green Cemetery) is located near Carney.[cdxxxiv]

The William and Lucy Barnett Family, Dudley, Oklahoma, 1918[cdxxv]

Fallis

Fallis, located two-and-a-half miles west and three-and-a-half miles north of Wellston, was the westernmost informal black community in Lincoln County. Three railroads passed through Fallis, facilitating the arrival of waves of black pioneers, some of whom chose Fallis simply because they did not have train fare to continue to other parts of Oklahoma.

Fallis produced a stunning number of writers, including children's stories author Blanche Seal Hunt; 1940 Oklahoma Poet Laureate Jenny Harris Oliver, who wrote books of poems and short stories; popular and detective short stories writer Beulah Rhodes Overman; prolific Western fiction writer Vingie Eve Roe; novelist and poetry editor in the 1930s and 1940s, Aletha Caldwell Conner; and 1963 Oklahoma Poet Laureate Delbert Davis. Most of these authors knew and worked with one another.[cdxxxvi]

African American notables produced by Fallis include Oklahoma educator Fredrick Douglass Moon, considered the dean of African American education in Oklahoma;[cdxxxvii] America's first black radio station owner, Jesse B. Blayton, Sr.;[cdxxxviii] and Vietnam War veteran and the first African American to receive the Congressional Medal of Honor, Riley Leroy Pitts.[cdxxxix] Some believe the *Fallis Blade*, briefly published in the early 1900s, to have been Lincoln County's first and only known newspaper with a black editor.[cdxl]

The 1900 and 1910 United States Censuses recorded no African American residents in Fallis. Later census data documented a black influx: In 1920, 24 black families (95 people); in 1930, 21 black families (57 people). Interviews with former Fallis residents indicate a number of black-owned dwellings and businesses in downtown Fallis during the 1930s.

Dunbar High School, a Rosenwald school[cdxli] primarily attended by students living in the Fallis-Wellston area, operated between 1922 and 1955. Located two-and-a-half miles northeast of Wellston, Dunbar began in a four-room brick building under the direction of its founder, Mr. G.M. Tuggle, as principal for the first twelve years. Dunbar expanded in 1927 with the addition of a principal's office and more classrooms.

Glover's Settlement

Glover's Settlement abutted Black Alley, sitting to the west and just south and west of the "white town" of Davenport.[cdxlii] The community's name came from the Glover family who settled there in the late 1800s. Indeed, some called the community "Gloversville" because there were so many Glovers living there.

Several members of the McCormick family, a well-known African American clan in Lincoln County, lived and farmed in and around

African American pioneers south of Davenport, Oklahoma, *circa* 1899[cdxliii]

Glover's Settlement. At one time, residents supported a Masonic Hall, a church, and a cemetery. School-age children from Glover's Settlement walked several miles to attend classes at the closest separate school, Lincoln School District #72, located in Black Alley.

All that remains of Glover's Settlement is Glover's Cemetery, a hard-to-access final resting place with visible-from-the-road headstones.[cdxliii]

Key West

Settlers formed Key West in the late 1890s. The community sits two-and-one-half miles south and two miles east of Stroud on the boundary line of Lincoln and Creek Counties. An African American man named Lemon Petty first settled the area, which was sold incorporated and named in 1907.

The status of Key West as an informal black community lasted until the discovery of oil in 1923. The black gold beneath Key West brought an influx of white oil field workers, swelling the white population and stalling the development of the area as a mostly black haven.

The enclave morphed into an oil town, but the economic benefits flowed unevenly based on race. Drillers reserved the better-paying oil field jobs for white workers, leaving only hard labor and pitchfork-and-wheel-barrow jobs for black laborers. George Hornbeak, the

Key West in the wake of a devastating 1927 tornado.[cdxiv]

first Lincoln County black professional oil field worker, shattered this petroleum ceiling in 1962.

In 1907 and 1927, tornados decimated Key West. After the second tornado, most black residents moved to other areas, with many landing in the southern part of nearby Stroud.

In its heyday (1923-1927), the prominent structures in Key West included oil derricks scattered throughout the town and the surrounding area. Sixty-eight oil pumps operated twenty hours a day. Shotgun houses pulled double duty, storing oil field maintenance equipment and providing housing for employees and their families.

Key West shone at night. Fifteen-foot-high, two-inch-diameter pipes stood like lampposts throughout the community, visible for miles in the darkness of night. Aglow twenty-four hours a day, the vessels funneled pockets of natural gas to an escape route from the underground oil fields to their fiery atmospheric ignition, sparking brightly colored flames that flickered several feet into the air.

Ms. Lizzy Davis of Key West (1910 – 1991)[cdxlviii]

The last black resident of Key West, Lizzy Davis, died in 1991. Bobby Baker and his sister, Arlene, natives of Key West, provided what little is known of its history.[cdxlvii] Bobby Baker eventually moved to nearby Stroud, but never fully abandoned Key West, where he maintained land. Key West Cemetery is located south of Stroud.[cdxlvii]

Kickapoo

Kickapoo, located four miles south and two miles west of Chandler, covered a one-mile length of the north/south section road, Miller Road, and extended for about a half-mile on either side of that road. Residents often called the nearby all-white town of Midlothian home. Some fifteen to twenty black families lived in Kickapoo.

The children of Kickapoo's earliest black pioneers attended an integrated school called the "Stockade," located about a quarter-of-a-mile south of the location of the later-built separate school, Dunbar School. Mount Moriah Church and the Mount Moriah Cemetery were co-located along Miller Road. "Sneed" and "Humphrey" are among the common surnames of persons buried in Mount Moriah Cemetery.

The Sneed farm, with a baseball diamond next to the farmhouse, occupied the space just north of Dunbar School on the east side of

Miller Road. It served as a community recreation area.

Several white families lived in Kickapoo. The white neighbors lived separate, but integrated, lives. They attended their own churches and social activities, but nonetheless maintained a presence in the black community, especially when it came time to plant and harvest crops. Black and white workers often broke bread together after a hard day's work during harvest season.

The Humphrey family held considerable sway in Kickapoo. Virginia Louise Hunter and Charley Humphrey married in Texas in the early 1880s. While there, Mrs. Humphrey bore five sons and three daughters. In 1903, the family moved to Lincoln County. Mrs. Humphrey bore two more children, Marcina and Jeffery Inman. Height became a Humphrey hallmark: Most of the women, including Virginia, stood five foot-seven inches or taller; two of the boys stood well over six-feet tall, one six-six, and another six-eight.

Payson

Payson is a diverse community located four miles south of Chandler on Highway 18. The community was sometimes confused with the nearby town of the same name, Payson. Geographically, most of Payson sits on the west side of Highway 18 and extends for about four miles to the west. Its southern boundary is the section road that crosses Highway 18 one mile south of Payson Road. Its northern boundary is about two miles north of the same intersection. The northwest corner of Payson, called "Galilee," was home to the Galilee Church and the Booker T. Washington Separate School.

Payson's oldest black residents, the Toliver family, arrived as part of the 1891 land opening. The oldest tombstone in the St. Paul's

St. Paul's Baptist Church, Payson, Oklahoma (2002)[cdliii]

Cemetery in Payson dates back to 1892. It is likely, however, that the community reached critical mass in the late 1920s (*i.e.*, the fifteen-black-family definitional criteria for an informal black community in Lincoln County). By the late 1930s, five white families and more than twenty black families lived in Payson.

While Payson's white families attended facilities and participated in activities that catered to them, they also engaged with their predominantly black neighbors. Poor farmers depended on one another, color notwithstanding.

In the 1940s, Payson's Spriggs Bar-B-Q became the community recreation center. Decades later, in 2001, both the St. Paul Baptist Church and the St. Paul Cemetery earned spots on the Oklahoma Register of Historic Places. Separate School for District #106 was located about a quarter mile east of St. Paul Baptist Church.

River Bend

As the smallest of Lincoln County's twelve informal black communities, River Bend, located five miles south and one mile east of Stroud (one mile east of the Sac and Fox Reservation), never grew beyond fifteen to twenty families.

The community derived its name from a sharp bend in the nearby Deep Fork River. River Bend began just after the river's sharp turn, and then followed the west bank of the Deep Fork River for about three miles.

Recurrent flooding of the Deep Fork River became both a burden and a blessing for the enclave. During rainy months, the cresting Deep Fork River flooded homes, but the flooding held one salutary effect: It spread silt over the farmland, providing essential nutrients and minerals for thirsty local crops.

Little is known about River Bend's history beyond the recollections of Ella B. Hargrove, whose ancestors, John and Mary Todd, arrived in River Bend in 1908. Over time, the Todds purchased more than 500 acres in the River Bend area. They joined several other black families already present, including the families of Willis Brooks, S.W.B. Mays, Willis Howell, and Henry Godwin.

In 1910, John Todd donated land to establish the River Bend Separate School, which served the community until its ultimate consolidation with the South Stroud Separate School in the mid-1950s.

In the early 1950s, prospectors discovered oil in the River Bend area. To the delight and financial enrichment of landowners, drillers launched some twenty wells.

River Bend gained unwelcome notoriety in the 1930s. Ted Cole, a white resident of Key West who grew up in River Bend, became one of only a few men to escape from Alcatraz prison in San Francisco.

Cole, convicted of kidnapping in Oklahoma and sentenced to fifty years incarceration, escaped with a companion on December 16, 1937. Presumed dead, he and his compatriot were never heard from again.[cdliii] The 1979 Clint Eastwood movie, *Escape from Alcatraz*, documented the tale.[cdliv]

Rock Springs

Rock Springs, founded in 1891 by George Washington Miller, an African American born into slavery in Tennessee, is located eight miles northwest of Chandler. Sometime in the 1860s, while still enslaved, George married Emeline Kell. They lived in Valley Mills, Texas, in a small community called Rock Springs. By 1891, twelve children had been born of that union.

In 1891, Miller struck out on one of the Oklahoma land runs. He secured a 160-acre section of land northwest of Chandler, and then returned to Rock Springs. He gathered his belongings and family, including his mother, and brought them to live in an Oklahoma community named after the place they left behind in Texas.

Miller built the family its first home, a log cabin, in Rock Springs. When fire destroyed the structure a few years later, Miller built a modern two-story frame house as its replacement. Two more chil-

George and Mary Miller (undated)[cdliv]

The Miller Family (undated)[cdlvi]

dren, Minnie and Aron, were born after the family's arrival in Oklahoma.

The Rock Springs community grew along a one-and-one-half mile strip of road. Dwellings sprang up on both sides of the road, extending about a mile-and-a-half. Miller donated land for a church, Rock Springs A.M.E., a school, Separate School District #36, and a cemetery, all adjacent to one another at about mid-point of the community's main road. Between its founding in 1891 and 1935, the community grew to about thirty families. The last resident departed Rock Springs before the end of World War II.

Sweet Home

In the early 1890s, the first black pioneers arrived in Sweet Home on the Otoe and McKinley township line, two-and-a-half miles north of Warwick and six miles south and one mile east of Carney. A one-and-one-half mile section road divided the community. Some of the earliest settlers, a number of whom hailed from Texas, included people with the surnames Coleman, Ester, West, Campbell, Allen, Gorstin, Arbuckle, Freeman, Epps, and Lewis families.

In 1890, Burl West donated one-and-one-half acres of land to establish the Sweet Home Baptist Church, rebuilt in 1918 on the original site. Some of the church's parishioners found their final resting places next to the church. At one time, Sweet Home also housed a Church of God and a Methodist church.

"Sweet Home" is believed to be the name of a Texas town or com-

Sweet Home Baptist Church, established 1930, *circa* 2009[cdlix]

munity from which a significant number of the first settlers originated. The pioneers never established a town site, and the small community never reached more than thirty families. The nearby community of Warwick provided basic support, including mail service and supplies. By the early 1950s, only a few homes remained. Sweet Home Cemetery is located south of Carney.

Sweet Home's one-room school once housed more than a hundred students taught by two teachers. That school closed in 1957. Beginning in 1922, high school students began attending the Dunbar Separate High School, located near Wellston.

Curious Chandlerites recently discovered the likely grave of an African American Civil War hero near Sweet Home. Frank Goldson, born in 1841 in Louisiana, served with the Louisiana Colored Infantry around 1863, and with the 47th Regiment, United States Colored Infantry in 1864. His name appears on the African American Civil War Memorial in Washington, D.C.

Goldson, who died in 1915, homesteaded land in McKinley Township north of Wellston, Oklahoma, obtaining outright ownership of the land in 1902. The Goldson family plot sits on an uncultivated corner of eighty acres. Among the gravestones found on the plot, only one, that of Goldson's daughter, Roxie, remains legibly marked. The other stones appear likely to be those of Goldson and his wife, Alice.[cdlviii]

Endnotes

[i]Mel Chatman, *Chandler: The Ellis Family Story*, chapter 8, http://www.ellis-familystory.com/contents.html (last visited August 21, 2013). Mel Chatman is the son of Ann Ellis, the youngest of the Whit and Maggie Ellis clan, a large African American family with deep roots in Chandler. Mr. Chatman has long taken a historical interest in the town. His extensive research and expertise have been of invaluable assistance in completing this project. For a listing of contributors to the project, see Appendix E.

[ii]http://www.ellisfamilystory.com/contents.html.

[iii]Correspondence from Mel Chatman to the author, February 2, 2015. In terms of family unity, Chatman recalled no instances of hearing shouting, harsh words, or name-calling among family members while growing up. As for oratory, he recalled being instructed on speaking proper English and avoiding black dialect.

[iv]Meeting with Jan Vassar, February 6, 2015, Tulsa, Oklahoma.

[v]*See* Timothy Taylor, "A History of the U.S. Economy in the Twentieth Century," The Great Courses, Business & Economics (course guidebook), http://anon.eastbaymediac.m7z.net/anon.eastbaymediac.m7z.net/teachingco/CourseGuideBooks/DG529_579A21.PDF (last visited September 5, 2014); http://www.2blowhards.com/archives/001378.html#001378 (last visited September 5, 2014).

[vi]Thomas Maloney, "African Americans in the Twentieth Century," EH.Net Encyclopedia (Robert Whaples, ed.), January 14, 2002, http://eh.net/encyclopedia/african-americans-in-the-twentieth-century/ (last visited June 30, 2014).

[vi]Telephone interview with George Sawner Ellis, October 18, 2013 (Ellis remembers a toy barking dog, a cherished gift given to him by his namesake, George Sawner, after the Sawners visited Montreal.)

[viii]Smitherman, Andrew Jackson. *The Tulsa Star* (Tulsa, Okla.), Vol. 8, No. 7, E. 1, Saturday, December 21, 1918. Tulsa, Oklahoma. The Gateway to Oklahoma History, http://gateway.okhistory.org/ark:/67531/metadc72777/ (last visited October 14, 2014).

[ix]"Passing," in racial parlance, generally referred to a person who, while classified as a member of a particular racial group, attempts to move surreptitiously into and be accepted by another racial group. In the American experience, passing often described the means by which some biracial or mixed race individuals, classified as black under the rule of hypodescent

(*i.e.*, the "one drop" rule), infiltrated white society to escape the ill effects of state-sanctioned segregation and discrimination and avoid distasteful private custom and usage that followed a racially hierarchical pattern.

[x]*See, e.g.*, Dunjee, Roscoe. *The Black Dispatch* (Oklahoma City, Okla.), Vol. 5, No. 8, Ed. 1 Friday, January 2, 1920. The Gateway to Oklahoma History. http://okhistory.org/ark:/67531/metadc152184/ (last visited October 15, 2014) ("[A]s everyone who knows him understands, [George Sawner] is so bright of complexion, that he is often mistaken for a white man.")

[xi]Dunjee, Roscoe. *The Black Dispatch* (Oklahoma City, Okla.), Vol. 5, No. 18, Ed. 1 Friday, May 30, 1919. The Gateway to Oklahoma History. http://okhistory.org/ark:/67531/metadc152132/ (last visited October 17, 2014).

[xii]*See, e.g.*, Hillary Crosley, "Is There Room for a Race Man Today?", *The Root*, August 19, 2013, http://www.theroot.com/articles/culture/2013/08/is_there_room_for_a_race_man_today.html (last visited May 31, 2015). The term "race man" generally refers to an African American fully committed to racial uplift.

[xiii]*In Memoriam: G. W. F. Sawner, Chandler News-Publicist Print*, May 2, 1924, at 10.

[xiv]"Sunset and Evening Star, In Memoriam: G. W. F. Sawner," *Chandler News-Publicist Print*, May 2, 1924, at 56.

[xv]In Memoriam: G. W. F. Sawner, *Chandler News-Publicist Print*, May 2, 1924, at 40 - 41.

[xvi]This adage dates *at least* back to 1945, and likely much earlier. *See, e.g.*, The Phrase Finder, http://www.phrases.org.uk/meanings/60500.html (last visited July 22, 2014).

[xvii]Mrs. Sawner worked within the legal and social confines of her era, including rigid school segregation. Her success educating rural black children, given the socio-cultural milieu, merits high praise. In general, however, school segregation is widely believed to have significantly disadvantaged black children. *See, e.g.*, Rucker C. Johnson, "Long-run Impacts of School Desegregation & School Quality on Adult Attainments," NBER Working Paper No. 16664, Issued in January 2011, available at http://www.nber.org/papers/w16664 (synopsis) (last visited September 4, 2014). In a 2011 paper investigating the long-run impacts of court-ordered school desegregation on an array of adult socioeconomic and health outcomes, Rucker C. Johnson, associate professor, Goldman School of Public Policy, University of California, Berkeley, found that:

> [F]or blacks, school desegregation significantly increased both educational and occupational attainments, college quality and adult earnings, reduced the probability of incarceration, and improved adult health status; desegregation had no effects on whites across each of these outcomes.

The results suggest that the mechanisms through which school desegregation led to beneficial adult attainment outcomes for blacks include improvement in access to school resources reflected in reductions in class size and increases in per-pupil spending.

[xviii]Sojourner Truth, born into slavery as Isabella Baumfree to James and Elizabeth Baumfree, circa 1797, was, among other things, an abolitionist, author, and human rights advocate. She died at age 86 on November 26, 1883, in Battle Creek, Michigan. *See, e.g.,* http://www.sojournertruthmemorial.org/ (last visited June 8, 2015).

[xix]Henry D. Spalding, Ed., *Encyclopedia Of Black Folklore And Humor* (Middle Village, NY: Jonathan David Publishers, Inc. 1990), at 46 (The piece is called "Sojourner Squelches A Squawker.")

[xx]Adapted from "I've Been to the Mountaintop" speech by Rev. Dr. Martin Luther King, Jr. (April 3, 1968).

[xxi]WE.B. Dubois, *The Souls Of Black Folk* (New York, NY: First Vintage Books/ The Library of America Edition 1990) (introduction by John Edgar Wideman), at The Forethought.

[xxii]*See* "United States in 1860: Free States, Slave States, and Territories," http://lincoln.lib.niu.edu/fimage/image.php?id=436 (last visited August 31, 2014).

[xxiii]European Americans considered these tribes "civilized" because they had adopted European ways—they had acculturated to a significant degree. See, *e.g.,* Andrew K. Frank, "Five Civilized Tribes," Oklahoma Historical Society's Encyclopedia of Oklahoma History & Culture, http://digital.library. okstate.edu/encyclopedia/entries/F/FI011.html (last visited September 9, 2014).

[xxiv]For more information on the Freedmen, the persons of African ancestry who lived among the Five Civilized Tribes, some free, others enslaved, *see* Hannibal B. Johnson, *Apartheid In Indian Country—Seeing Red Over Black Disenfranchisement* (Waco, TX: Eakin Press 2012).

[xxv]*See, e.g.,* Academy of American Franciscan History, "Black Conquistadors: Armed Africans in Early Spanish America (1500's)," The Americas, 57:2 October 2000, at 171 – 2015, available online at http://originalpeople.org/ black-conquistadors-armed-africans-in-early-spanish-america-1500s/ (last visited September 5, 2014); Donald N. Brown, "Immigration," Oklahoma Historical Society's Encyclopedia of Oklahoma History & Culture, http:// digital.library.okstate.edu/encyclopedia/entries/I/IM001.html (last visited September 5, 2014); Schomburg Center for Research in Black Culture Presents "IN MOTION: The African-American Migration Experience" (The Western Migration) http://www.inmotionaame.org/migrations/topic. cfm?migration=6&topic=5 (last visited September 2, 2014); Hannibal B.

Johnson, *Apartheid In Indian Country: Seeing Red Over Black Disenfranchise-ment* (Fort Worth, TX: Eakin Press 2012).

[xxvi]"Oklahoma" means "territory of the red people" in the Choctaw language. *See, e.g., Chahta Anumpa Aiikhvna*, School of Choctaw Language, http://www.choctawschool.com/home-side-menu/history/choctaw-place-names-in-oklahumma.aspx (an authorized website of the Choctaw Nation of Oklahoma), last visited March 5, 2015.

[xxvii]Kenny L. Brown, "Oklahoma Territory," Oklahoma Historical Society's Encyclopedia of Oklahoma History & Culture, http://digital.library.okstate.edu/encyclopedia/entries/O/OK085.html (last visited October 31, 2014).

[xxviii]*See, e.g.*, "The Unassigned Lands of Oklahoma Territory," http://www.rootsweb.ancestry.com/~itunassi/, last visited March 15, 2015.

[xxix]*See, e.g.*, J. F. Holden, "THE B.I.T.: The Story of an Adventure in Railroad Building," *Chronicles of Oklahoma* (vol. 11, no. 1. March 1933): 643 – 645:

> There had been no railroads in the Indian country up to 1870, but beginning in that year the steel rails began to push their way into the Territory. . . . The coming of the railroads into the Indian country was the beginning of the disintegration of the Indian nations, and foreshadowed the ending of the isolation of the Indian Territory. As the long lines of rail pushed their way farther and farther into the country white people followed them. Stations and towns were located, coal mines opened up, and merchants and tradesmen began doing business—all spelling the doom of the old free and self-governing national life and existence of the Indians.

[xxx]*See, e.g.*, "Native American Tribes of Oklahoma," http://www.native-languages.org/oklahoma.htm (last visited September 9, 2014).

[xxxi]*See, e.g.*, Schomburg Center for Research in Black Culture Presents *In Motion: The African-American Migration Experience* (The Western Migration) http://www.inmotionaame.org/migrations/topic.cfm?migration=6&topic=5 (last visited September 2, 2014).

[xxxii]Hannibal B. Johnson, *Imagine*, 2010 (unpublished).

[xxxiii]Postcard courtesy of Mel Chatman, presented to Mr. Chatman by Jan Vassar in 2009. The postcard was published in Kansas City, Missouri. According to Jan Vassar, black Oklahoma boosters targeted African Americans in the area, encouraging them to seek their fortunes and better lives in Oklahoma Territory (*i.e.*, the western portion of pre-statehood Oklahoma). E-mail from Jan Vassar to Mel Chatman dated February 10, 2015.

[xxxiv]Photo courtesy Mel Chatman.

[xxxv]Photo courtesy Mel Chatman.

xxxviLincoln County Historical Society, available at www.rootsweb.ancestry. com/~oklincol/land.html,, (last visited September 12, 2013).

xxxviiPopulation of Oklahoma and Indian Territory, 1907 (Washington, D.C.: Government Printing Office), at 16 (publication of the Department of Commerce and Labor, Bureau of The Census, S.N.D. North, Director), at 7, available at http://www2.census.gov/prod2/decennial/documents/1907pop_ OK-IndianTerritory.pdf (last visited August 8, 2014).

xxxviiiSamuel Francis Smith, My Country, 'Tis of Thee (aka, America) (1831).

xxxix*See* Hannibal B. Johnson, *Acres Of Aspiration — The All-Black Towns In Oklahoma* (Austin, TX: Eakin Press 2002).

xlen.wikipedia.org/wiki/Five_CivilizedTribes (last visited August 13, 2013).

xliTripadvisor, www.tripadvisor.com/Attraction_Review-g51535-d578636- Reviews-F... (last visited August 13, 2013).

xlii*See, e.g.,* Jere Roberson, McCabe, Edward P. (1850 – 1920), Oklahoma Historical Society's Encyclopedia of Oklahoma History & Culture, http://digital.library.okstate.edu/ENCYCLOPEDIA/ENTRIES/M/MC006.html (last visited October 31, 2014).

xliii*See* Hannibal B. Johnson, *Black Wall Street — From Riot To Renaissance In Tulsa's Historic Greenwood District* (Austin, TX: Eakin Press 1998).

xliv*See* Hannibal B. Johnson, *Acres Of Aspiration — The All-Black Towns In Oklahoma* (Austin, TX: Eakin Press 2002), at 159 - 163.

xlv*See, e.g.,* Eric Foner, *Reconstruction: America's Unfinished Revolution* (New York, NY: Harper & Row 1988).

xlviJohn G. Van Deusen, *The Exodus of 1879*, 21:2 *The Journal Of Negro History* (April 1936).

xlvii*See, e.g.,* Booker T. Washington, *Up From Slavery: An Autobiography* (Garden City, NY: Doubleday & Co. 1901).

> The term was first used to designate a part of the country which was distinguished by the colour of the soil. The part of the country possessing this thick, dark, and naturally rich soil was, of course, the part of the South where the slaves were most profitable, and consequently they were taken there in the largest numbers. Later and especially since the war, the term seems to be used wholly in a political sense— that is, to designate the counties where the black people outnumber the white.

xlviiiKathy Weiser, *Legends of America, Legends of Kansas: Nicodemus — A Black Pioneer Town*, www.legendsofamerica.com/ks-nicodemus.html (updated May 2012) (last visited August 12, 2013).

xlixKathy Weiser, *Legends of America, Legends of Kansas: Nicodemus — A Black Pi-*

oneer Town, www.legendsofamerica.com/ks-nicodemus.html (updated May 2012) (last visited August 12, 2013).

[l]"Edward P. McCabe,"*Kansapedia,* Kansas Historical Society, http://www.kshs.org/kansapedia/edward-p-mccabe/12142 (last visited October 26, 2014).

[li]"Legends of Kansas: History, Tales and Destinations in the Land of Ahs," http://www.legendsofkansas.com/people-m.html (last visited October 26, 2014); *see also,* Simmie Knox, "Edward P. McCabe, 1850 – 1923)," Oklahoma Arts Council, http://www.arts.ok.gov/Teaching_with_Capitol_Art.php?c=cac&awid=66 (photo of oil portrait of McCabe commissioned for the Oklahoma State Capitol, with information and resources for educators on McCabe's life and legacy) (last visited October 26, 2104).

[lii]The establishment of what is now Langston University pursuant to Oklahoma Territorial Bill 151, March 12, 1897, demonstrates E.P. McCabe's understanding of the centrality of education to black progress. The institution had as its stated mission the instruction of "both male and female Colored persons in the art of teaching various branches which pertain to a common school education and in such higher education as may be deemed advisable, and in the fundamental laws of the United States in the rights and duties of citizens in the agricultural, mechanical and industrial arts." Moreover, the land on which Langston University would be built came conditionally: it would be available for such use only if the citizens of Langston became stakeholders—only if they purchased it outright. They did. They held picnics, auctions, and bake sales to raise money. They purchased the land within a year. These black trailblazers, committed to education and advancement for their children, bought into the quintessentially American dream of educational uplift. *See* http://www.langston.edu/about-us/resources/history-langston-university (last visited August 20, 2014).

[liii]Photo available at digital.library.okstate.edu/ENCYCLOPEDIA/ENTRIES/M/MC006.html (last visited October 20, 2014).

[liv]Oklahoma Historical Society, gateway.okhistory.org/ark:/67531/metadc69896/m1/1/ (last visited August 8, 2013).

[lv]Oklahoma Historical Society's Encyclopedia of Oklahoma History & Culture, http://digital.library.okstate.edu/encyclopedia/entries/L/LA021.html (last visited August 19, 2013).

[lvi]George Sawner quoted in the *Langston City Herald,* date uncertain.

[lvii]*New York Times,* March 1, 1890, p. 4, c. 4.

[lviii]*See, e.g.,* James W. Loewen, *Sundown Towns: A Hidden Dimension Of American Racism* (New York, NY: Touchstone 2005).

[lix]Perkins, G. N. *The Oklahoma Guide* (Guthrie, Okla. Terr.), Vol. 15, No. 8, Ed. 1 Thursday, July 13, 1905. The Gateway to Oklahoma History. http://gateway.okhistory.org/ark:/67531/metadc95831/ (last visited October 17, 2014).

[lx]*See, e.g., Jimmie Lewis Franklin, The Blacks In Oklahoma* (Norman, OK: University of Oklahoma Press 1980), p. 40.

[lxi]Roy E. Stafford, *Gives Justice to Both the Races: Negro Must be Made to Know His Place—Should Have Equal Privileges But Entirely Separate, The Daily Oklahoma*, September 13, 1907, p. 1.

[lxii]Indian Territory to the east and Oklahoma Territory to the west comprised the Twin Territories prior to Oklahoma statehood in 1907.

[lxiii]*The Guthrie Leader* (Guthrie, Okla. Terr.), Vol. 30, No. 10, Ed. 1 Friday, November 15, 1907. Guthrie, Oklahoma Territory. The Gateway to Oklahoma History. http://gateway.okhistory.org/ark:/67531/metadc76901/ (last visited October 22, 2014).

[lxiv]Shepard, Susie W. & Shepard, Horace W., *The Altus Times* (Altus, Okla.), Vol. 6, No. 45, Ed. 1 Thursday, November 21, 1907. Altus, Oklahoma. The Gateway to Oklahoma History. http://gateway.okhistory.org:/ark67531/metadc405056/ (last visited October 23, 2014); *see also*, http://gateway.okhistory.org/ark:/67531/metadc340897/ (last visited October 23, 2014) (photograph used for a story in *The Oklahoma Times* newspaper captioned: "Statue in front of the Oklahoma Territorial Museum in Guthrie represents the marriage of the Oklahoma and Indian Territories with statehood in 1907" (Photograph 2012.201.B0232.0278, 1980, Oklahoma Historical Society, Oklahoma City, Oklahoma).

[lxv]Oklahoma statehood photographs, blog.newsok.com/newsroom/2008/02/25 facial-fire-tops-statehood/ (last visited August 10, 2013).

[lxvi]*See, e.g.*, Art. XIII, Sec. 3 of the 1907 Oklahoma Constitution (regarding education), *The Constitution of the State of Oklahoma* (1907), https://archive.org/stream/constitutionofst00okla#page/24/mode/2up (last visited August 26, 2014).

[lxvii]Frank A. Balyeat, "Segregation in the Public Schools of Oklahoma Territory," *The Chronicles Of Oklahoma*, AT 180.

[lxviii]*McCabe v. Atchison, Topeka, & Santa Fe Railway Company*, 186 F. Supp. 966 (8th Cir. 1911).

[lxix]*Plessy v. Ferguson*, 163 U. S. 537 (1896).

[lxx]*See* Kansas Historical Society, Topeka Cemetery Records, http://www.kshs.org/p/topeka-cemetery-records/13804 (last visited August 7, 2013).

[lxxi]*See, e.g., Arthur L. Tolson, The Black Oklahomans: A History, 1541–1972* (New Orleans, LA: Edwards Printing Company 1974), at 102; Hannibal B. Johnson, *Acres Of Aspiration—The All-Black Towns In Oklahoma* (Austin, TX: Eakin Press 2002), at 142.

[lxxii]Bruce Fisher and Jerome Holmes, "African American Lawyers in Oklahoma," 75 *Oklahoma Bar Journal* 66 (September 11, 2007) (Special Centennial Issue of the Oklahoma Bar Journal), at 1.

[lxxii]Jimmie L. White, Jr., Twine, William Henry (1864 – 1933), *The Chronicles*

Of Oklahoma, Oklahoma Encyclopedia of History & Culture, http://digital. library.okstate.edu/encyclopedia/entries/T/TW006.html (last visited October 22, 2014).

[lxxiv]W. E. B. Du Bois Papers, Dunjee, Roscoe, Letter from Roscoe Dunjee to W. E. B. Du Bois, March 8, 1928, http://oubliette.library.umass.edu/view/full/mums312-b043-i136 (last visited August 19, 2013).

[lxxv]*Guinn v. United States,* 238 U.S. 347 (1915).

[lxxvi]*Lane v. Wilson,* 307 U.S. 268 (1939).

[lxxvii]A "whipping party" was a mass, celebratory event during which a white mob whipped or beat an African American accused or suspected of some criminal offense or social slight. *See, e.g.,* Diana Everett, "Lynching," *Oklahoma Historical Society's Encyclopedia of Oklahoma History & Culture* http://digital.library.okstate.edu/encyclopedia/entries/l/ly001.html (last visited August 6, 2013).

[lxxviii]*See* Hannibal B. Johnson, *Acres Of Aspiration — The All-Black Towns In Oklahoma* (Austin, TX: Eakin Press 2002), at 98. The efforts of Chief Sam bring to mind the work of a contemporary, Jamaican-born Marcus Garvey (August 17, 1887 – June 10, 1940), a leading figure in the early twentieth century Black Nationalism and Pan-Africanism (eponymously referred to as "Garveyism") movements. Among other ventures, Garvey founded the Universal Negro Improvement Association ("UNIA") in 1912. UNIA sought to unite the African diaspora, perhaps mostly notably by resettling African Americans in the African homeland. Garvey used his newspaper, the *Negro World,* as a propaganda vehicle for his political and philosophical sentiments. By 1919, he had launched the Black Star Line, a shipping company intended to establish trade and commerce between and among Africans in America, the Caribbean, South and Central America, Canada and Africa. See http://www.biography.com/people/marcus-garvey-9307319#death-and-legacy (last visited June 25, 2015).

[lxxix]*See generally,* Diana Everett, "Lynching," *Oklahoma Historical Society's Encyclopedia of Oklahoma History & Culture*http://digital.library.okstate.edu/encyclopedia/entries/l/ly001.html (last visited August 9, 2014).

[lxxx]For factors underlying the phenomenon, *see, e.g.,* Jana Evans Braziel, History of Lynching in the United States, http://www.umass.edu/complit/aclanet/USLynch.html (last visited August 6, 2013).

[lxxxi]Woody Guthrie Center, Tulsa, Oklahoma, http://woodyguthriecenter.org/about-woody/ (last visited November 6, 2014).

[lxxxii]*See, e.g.,* "The Nelson Lynching of 1911 @ Okemah, Oklahoma, http://lauranelsonlynching.weebly.com/ (last visited September 9, 2014); "Lynchings and Hangings," http://www.legendsofamerica.com/ah-lynching7.html (last visited September 9, 2014).

James Allen, Hilton Als, Congressman John Lewis, & Leon F. Litwack, Without Sanctuary: Lynching Photography In America (Sante Fe, NM: Twin Palms Publishers 2008)

[lxxxiv]Wikimedia Commons, http://commons.wikimedia.org/wiki/File:Lynching_of_Laura_Nelson_and_her_son_1.jpg (last visited August 10, 2013).

[lxxxv]Abel Meeropol, *aka* Lewis Allan, *Strange Fruit. Strange Fruit* was originally published as a poem in *The New York Teacher*, a union magazine, in 1936, and then set to music by Meeropol. As performed by Billie Holliday, credits include: Lewis Allan (*i.e.*, Meeropol), songwriter; Maurice Pearl, songwriter; Dwayne P. Wiggins, songwriter; Dwayne Wiggins Pub Designee, publisher; and WB Music Corp., publisher.

> *Southern trees bear a strange fruit,*
> *Blood on the leaves, blood at the root,*
> *Black bodies swinging in the southern breeze,*
> *Strange fruit hanging from the poplar trees.*
>
> *Pastoral scene of the gallant south,*
> *The bulging eyes and the twisted mouth,*
> *Scent of magnolia sweet and fresh,*
> *Then the sudden smell of burning flesh.*
>
> *Here is a fruit for the crows to pluck,*
> *For the rain to gather, for the wind to suck,*
> *For the sun to rot, for the trees to drop,*
> *Here is a strange and bitter crop.*

[lxxxvi]*See, e.g.*, http://www.history.com/topics/roaring-twenties (last visited June 8, 2015).

[lxxxvii]F. Scott Fitzgerald, *The Great Gatsby* (New York, NY: Charles Scribner's Sons, First Edition, 1925).

[lxxxviii]*See* Hannibal B. Johnson, *Black Wall Street—From Riot To Renaissance In Tulsa's Historic Greenwood District* (Austin, TX: Eakin Press 1998); *see also Final Report Of The Oklahoma Commission To Study The Tulsa Race Riot Of 1921* (Oklahoma Historical Society 2001), www.okhistory.org/trrc/freport.htm. The Lincoln County Republican provided contemporaneous coverage of the 1921 Tulsa Race Riot. That a county newspaper reported such events in may itself be news. "Hundreds Killed Tulsa Race Riot," *Lincoln County Republican*, June 2, 1921. (Note: *Circa* 1955, The *Lincoln County Republican* became the *Lincoln County News*.)

[lxxxix]100 Years of Oklahoma Governors, http://www.odl.state.ok.us/oar/governors/Walton.htm (last visited September 12, 2013); Oklahoma Historical Society's Encyclopedia of Oklahoma History and Culture, http://digital.library.okstate.edu/ENCYCLOPEDIA/entries/W/WA014.html (last visited September 12, 2013).

[xc]*See* Hannibal B. Johnson, *Acres Of Aspiration — The All-Black Towns In Okla-homa* (Austin, TX: Eakin Press 2002).

[xci]Boley, Oklahoma, historic marker, www.lwfaam.net/wf/ (last visited September 15, 2013).

[xcii]Oklahoma Historical Society, www.blackpast.org/?q=aaw/boley-oklahoma-1903 (photo courtesy of William L. Katz), (last visited August 8, 2013).

[xciii]A significant number of African Americans in Oklahoma claim Native American roots. Indeed, the present day wrangling over the status of the Freedmen— persons of African ancestry who claim citizenship in the one of the Five Civilized Tribes based on blood relationships, affinity ties, and/or treaty obligations—stems from this complex web of relationships. For a full discussion of the status of the Freedmen of the Five Civilized Tribes, *see* Hannibal B. Johnson, *Apartheid In Indian Country: Seeing Red Over Black Disenfranchisement* (Fort Worth, TX: Eakin Press 2012).

[xciv]*See* Hannibal B. Johnson, *Acres Of Aspiration — The All-Black Towns In Okla-homa* (Austin, TX: Eakin Press 2002).

[xcv]Oklahoma County Map—Oklahoma Map, http://www.digital-topo-maps.com/county-map/oklahoma.shtml (last visited August 12, 2013).

[xcvi]Mel Chatman and Jan Vassar, "The 'Negro Problem' in Lincoln County, Oklahoma (1889 – 1954)" (unpublished manuscript based on interviews with Lincoln County pioneers and historical information and documentation relevant to Lincoln County), 2005.

[xcvii]The Chandler post office commenced service on September 21, 1891. Sally Bourne Ferrell and Donald F. Ferrell, Oklahoma Historical Society's Encyclopedia of Oklahoma History & Culture, http://digital.library.okstate.edu/encyclopedia/entries/C/CH002.html (last visited July 23, 2013).

[xcviii]Sally Bourne Ferrell and Donald F., Ferrell, Oklahoma Historical Society's Encyclopedia of Oklahoma History & Culture, http://digital.library.okstate.edu/encyclopedia/entries/C/CH002.html (last visited July 13, 2014); e-mail correspondence from Jan Vassar, Lincoln County historian, July 10, 2014 (on file with the author).

[xcix]*See, e.g.,* http://www.legendsofamerica.com/ok-chandler.html(last visited January 25, 2015) ("On March 30, 1897, young Chandler would suffer a devastating blow when a tornado completely wiped out the business area and many of the new homes constructed near it. Within a just a few minutes, every building that lay within a four-block-wide area was leveled."); *A Terrific Cyclone. Works Frightful Havoc at Chandler. The Little Town Demolished and Many People Killed.*, The *St. Albans Daily Messenger*, St. Albans, Vermont, March 31, 1897, available at http://www3.gendisasters.com/oklahoma/7853/chandler-ok-tornado-mar-1897, last viewed July 12, 2010.

A TERRIFIC CYCLONE.

Works Frightful Havoc at Chandler, Oklahoma.
The Little Town [sic] Demolished and Many People Killed.

GUTHRIE, O. T., March 31. - A terrific cyclone struck the town of Chandler, 40 miles east of here, last evening, and the lastest [sic] news is that 45 people were killed and more than 20 injured, a dozen of them fatally. A despatch [sic] received here at 2 a. m. reported the ruins on fire and many of the injured people burned to death. So far 24 dead bodies have been taken from the ruined buildings.

Chandler is a town of 1,500 inhabitants and was almost completely devastated, only two buildings being left standing.

[c]Kathy Weiser, *Legends of America, Oklahoma Legends—Chandler, Last Gunfight of the Old West*, http://www.legendsofamerica.com/ok-chandler.html (updated May 2013) (last visited August 20, 2014).

[ci]Created on November 11, 1926, Route 66 has been variously known as the Will Rogers Highway, the Main Street of America, the Ozark Trail, and the Mother Road. Route 66 became an iconic thoroughfare, originally running from Chicago, Illinois, through Missouri, Kansas, Oklahoma, Texas, New Mexico, and Arizona to its endpoint, Los Angeles, California. Popular culture celebrated the Route 66, this 2,448 mile stretch of asphalt, with a hit song and television show in the 1960s.

[cii]http://s1.favim.com/orig/6/black-and-white-road-route-66-Favim.com-162207.jpg (last visited September 9, 2013).

[ciii]*Lincoln Log*, Chandler, Oklahoma, newsletter (Summer and Spring 2014).

[civ]*See, e.g.*, William D. Wyatt, http://joannmcmillan.tripod.com/benny-kentfilmfestival/id2.html (last visited October 31, 2014). The filmmaker's "Early Days," footage chronicling Oklahoma in her infancy, begins with a personal note: "For your appreciation and cooperation, I am profoundly grateful. Benny Kent". Benny Kent, a former cameraman for Pathe' News, a newsreel producer from 1910 – 1956, spent some thirty-five years taking footage in Oklahoma. His videography spans a period from the turn of the twentieth century until 1937. Benny Kent gathered and captured images that revealed the conception and birth of America's forty-sixth state, beginning with the land openings in Oklahoma Territory and including gubernatorial inaugurations, droughts, floods, patriotic events, beauty contests, oil booms, cotton picking outings, religious rituals and figures, Native American culture, and much more. Through his black-and-white moving footage set to music, often marches like John Philip Sousa's 1897 masterpiece, "The Stars and Stripes Forever," he tells the Oklahoma story with the vim and vigor of a bullish booster.

[cv]Benny Kent, "Early Days," (newsreel footage of Oklahoma taken, roughly, between 1900 and 1937) (on file with the author). A screenshot in *Early Days* notes: "Following the opening of Old Oklahoma, April 22, 1889 The Iowa, Sac and Fox Country opened SEPT. 22nd, 1901 [sic]." Footage of a wagon is captioned: "Waiting for the opening guns Sept. 22nd 1891." The Sac and Fox land opening on September 22, 1891, became the first opening of Oklahoma Territory lands previously settled by Native Americans. Linda D. Wilson, "Sac and Fox Opening," Oklahoma Historical Society's Encyclopedia of Oklahoma History & Culture, http://digital.library.okstate.edu/encyclopedia/entries/S/SA002.html (last visited October 31, 2014).

[cvi]Workmen in Chandler produced bricks stamped "Chandler, Okla" after Oklahoma statehood in 1907. The brick plant closed in 1908, and only a few bricks were made. This scarcity has made the post-statehood bricks more valuable than the older Oklahoma Territory bricks. E-mail from Jan Vassar to Mel Chatman, September 12, 2014 (on file with author).

[cvii]Abraham Lincoln (February 12, 1809 – April 15, 1865), served as the 16th President of the United States of America from March 1861 until his assassination in April 1865.

[cviii]State legislatures or officials at the state or federal level typically name counties, not voters.

[cix]*See* http://oklahoma.hometownlocator.com/ok/lincoln/ (last visited August 16, 2014). Chandler historian Jan Vassar concluded that a few of the towns were likely something less than that. She notes that Emsey, for example, existing merely as a railroad loading dock and not an official town. Wild Horse and South Village are unfamiliar as towns to Ms. Vassar as well. E-mail from Jan Vassar to Mel Chatman, September 12, 2014 (on file with author). *See also*, George H. Shirk, *Oklahoma Place Names* (Norman, Oklahoma: University of Oklahoma Press 1987) (wherein the author catalogues some 3,600 counties, cities, mountains, and lakes, chronicling such information as origin of name, date of founding and abandonment of towns, and the existence/nonexistence of a post office).

[cx]*See, e.g.*, *Population of Oklahoma and Indian Territory, 1907* (Washington, D.C.: Government Printing Office), at 16 (publication of the Department of Commerce and Labor, Bureau of The Census, S.N.D. North, Director), at 16, available at http://www2.census.gov/prod2/decennial/documents/1907pop_OK-IndianTerritory.pdf (last visited August 8, 2014) (33,099 white persons and 3,856 black persons lived in Lincoln County; in Chandler, the numbers were 1,942 and 292, respectively).

[cxi]Persons of African ancestry connected to the Five Civilized Tribes forced to migrate to Indian Territory (present-day Oklahoma) earlier in the nineteenth century are not included for purposes of this discussion of the settlement of Lincoln County.

[cxii]An undated listing of Lincoln County, Oklahoma, Separate Schools may be found at the Pioneer Museum of History in Chandler, Oklahoma. Jan Vassar, Chandler historian, provided the author with this list of seemingly official, but unknown, origin.

[cxiii]Mel Chatman, Chandler historian and researcher, established these criteria.

[cxiv]One Lincoln County Oklahoma area, "Wellston Colony," supposedly located three miles from Wellston, Oklahoma, is often cited as all-black town, though there appears to be scant support for its existence. Some suggest that no such place as Wellston Colony ever existed in Lincoln County, Oklahoma. From 2005 through 2008, Mel Chatman and Jan Vassar conducted onsite interviews and researched Lincoln County archives, including local newspapers and government documents. They determined that Lincoln County never contained a formally designated all-black town.

[cxv]*See, e.g.*, Hannibal B. Johnson, *Acres Of Aspiration: The All-Black Towns In Oklahoma* (Austin, TX: Eakin Press 2002).

[cxvi]Photo courtesy of Mel Chatman.

[cxvii]Mel Chatman and Jan Vassar, *The 'Negro Problem' in Lincoln County, Oklahoma (1889 – 1954)* (unpublished manuscript based on interviews with Lincoln County pioneers and historical information and documentation relevant to Lincoln County), 2005.

[cxviii]Map courtesy of Mel Chatman.

[cxix]The principal text contains an overview of the informal black community in Chandler proper, known as The Bottom. Informational summaries of the other such communities may be found in Appendix F.

[cxx]The United States Census only indicates the total numbers for black residents beginning in 1930. Black resident total numbers for previous years are based on count made by Mel Chatman.

[cxxi]Not included in these totals is a special pre-statehood census completed in 1907. In this special census, cited above, a total of 2,234 persons were recorded. Of those, 292, or 13 percent, were listed as black.

[cxxii]"From Maine to California, thousands of communities kept out African Americans (or sometimes Chinese Americans, Jewish Americans, etc.) by force, law, or custom. These communities are sometimes called "sundown towns" because some of them posted signs at their city limits reading, typically, 'Nigger, Don't Let The Sun Go Down On You In [Name of City or Town].'" James W. Loewen, http://sundown.afro.illinois.edu/sundown-towns.php (last visited August 21, 2014); see also James, W. Loewen, *Sundown Towns: A Hidden Dimension Of American Racism* (New York, NY: The New Press 2005).

[cxxiii]E-mail to author from Jan Vasser, August 21, 2014 (on file with author).

[cxxx]Mel Chatman and Jan Vassar, *The 'Negro Problem' in Lincoln County, Okla-*

homa (1889 – 1954) (unpublished manuscript based on interviews with Lincoln County pioneers and historical information and documentation relevant to Lincoln County), 2005.

[cxxv]Notes from George Sawner Ellis, January 26, 2015 (on file with author).

[cxxvi]*See* Chapter 3, *Chandler, Oklahoma: The Location (1890 – 1940), Chandler: The Ellis Family Story,* http://www.ellisfamilystory.com/chapter03.html.

[cxxvii]Photo courtesy Mel Chatman.

[cxxviii]Reverend S. R. Glover and his wife, Sylvia, organized Mount Calvary First Baptist Church, originally, First Baptist Church, in 1890. Central Methodist Episcopal Church (Lane Chapel), organized in 1907 by Reverend J. R. McClain, offered another opportunity for worship in The Bottom. Reverend J. W. Wiley later assumed the pastorate. Central Baptist Church, founded in 1917 by Mr. and Mrs. Charles Sneed and several others, also became a fixture in The Bottom. The Sneeds hosted numerous church activities during the early years until the construction of the first church building at 215 West 14th Street in 1928. In February 1993, a new structure replaced the original structure.

[cxxix]Photo courtesy Mel Chatman.

[cxxx]Mel Chatman and Jan Vassar, *The 'Negro Problem' in Lincoln County, Oklahoma (1889 – 1954)* (unpublished manuscript based on interviews with Lincoln County pioneers and historical information and documentation relevant to Lincoln County), 2005. Mel Chatman and Jan Vassar collaborated on *The Negro Problem in Lincoln County, Oklahoma (1889-1954),* a brief history of the black pioneers who first settled in Lincoln County, Oklahoma. Research for the initiative took place between 2002 and 2005, with a focus the life and times of black families in Lincoln County. The researchers conducted personal interviews with firsthand and secondhand observers to the history. Most interviews were recorded, but not transcribed. Over one hundred audio tape recordings from more than one hundred thirty contributors were collected. Most interviews lasted 30 to 90 minutes and were conducted in private homes. Most interviewees were 70 years-old, and many were 80 years-old and older. Newspaper articles, historical documents, and photos supplemented the recorded interviews. Chatman and Vassar presented the results of their research on March 5, 2005, at the Lincoln County Historical Society Museum.

[cxxxi]"Last Rites For Mrs. L. L. Sawner Here Saturday: Burial Newkirk", *The Lincoln County News,* March 2, 3, or 4, 1949.

[cxxxii]Kathy Weiser, *Legends of America, Oklahoma Legends—Chandler, Last Gunfight of the Old West,* http://www.legendsofamerica.com/ok-chandler.html (updated May 2013) (last visited August 21, 2013).

[cxxxiii]Jan Vassar, *Only 'Near' Lynchings in Lincoln County* (February 2004); Jan Vassar, *Only 'Near' Lynchings in Lincoln County's History,* The *Stroud Amer-*

ican, March 4, 2004, at 5; correspondence from Jan Vassar to author, July 14, 2014 (on file with author). Following are the three incidents sometimes thought to be Lincoln County lynchings.

- The September 26, 1894, lynching of Perry Cook, a purported horse thief and an alleged perpetrator of the July 23, 1894, robbery of the Chandler National Bank, likely occurred in Lincoln, Oklahoma, not in Lincoln County. At the time, there were two towns in Oklahoma named Lincoln, one in Jackson County (the likely site of the lynching), and the other in Kingfisher County.

- On the night of December 13, 1904, a black man burned to death when the Wellston jail burned to the ground with him inside. The flimsy, kindling jail had been the site of several fires, allegedly started by inmates. Local newspapers reported that firemen made a gallant effort to extinguish the blaze. There were no reports of suspicious or malicious activity surrounding the tragic event, and thus no evidence that the death should be characterized as a lynching.

- On April 28, 1920, a man assaulted Willa Harvey, a teacher at Golden Valley School southeast of Stroud, as she walked home. A large posse, including members of local law enforcement, assembled to track the alleged perpetrator, Marion Davis, a black teen. Also joining the posse were members of a movie crew in town to film *A Debtor to the Law*. The crew included a former notorious bank robber, Henry Starr, famed United States Marshall Bill Tilghman, and well-known news photographer Bennie Kent. Sheriff Brown soon arrested Davis, took him to the county jail in Chandler, and arranged for him to plead guilty in a special district court session presided over by Judge Hal Johnson. Lynch talk persisted. Scores of armed men surrounded the courthouse after having learned of the plea. One step ahead of the game, the Sheriff spirited young Davis out of town, first to Shawnee, then to Wewoka, and finally to McAlester. The lynch mob pursued the Sheriff and his prisoner to Shawnee and Wewoka, always a step behind. Davis survived, and wound up in the state penitentiary in McAlester.

cxxxivChandler historian Mel Chatman noted that white-to-black courtesies were more likely to be shown by white citizens in their interactions with black "elites" (as opposed to workaday black residents). Correspondence with Mel Chatman, February 10, 2105.

cxxxvSee, *e.g.*, Erica Frankenberg, Chungmei Lee, and Gary Orfield, "A Multiracial Society with Segregated Schools: Are We Losing the Dream?" The Civil Rights Project, Harvard University, January 2003, http://civilrightsproject.ucla.edu/research/k-12-education/integration-and-diversity/a-multiracial-society-with-segregated-schools-are-we-losing-the-dream/frankenberg-multiracial-society-losing-the-dream.pdf (last visited September 14, 2014).

cxxxviBrown v. Board of Education, 347 U.S. 483 (1954).

cxxxviiE-mail from Jan Vassar to Mel Chatman, September 12, 2014 (on file with author). Ms. Vassar noted that the Klan once burned a cross on the near-downtown lawn of Constance Wolcott, a member of the local Catholic church and the first female pharmacist educated at the University of Oklahoma. The Klan eventually ran Wolcott out of town, forcing her to close her main street drugstore and flee to Guthrie, where she secured employment at a Catholic school.

cxxxviiiSee Chandler: The Ellis Family Story, "Chandler, Oklahoma: The Location (1890 – 1940)", http://www.ellisfamilystory.com/ (last visited July 31, 2015).

cxxxixSee Chandler: The Ellis Family Story, "Chandler, Oklahoma: The Location (1890 – 1940)", http://www.ellisfamilystory.com/ (last visited July 31, 2015).

cxlE-mail from Mel Chatman to the author, July 31, 2014 (on file with author).

dxiSee Chandler: The Ellis Family Story, http://www.ellisfamilystory.com/ (last visited September 14, 2014).

cxliiPhoto courtesy of Mel Chatman.

cxliiiThe Monrovia restaurant was named for Monrovia, Liberia, one of Whit Ellis's favorite places. Prior to his arrival in Oklahoma, Ellis served as a galley cook on an international trade ship that took him to West Africa and other far-flung destinations. See Chandler: The Ellis Family Story, http://www.ellisfamilystory.com/ (last visited October 10, 2014).

cxlivPhoto courtesy of Mel Chatman. This 1906 photo shows a seldom-seen side of African American life in that era. The well-dressed photo subjects in this sophisticated scene stand in stark contrast to more typical images of rural African Americans in squalid settings.

cxlvMel Chatman and Jan Vassar, The 'Negro Problem' in Lincoln County, Oklahoma (1889 – 1954) (unpublished manuscript based on interviews with Lincoln County pioneers and historical information and documentation relevant to Lincoln County)

cxlviMel Chatman and Jan Vassar, The 'Negro Problem' in Lincoln County, Oklahoma (1889 – 1954) (unpublished manuscript based on interviews with Lincoln County pioneers and historical information and documentation relevant to Lincoln County), 2005.

cxlviiMel Chatman and Jan Vassar, The 'Negro Problem' in Lincoln County, Oklahoma (1889 – 1954) (unpublished manuscript based on interviews with Lincoln County pioneers and historical information and documentation relevant to Lincoln County)

cxlviiiPhoto courtesy of Mel Chatman.

[cxlix]Mel Chatman and Jan Vassar, *The 'Negro Problem' in Lincoln County, Oklahoma (1889 – 1954)* (unpublished manuscript based on interviews with Lincoln County pioneers and historical information and documentation relevant to Lincoln County), 2005.

[cl]Mel Chatman and Jan Vassar, *The 'Negro Problem' in Lincoln County, Oklahoma (1889 – 1954)* (unpublished manuscript based on interviews with Lincoln County pioneers and historical information and documentation relevant to Lincoln County)

[cli]Mel Chatman and Jan Vassar, *The 'Negro Problem' in Lincoln County, Oklahoma (1889 – 1954)* (unpublished manuscript based on interviews with Lincoln County pioneers and historical information and documentation relevant to Lincoln County), 2005.

[clii]LCHS Museum of Pioneer History.

[cliii]*See* Chapter 3, *Chandler, Oklahoma: The Location (1890 – 1940), Chandler: The Ellis Family Story,* http://www.ellisfamilystory.com/chapter03.html.

[cliv]*See* Chapter 3, *Chandler, Oklahoma: The Location (1890 – 1940), Chandler: The Ellis Family Story,* http://www.ellisfamilystory.com/chapter03.html.

[clv]Fifty dollars in 1930 would be worth some $680 dollars in 2015. *See, e.g.,*http://www.dollartimes.com/inflation/inflation.php?amount=1&year=1930 (last visited June 2, 2015).

[clvi]Telephone interview with Mel Chatman, Whit Ellis's grandson, August 1, 2015.

[clvii]Telephone interview with Mel Chatman, Whit Ellis's grandson, October 6, 2014.

[clviii]*See* Chapter 5, *Whit Ellis' Restaurants: (1894 – 1932), Chandler: The Ellis Family Story,* http://www.ellisfamilystory.com/chapter05.html.

[clix]The Turner Turnpike opened in 1953 as Oklahoma's first turnpike, running parallel to historic Route 66 (now State Highway 66), and connecting the state largest cities, Tulsa and Oklahoma City. The Turner Turnpike covers almost a ninety-mile stretch of Interstate 44, and is named in honor of the state's thirteenth governor, Roy J. Turner, who served from 1947 – 1951. *See, e.g.,* "Interstate Highways," http://www.okhighways.com/i44tt.html (last visited October 9, 2014); "Oklahoma Turnpike Authority—History," https://www.pikepass.com/about/History.aspx (last visited October 10, 2014); Leroy H. Fischer, *Oklahoma's Governors, 1929 - 1955* (Oklahoma Series Volume 19) (Oklahoma City, OK: Oklahoma Historical Society 1983).

[clx]Jimmie L. Franklin, "Prohibition," Oklahoma Historical Society's Encyclopedia of Oklahoma History & Culture, http://digital.library.okstate.edu/encyclopedia/entries/p/pr018.html (last visited October 9, 2014).

[clxi]Telephone interview with Victor Brown, son of Edward Marshall Brown, October 9, 2014.

[clxii]Telephone interview with Mel Chatman, October 17, 2013; Telephone interview with George Sawner Ellis, October 18, 2013; Newspaper summary of Lincoln County Commissioners' Proceedings on July 4, 1904, showing claims allowed, including a claim for house rent owed to G. W. F. Sawner. Gilstrap, H. B. The *Chandler News* (Chandler, Okla. Terr.), Vol. 13, No. 42, Ed. 1 Thursday, July 7, 1904. Chandler, Oklahoma Territory. The Gateway to Oklahoma History. http://gateway.okhistory.org/ark:/67531/metadc160234/ (last visited October 19, 2014).

[clxiii]Mel Chatman and Jan Vassar, *The 'Negro Problem' in Lincoln County, Oklahoma (1889 – 1954)* (unpublished manuscript based on interviews with Lincoln County pioneers and historical information and documentation relevant to Lincoln County), 2005.

[clxiv]Mel Chatman and Jan Vassar, *The 'Negro Problem' in Lincoln County, Oklahoma (1889 – 1954)* (unpublished manuscript based on interviews with Lincoln County pioneers and historical information and documentation relevant to Lincoln County), 2005.

[clxv]See Chapter 3, *Chandler, Oklahoma: The Location (1890 – 1940), Chandler: The Ellis Family Story,* http://www.ellisfamilystory.com/chapter03.html (last visited September 10, 2014).

[clxvi]E-mail from Mel Chatman to the author, July 31, 2014.

[clxvii]Telephone interview with George Sawner Ellis, October 18, 2013.

[clxviii]Map courtesy of the Oklahoma Department of Libraries. The map is a Sanborn Fire Insurance Map, Chandler, Oklahoma, March 1920 (Database and software copyright (c) 2001-2013 ProQuest, LLC. All rights reserved. All copyright in the Sanborn Maps are held by Environmental Data Resources, Inc. or its affiliates. Sanborn Map Company logo used with permission.).

[clxix]Map courtesy of Mel Chatman, *Chandler, Oklahoma: The Location (1890 – 1940), Chandler: The Ellis Family Story,* http://www.ellisfamilystory.com/chapter03.html.

[clxx]Mel Chatman and Jan Vassar, *The 'Negro Problem' in Lincoln County, Oklahoma (1889 – 1954)* (unpublished manuscript based on interviews with Lincoln County pioneers and historical information and documentation relevant to Lincoln County), 2005.

[clxxi]Photo courtesy of Mel Chatman.

[clxxii]Civil War Trust, "John Brown's Harpers Ferry Raid," http://www.civilwar.org/150th-anniversary/john-browns-harpers-ferry.html (last visited August 31, 2014).

[clxxiii]William McWillie served as Mississippi's twenty-second Governor, in office from 1857 – 1859.

[clxxiv]Mississippi History Timeline, http://mdah.state.ms.us/timeline/zone/1859/ (last visited July 30, 2013)

^{clxxv}State of Texas, Certificate of Vital Record, County of Fayette (death certificate for Ida F. Sawner), filed December 27, 1927, Albert F. Mach, Registrar (certified copy dated November 10, 2014, on file with author).

^{clxxvi}Marriage Record, State of Texas, Fayette County, April 17, 1888, Joseph Ehlinger, County Clerk, returned and filed April 27, 1888 (certified copy dated November 10, 2014, on file with author).

^{clxxvii}George Sawner's will also lists another daughter, Bessie Allen. In the Matter of the Estate of G.W.F. Sawner, Deceased, Final Decree and Order Discharging Executrix, filed March 26, 1927, Allen Brugess, County Clerk, County Court of Lincoln County, State of Oklahoma, No. 2882.

^{clxxviii}Pellagra is a condition caused by a dietary deficiency of one of the B vitamins, called niacin, http://medical-dictionary.thefreedictionary.com/Pellegra (last visited June 3, 2015).

^{clxxix}State of Texas, Certificate of Vital Record, County of Fayette (death certificate for Ida F. Sawner), filed December 27, 1927, Albert F. Mach, Registrar (certified copy dated November 10, 2014, on file with author).

^{clxxx}State of Texas, Certificate of Vital Record, County of Fayette (death certificate for Ida F. Sawner), filed December 27, 1927, Albert F. Mach, Registrar (certified copy dated November 10, 2014, on file with author).

^{clxxxi}The death certificate required that one of the following designations be chosen: single, married, widowed, or divorced. State of Texas, Certificate of Vital Record, County of Fayette (death certificate for Ida F. Sawner), filed December 27, 1927, Albert F. Mach, Registrar (certified copy dated November 10, 2014, on file with author).

^{clxxxii}*See, e.g.*, Social Security Handbook, Section 401. When is a widow(er) entitled to widow(er)'s insurance benefits?, https://www.socialsecurity.gov/OP_Home/handbook/handbook.04/handbook-0401.html (defining "widow" for purposes of Social Security benefits) (last visited August 15, 2015).

^{clxxxiii}Stan Hoig, "Land Run of 1889," Oklahoma Historical Society's Encyclopedia of Oklahoma History & Culture, http://digital.library.okstate.edu/encyclopedia/entries/l/la014.html (last visited July 30, 2013)

^{clxxxiv}Golobie, John. *Oklahoma State Register* (Guthrie, Okla.), Vol. 26, No. 28, Ed. 1 Thursday, November 16, 1916. Guthrie, Oklahoma. The Gateway to Oklahoma History. http://gateway.okhistory.org/ark:/67531/metadc281238 (last visited October 19, 2014). Mrs. Farmer transferred property to George Sawner just weeks before her death. The *Oklahoma Leader* (Guthrie, Okla.), Vol. 26, No. 42, Ed 1 Thursday, October 19, 1916. Guthrie, Oklahoma. The Gateway to Oklahoma History. http://gateway.okhistory.org/ark:/67531/metadc122130 (last visited October 19, 2014).

^{clxxxv}Messrs. Sawner and Twine received high praise for their handling of a case in Guthrie in 1894. They represented the defendant in a gun theft case and ultimately lost, but one newspaper described their defense effort

as "magnificent." Greer, Frank H. *The Daily Oklahoma State Capital* (Guthrie, Okla.), Vol. 6, No. 15, Ed. 1 Wednesday, May 9, 1894. Guthrie, Oklahoma. The Gateway to Oklahoma History. http://gateway.okhistory.org/ark:/67531/metadc122416 (last visited October 16, 2014). E. I. Saddler and W.H. Twine practiced law in Muskogee as well. Saddler also practiced in Tulsa. Mr. Sawner continued to be active in the legal profession, serving as court-appointed counsel in a criminal case in Guthrie in 1906 and taking a leading role in the Negro Bar Association throughout his life. Greer, Frank H. The Oklahoma State Capital (Guthrie, Okla. Terr.), Vol. 18, No. 20, Ed. 1 Wednesday, May 16, 1906. Guthrie, Oklahoma Territory. The Gateway to Oklahoma History. http://gateway.okhistory.org/ark:/67531/metadc126140/(last visited October 19, 2014) (court-appointed counsel); Dunjee, Roscoe. *The Black Dispatch* (Oklahoma City, Okla.), Vol. 7, No. 10, Ed. 1 Thursday, February 9, 1922. Oklahoma City, Oklahoma. The Gateway to Oklahoma History. http://gateway.okhistory.org/ark:/67531/metadc/152371/ (last visited October 19, 2014) (Negro Bar Association).

[clxxxvi]Buck Colbert Franklin is the father of eminent American historian Dr. John Hope Franklin (January 2, 1915 – March 25, 2009).

[clxxxvii]Bruce Fisher and Jerome Holmes, *African American Lawyers in Oklahoma*, 75 *Oklahoma Bar Journal* 66 (September 11, 2007) (Special Centennial Issue of the *Oklahoma Bar Journal*), at 1; *John Hope Franklin And John Whittington Franklin, Eds., My Life And An Era—The Autobiography Of Buck Colbert Franklin* (Baton Rouge, Louisiana: Louisiana State University Press, 1997), at 51.

[clxxxviii]African American Registry, www.aaregistry.org/historic_events/view/black-indian-power-jam... (last visited August 19, 2013). *See also,* James Coody Johnson (1864 – 1927), http://www.blackpast.org/aaw/johnson-james-coody-1864-1927 (last visited August 15, 2015), citing Gary Zellar, *African Creeks: Estelvste And The Creek Nation* (Norman, OK: University of Oklahoma Press 2007).

> James Coody Johnson, a Muscogee (Creek) Freedman lawyer, politician and entrepreneur, championed black rights in pre and post-statehood Oklahoma. Born in 1864 at Fort Gibson, he received his early education at the Presbyterian Mission north of Wewoka, and his later schooling at Lincoln University in Chester, Pennsylvania, courtesy of the Seminole Nation, for whom his father had served as an interpreter.
>
> Johnson returned to the Indian Territory in 1884 after his graduation. He joined the ranks of the black cowboys riding the range in the Southwest. A few years later, he tapped his bilingual abilities and education, snaring a job as interpreter for Judge Isaac Parker, the infamous "Hanging Judge" who presided over the Federal District Court for Western Arkan-

sas, then having jurisdiction over the Indian Territory.

Johnson studied law under Judge Parker and was admitted to practice in the federal courts. He became one of the few Freedmen accorded dual citizenship in both the Creek and Seminole Nations. He served as the official interpreter for the Seminole Nation and as an advisor to Seminole Chief Halputta Micco. Johnson emerged as a central figure in Muscogee (Creek) politics. He served in the House of Warriors and on several official delegations to Washington, D.C., during the allotment period. He died at his home in Wewoka, Oklahoma, in February of 1927.

[clxxxix]John Hope Franklin And John Whittington Franklin, Eds., *My Life And An Era—The Autobiography Of Buck Colbert Franklin* (Baton Rouge, LA: Louisiana State University Press, 1997), at 51.

[cxc]Bruce Fisher and Jerome Holmes, African American Lawyers in Oklahoma, 75 *Oklahoma Bar Journal* 66 (September 11, 2007) (Special Centennial Issue of the Oklahoma Bar Journal).

[cxci]A 1916 gathering of the group summons members with particular urgency: "The Negro Bar Association of the State of Oklahoma is hereby called in annual session....Business of great importance will claim the attention of the association at this session. No excuses, the business is that which affects the race and the braves are called in council." Smitherman, Andrew Jackson. The Tulsa Star (Tulsa, Okla.), Vol. 4, No. 9, ed. 1 Saturday, January 8, 1916. Tulsa, Oklahoma. The Gateway to Oklahoma History. http://gateway.okhistory.org/ark:/67531/metadc72738/ (last visited October 16, 2014).

[cxcii]Greer, Frank H. The Daily Oklahoma State Capital (Guthrie, Okla.), Vol. 6, No. 38, Ed. 1 Thursday, June 7, 1894. Guthrie, Oklahoma. The Gateway to Oklahoma History. http://gateway.okhistory.org/ark:/67531/metadc1122439/ (last visited October 16, 2014).

[cxciii]French, W. H. *The Chandler Publicist* (Chandler, Okla. Terr.), Vol. 2, No. 35, Ed. 1 Friday, November 11, 1898. Chandler, Oklahoma Territory. The Gateway to Oklahoma History. http://gateway.okhistory.org/ark:/67531/metadc147209/ (last visited October 18, 2014). Mr. Sawner received a third-grade teaching certificate at the regularly quarterly examination held in Chandler; *see also*, French, W. H. The *Chandler Publicist* (Chandler, Okla. Terr.), Vol. 2, No. 47, Ed. 1 Friday, March 20, 1896. Chandler, Oklahoma Territory. The Gateway to Oklahoma History. http://gateway.okhistory.org/ark:/67531/metadc147227/ (last visited October 19, 2014). "G. W. F. Sawner closed his school in district No. 59 last Friday. He may teach again this year in the southeast part of the county."

[cxciv]Gilstrap, H. B. & Gilstrap, Effie, The Chandler News (Chandler, Okla. Terr.), Vol. 4, No. 24, Ed. 1 Friday, March 8, 1895. Chandler, Oklahoma Ter-

ritory. The Gateway to Oklahoma History. http://gateway.okhistory.org/ark:/67531/metadc115246/ (last visited October 18, 2014).

cxcvGilstrap, H. B. & Gilstrap, Effie, The *Chandler News* (Chandler, Okla. Terr.), Vol. 5, No. 40, Ed. 1 Friday, June 26, 1896. Chandler, Oklahoma Territory. The Gateway to Oklahoma History. http://gateway.okhistory.org/ark:/67531/metadc115296/ (last visited October 18, 2014).

cxcviGreer, Frank H. The *Daily Oklahoma State Capital* (Guthrie, Okla. Terr.), Vol. 9, No. 32, Ed. 1 Thursday, May 27, 1897. Guthrie, Oklahoma Territory. The Gateway to Oklahoma History. http://gateway.okhistory.org/ark:/67531/metadc122756/ (last visited October 18, 2014).

cxcviiGreer, Frank H. The *Weekly Oklahoma State Capital* (Guthrie, Okla. Terr.), Vol. 8, No. 1, Ed. 1 Saturday, March 14, 1896. Guthrie, Oklahoma Territory. The Gateway to Oklahoma History. http://gateway.okhistory.org/ark:/67531/metadc352781/ (last visited October 19, 2014).

cxcviiiFrench, W. H. The *Chandler Publicist* (Chandler, Okla. Terr.), Vol. 5, No. 28, Ed. 1 Friday, November 11, 1898. Chandler, Oklahoma Territory. The Gateway to Oklahoma History. http://gateway.okhistory.org/ark:/67531/metadc150699/ (last visited October 18, 2014).

cxcix*See, e.g.,* "Justice of the Peace," http://legal-dictionary.thefreedictionary.com/Justice+of+the+Peace (last visited August 15, 2015).

ccIsenberg, J. L. The *Enid Weekly Wave* (Enid, Okla. Terr.), Vol. 5, No. 47, Ed. 1 Thursday, November 24, 1898. Enid, Oklahoma Territory. The Gateway to Oklahoma History. http://gateway.okhistory.org/ark:/67531/metadc112091/ (last visited October 17, 2014).

cciMr. Sawner helped organize a league for the social and commercial advancement of Africans in Lincoln County in 1899. Gilstrap, H. B. The *Chandler News* (Chandler, Okla. Terr.), Vol. 9, No. 6, Ed. 1 Friday, October 27, 1899. Chandler, Oklahoma Territory. The Gateway to Oklahoma History. http://gateway.okhistory.org/ark:/67531/metadc115439/ (last visited October 16, 2014). Mr. Sawner spoke to African Americans in Lincoln County about the importance of black/white friendship and peace in 1904. French, Mrs. W. H. The *Chandler Publicist* (Chandler, Okla. Terr.), Vol. 11, No. 20, Ed. 1 Friday, September 23, 1904. Chandler, Oklahoma Territory. The Gateway to Oklahoma History. http://gateway.okhistory.org/ark:/67531/metadc151000/ (last visited October 16, 2014).

cciiGilstrap, H. B. The *Chandler News*. (Chandler, Okla. Terr.), Vol. 10, No. 3, Ed. 1 Thursday, October 4, 1900. Chandler, Oklahoma Territory. The Gateway to Oklahoma History. http://gateway.okhistory.org/ark:/67531/metadc115944/ (last visited October 18, 2014).

cciiiMcCormick, H. W. *Mulhall Enterprise* (Mulhall, Okla. Terr.), Vol. 10, No. 24, Ed. 1 Friday, June 13, 1902. Mulhall, Oklahoma Territory. The Gateway to Oklahoma History. http://gateway.okhistory.org/ark:/67531/

metadc285868/ (last visited October 15, 2014); Niblack, Leslie G. The Guthrie Guide (Guthrie, Okla. Terr.), Vol. 19, No. 156, Ed. 1 Wednesday, June 4, 1902. Guthrie, Oklahoma Territory. The Gateway to Oklahoma History. http://gateway.okhistory.org/ark:/67531/metadc75938/ (last visited October 18, 2014); Niblack, Leslie G. *Oklahoma Leader* (Guthrie, Okla. Terr.), Vol. 10, No. 19, Ed. 1 Thursday, June 5, 1902. Guthrie, Oklahoma Territory. The Gateway to Oklahoma History. http://gateway.okhistory.org/ark:/67531/metadc121573/ (last visited October 19, 2014); Burke, J. J. The *Norman Transcript* (Norman, Okla. Terr.), Vol. 13, No. 31, Ed. 1 Thursday, June 12, 1902. Norman, Oklahoma Territory. The Gateway to Oklahoma History. http://gateway.okhistory.org/ark:/67531/metadc186393/ (last visited October 19, 2014)

[cciv]French, Mrs. W. H. The *Chandler Publicist* (Chandler, Okla. Terr.), Vol. 12, No. 27, Ed. 1 Friday, November 24, 1905. Chandler, Oklahoma Territory. The Gateway to Oklahoma History. http://gateway.okhistory.org/ark:/67531/metadc151082/ (last visited October 18, 2014).

[ccv]"Men and Women of Both Races Honor Fallen Leader. Body Is Interred at Newkirk. Masons Have Charge of Funeral," *In Memoriam: G. W. F. Sawner, Chandler News-Publicist Print*, May 2, 1924, at 7 - 8.

[ccvi]W.E.B. Du Bois, *The Talented Tenth*, featured in *The Negro Problem* (New York, NY: James Pott and Company 1903) (text available at TeachingAmericanHistory.org, Ashland University, accessed July 13, 2010). See also, Philip S. Foner, ed., *W.E.B. Du Bois Speaks: Speeches And Addresses 1890 – 1919*, (New York, NY: Pathfinder, 1970), at 86; David Levering Lewis, W.E.B. Du Bois: *Biography Of A Race, 1868 – 1919* (New York, NY: Henry Holt and Company, Inc., 1993), at 73.

[ccvii]"Open Letter to Woodrow Wilson," TeachingAmericanHistory.org, http://teachingamericanhistory.org/library/document/open-letter-to-woodrow-wilson/ (published in the March 1913 issue of The Crisis) (last visited June 26, 2015).

[ccviii]W.E.B. Du Bois, "The Talented Tenth," from *The Negro Problem: A Series of Articles by Representative Negroes of Today* (New York, 1903), available online at http://www.yale.edu/glc/archive/1148.htm (last visited April 27, 2015).

[ccix]Michael John Gerson, chief speechwriter for President George W. Bush from 2001 until mid-2006, coined the phrase "the soft bigotry of low expectations."

[ccx]www.biography.com/people/web-du-bois-9279924 (last visited August 12, 2013). Dr. Du Bois' views on African American intellectualism and educational parity, often juxtaposed against Booker T. Washington's advocacy for vocational education for African Americans, shaped debate on educational policy for decades. The following quotes on education offer a glimpse of this philosophical tussle:

- "I should recommend for the average colored child the same course of study as for the average white child." (1926)

- "The question as to whether American Negroes were capable of education was no longer a debatable one in 1876. The whole problem was simply one of opportunity." (1935)

- "We cannot base the education of future citizens on the present inexcusable inequality of wealth nor on physical differences of race. We must seek not to make men carpenters but to make carpenters men." (1920)

- "The chief difficulty with Hampton is that its ideals are low. It is ...deliberately educating a servile class for a servile place. It is substituting the worship of philanthropists like Samuel Armstrong (excellent man though he was) for worship of manhood ... The fact of the matter is, that if the Negro race survives in America and in modern civilization it will be because it assimilates that civilization and develops leaders of large intelligent caliber. The people back of Hampton do not propose that any such thing take place. Consciously or unconsciously they propose to develop the Negro race as a caste of efficient workers, do not expect them to be co-workers in a modern cultured state. It is that underlying falsehood and heresy, the refusing to recognize Negroes as men, which is the real basic criticism of Hampton." (1916)

- "[Hampton is] probably the best center of trade-teaching for Negroes in the United States .... We do not feel, at present, that Hampton is our school - on the contrary, we feel that she belongs to the white South and to the reactionary North, and we fear that she is a center of that underground and silent intrigue which is determined to perpetuate the American Negro as a docile peasant and peon, without political rights of social standing, working for little wages, and heaping up dividends to be doled out in future charity to his children." (1917)

William Edward Burghardt Du Bois on Education, http://northbysouth. kenyon.edu/1998/edu/home/web.htm (last visited June 10, 2014).

ccxi"Bank Closes in Sawner's Honor," *The Black Dispatch*, May 8, 1924, at 1.

ccxiiPhoto courtesy of Mel Chatman.

ccxviiiGreer, Frank H. The *Daily Oklahoma State Capital* (Guthrie, Okla.), Vol. 6, No. 38, Ed. 1 Thursday, June 7, 1894. Guthrie, Oklahoma. The Gateway to Oklahoma History. http://gateway.okhistory.org/ark:/67531/metadc1122439/ (last visited October 15, 2014).

ccxivGreer, Frank H. The *Weekly Oklahoma State Capital* (Guthrie, Okla. Terr.), Vol. 6, No. 10, Ed. 1 Saturday, July 7, 1894. Guthrie, Oklahoma Territory. The Gateway to Oklahoma History. http://gateway.okhistory.org/ark:/67531/

metadc352401/ (last visited October 19, 2014).

ccxvGreer, Frank H. *The Daily Oklahoma State Capital* (Guthrie, Okla. Terr.), Vol. 6, No. 219, Ed. 1 Monday, January 7, 1895. Guthrie, Oklahoma Territory. The Gateway to Oklahoma History. http://gateway.okhistory.org/ark:/67531/metadc122613/ (last visited October 16, 2014).

ccxviGilstrap, H. B. *The Chandler News.* (Chandler, Okla. Terr.), Vol. 9, No. 50, Ed. 1 Thursday, August 30, 1900. Chandler, Oklahoma Territory. The Gateway to Oklahoma History. http://gateway.okhistory.org/ark:/67531/metadc115939/ (last visited October 16, 2014).

ccxviiFrench, Mrs. W. H. *The Chandler Publicist* (Chandler, Okla. Terr.), Vol. 9, No. 4, Ed. 1 Friday, June 20, 1902. Chandler, Oklahoma Territory. The Gateway to Oklahoma History. http://gateway.okhistory.org/ark:/67531/metadc150884/ (last visited October 16, 2014).

ccxviiiGreer, Frank H. *The Weekly Oklahoma State Capital* (Guthrie, Okla. Terr.), Vol. 6, No. 45, Ed. 1 Saturday, March 9, 1895. Guthrie, Oklahoma Territory. The Gateway to Oklahoma History. http://gateway.okhistory.org/ark:/67531/metadc353156/ (last visited October 19, 2014).

ccxix*The Daily Times-Journal* (Oklahoma City, Okla. Terr.), Vol. 7, No. 238, Ed. 1 Friday, March 27, 1896. Oklahoma City, Oklahoma Territory. The Gateway to Oklahoma History. http://gateway.okhistory.org/ark:/67531/metadc95228/ (last visited October 18, 2014).

ccxx*The Daily Times-Journal* (Oklahoma City, Okla. Terr.), Vol. 12, No. 148, Ed. 1 Monday, October 19, 1900. Oklahoma City, Oklahoma Territory. The Gateway to Oklahoma History. http://gateway.okhistory.org/ark:/67531/metadc95634/ (last visited October 19, 2014).

ccxxiGilstrap, H. B. *The Chandler News.* (Chandler, Okla. Terr.), Vol. 13, No. 30, Ed. 1 Thursday, April 14, 1904. Chandler, Oklahoma Territory. The Gateway to Oklahoma History. http://gateway.okhistory.org/ark:/67531/metadc117770/ (last visited October 15, 2014).

ccxxiiGilstrap, H. B. *The Chandler News* (Chandler, Okla. Terr.), Vol. 13, No. 28, Ed. 1 Thursday, March 31, 1904. Chandler, Oklahoma Territory. The Gateway to Oklahoma History. http://gateway.okhistory.org/ark:/67531/metadc117766/ (last visited October 15, 2014).

ccxxiiiPerkins, G. N. *The Oklahoma Guide* (Guthrie, Okla. Terr.), Vol. 15, No. 8, Ed. 1 Thursday, July 13, 1905. Guthrie, Oklahoma Territory. The Gateway to Oklahoma History. http://gateway.okhistory.org/ark:/67531/metadc95831/ (last visited October 18, 2014).

ccxxivTwine, W. H. *The Muskogee Cimeter*(Muskogee, Indian Terr.), Vol. 6, No. 42, Ed. 1 Thursday, July 27, 1905. Muskogee, Indian Territory. The Gateway to Oklahoma History. http://gateway.okhistory.org/ark:/67531/metadc70005/ (last visited October 18, 2014); Halpin, Harry E. *The Shawnee News* (Shawnee, Okla. Territory), Vol. 9, No. 110, Ed. 1 Tuesday, August

22, 1905. Shawnee, Oklahoma Territory. The Gateway to Oklahoma History. http://gateway.okhistory.org/ark:/67531/metadc137878/ (last visited October 18, 2014); Greer, Frank H. *The Weekly Oklahoma State Capital* (Guthrie, Okla. Terr.), Vol. 17, No. 23, Ed. 1 Saturday, September 2, 1905. Guthrie, Oklahoma Territory. The Gateway to Oklahoma History. http://gateway.okhistory.org/ark:/67531/metadc352968/ (last visited October 19, 2014).

ccxxv*The Daily Ardmoreite* (Ardmore, Indian Terr.), Vol. 12, No. 429, Ed. 1 Monday, August 28, 1905. Ardmore, Indian Territory. The Gateway to Oklahoma History. http://gateway.okhistory.org/ark:/67531/metadc79919/ (last visited October 18, 2014).

ccxxviGilstrap, H. B. *The Chandler News* (Chandler, Okla. Terr.), Vol. 15, No. 17, Ed. 1 Thursday, January 18, 1906. Chandler, Oklahoma. Chandler, Oklahoma Territory. The Gateway to Oklahoma History. http://gateway.okhistory.org/ark:/67531/metadc160405/ (last visited October 18, 2014).

ccxxviiGilstrap, H. B. *The Chandler News* (Chandler, Okla. Terr.), Vol. 15, No. 26, Ed. 1 Thursday, March 22, 1906. Chandler, Oklahoma Territory. The Gateway to Oklahoma History. http://gateway.okhistory.org/ark:/67531/metadc160414/ (last visited October 18, 2014).

ccxxviiiUlam, P. L. *The Chandler Publicist* (Chandler, Okla. Terr.), Vol. 14, No. 11, Ed. 1 Friday, July 12, 1907. Chandler, Oklahoma Territory. The Gateway to Oklahoma History. http://gateway.okhistory.org/ark:/67531/metadc151242/ (last visited October 18, 2014).

ccxxixUlam, P. L. *The Chandler Publicist* (Chandler, Okla. Territory), Vol. 14, No. 11, Ed. 1 Friday, July 12, 1907. Chandler, Oklahoma Territory. The Gateway to Oklahoma History. http://gateway.okhistory.org/ark:/67531/metadc151242/ (last visited October 18, 2014).

ccxxxGeorge Sawner played an active role in the Republican State Convention in Oklahoma City in 1922. Held at the Coliseum, the event drew throngs, with estimated attendance at 3,000. Some seventy-five African American delegates attended. Mr. Sawner led an informal side meeting at which a resolution protesting the seating of Congressional Representative Alice Robinson as chair of the convention was drafted and forwarded to the Republican Party organization committee. Congresswoman Robinson had voted against the Dyer Anti-Lynching Bill, an unsuccessful 1922 Congressional effort to pass federal legislation to address and otherwise provide federal prosecution of nationwide lynchings, particularly those in the southern states. Attorney W. H. Twine of Muskogee lobbied vehemently against her seating as chair. Dunjee, Roscoe. *The Black Dispatch* (Oklahoma City, Okla.), Vol. 7, No. 39, Ed. 1 Thursday, August 31, 1922. Oklahoma City, Oklahoma. The Gateway to Oklahoma History. http://gateway.okhistory.org/ark:/67531/metadc/152400/ (last visited October 18, 2014).

ccxxxiThe Negro Protective League operated as a black self-help and anti-racism organization. The Negro Protective Party Platform, adopted at the Columbus, Ohio, convention on September 22, 1897, expounded upon these principles:

> [W]e demand an immediate recognition of our rights as citizens such as have been repeatedly pledged and as often violated, and which are guaranteed by the constitution and laws of the land. A decent regard for our own feelings, of those we love and cherish, compels us to take immediate political action that we may show to the world that we are no longer the plaything of politicians or chattels for sale to the highest bidder.
>
> Whereas, The Negroes of the United States are deprived of the enjoyment of their constitutional and legal rights, the gates of industry being closed against us, the right of public travel and equal accommodation being restricted in many localities, mob law, having supplanted the law of the land in many states, not excepting the state of Ohio, our cries for justice being disregarded by those in power, and having appealed in vain to both of the dominant political parties for redress of grievances; therefore,
>
> Resolved, That the time has come for independent action on the part of the Negro citizens of Ohio.
>
> Resolved, That this party shall be known as the Negro Protective Party.

Negro Protective League Party Platform, September 22, 1897, http://commons.wikimedia.org/wiki/File:Negro_Protective_League_Platform.jpg#-file, (last visited July 25, 2013).

[ccxxxii]Timothy Thomas Fortune formed The National Afro-American League on January 25, 1890. A forerunner to the NAACP, the league advocated for black civil and political rights. It dissolved in 1893, but reemerged in 1898, albeit under a slightly different name, the National Afro-American Council. The council continued for about ten years. See, e.g., Emma Lou Thornbrough, "The National Afro-American League, 1887-1908," THE JOURNAL OF SOUTHERN HISTORY, Vol. 27, No. 4, November 1961, pp. 494-512, http://www.jstor.org/stable/2204311 (last visited July 25, 2013).

[ccxxxiii]"Oklahoma Negro Issue Put Up To Roosevelt," *New York Times*, February 2, 1907, at 4.

[ccxxxiv]Williams, M. W. *The Wewoka and Lima Courier* (Wewoka, Okla.),Vol. 1, No. 18, Ed. 1 Friday, November 21, 1913. Wewoka, Oklahoma. The Gateway to Oklahoma History. http://gateway.okhistory.org/ark:/67531/metadc/167760/ (last visited October 19, 2014)

[ccxxxv]*Guinn v. United States*, 238 U.S. 347 (1915.)

[ccxxxvi]Alfred L. Brophy, *Guinn V. United States (1915), Oklahoma Historical So-*

ciety's *Encyclopedia Of Oklahoma History & Culture*, http://digital.library.ok-state.edu/encyclopedia/entries/G/GU001.html (last visited October 19, 2014).

ccxxxv*Lane v. Wilson*, 307 U.S. 268 (1939).

ccxxxviiiSmitherman, Andrew Jackson. *The Tulsa Star* (Tulsa, Okla.), Vol. 2, No. 19, E. 1, Saturday, February 28, 1914. Tulsa, Oklahoma. The Gateway to Oklahoma History, http://gateway.okhistory.org/ark:/67531/metadc72830/ (last visited October 19, 2014).

ccxxxixExcerpts from Booker T. Washington address to the National Negro Business League conference in Muskogee, Oklahoma, on August 14, 1914, Booker T. Washington Society, http://www.btwsociety.org/library/speeches/11.php (last visited June 25, 2015)

ccxlA copy of George Sawner's National Negro Business League membership certificate is on file with the author. Twenty-five of 1900 dollars would be worth $714.29 in 2014. http://www.davemanuel.com/inflation-calculator.php (last visited May 25, 2015).

ccxliNational Negro Business League Executive Committee, circa 1917, New York Public Library Digital Gallery, digitalgallery.nypl.org/nypldigital/dgkeysearchdetail.cfm?trg=... (last visited August 12, 2013).

ccxliiJohn H. Bracey, Jr. and August Meier, eds., A Guide to the Microfilm Edition of Black Studies Research Sources Microfilms from Major Archival and Manuscript Collections Records of the National Negro Business League: Part 1: Annual Conference Proceedings and Organizational Records, 1900-1919; Part 2: Correspondence and Business Records, 1900-1923 (Bethesda, Maryland: University Publications of America 1995) (introduction by Kenneth Hamilton Department of History, Southern Methodist University).

ccxliii Dunjee, Roscoe. *The Black Dispatch* (Oklahoma City, Okla.), Vol. 4, No. 41, Ed. 1 Friday, November 2, 1917. Oklahoma City, Oklahoma. The Gateway to Oklahoma History. http://gateway.okhistory.org/ark:/67531/metadc/152053/ (last visited November 17, 2014).

ccxlivTwine, W. H. *The Muskogee Cimeter* (Muskogee, Okla.), Vol. 18, No. 38, Ed. 1 Saturday, May 4, 1918. Muskogee, Oklahoma. The Gateway to Oklahoma History. http://gateway.okhistory.org/ark:/67531/metadc70241/ (last visited October 16, 2014).

ccxlv*The Dallas Express* (Dallas, Texas), Vol. 28, No. 1, Ed. 1 Saturday, October 9, 1920. Dallas, Texas. The Portal to Texas History. http://texashistory.unt.edu/ark/67531/ (last visited July 1, 2015).

ccxlvi*The Dallas Express* (Dallas, Texas), Vol. 28, No. 1, Ed. 1 Saturday, October 9, 1920. Dallas, Texas. The Portal to Texas History. http://texashistory.unt.edu/ark/67531/ (last visited July 1, 2015).

ccxlviiState of Oklahoma certificate of appointment signed by J.B.A. Robertson, Governor of the State of Oklahoma, June 13, 1921.

ccxlviiiDunjee, Roscoe. *The Black Dispatch* (Oklahoma City, Okla.), Vol. 6, No. 3, Ed. 1 Friday, December 20, 1920. Oklahoma City, Oklahoma. The Gateway to Oklahoma History. http://gateway.okhistory.org/ark:/67531/metadc/152315/ (last visited October 18, 2014); Smitherman, Andrew Jackson. *The Tulsa Star* (Tulsa, Okla.), Vol. 10, No. 48, E. 1, Saturday, February 21, 1920. Tulsa, Oklahoma. The Gateway to Oklahoma History, http://gateway.okhistory.org/ark:/67531/metadc72830/ (last visited October 18, 2014); Dunjee, Roscoe. *The Black Dispatch* (Oklahoma City, Okla.), Vol. 5, No. 41, Ed. 1 Friday, September 17, 1920. Oklahoma City, Oklahoma. The Gateway to Oklahoma History. http://gateway.okhistory.org/ark:/67531/metadc/152288/ (last visited October 19, 2014); Dunjee, Roscoe. *The Black Dispatch* (Oklahoma City, Okla.), Vol. 5, No. 50, Ed. 1 Friday, November 19, 1920. Oklahoma City, Oklahoma. The Gateway to Oklahoma History. http://gateway.okhistory.org/ark:/67531/metadc/152310/ (last visited October 19, 2014); Newdick, Edwin. *Oklahoma Leader* (Oklahoma City, Okla.), Vol. 1, No. 35, Ed. 2 Friday, September 24, 1920. Oklahoma City, Oklahoma. The Gateway to Oklahoma History. http://gateway.okhistory.org/ark:/67531/metadc/149186/ (last visited October 19, 2014); Dunjee, Roscoe. *The Black Dispatch* (Oklahoma City, Okla.), Vol. 6, No. 24, Ed. 1 Friday, May 20, 1921. Oklahoma City, Oklahoma. The Gateway to Oklahoma History. http://gateway.okhistory.org/ark:/67531/metadc/152333/ (last visited October 19, 2014).

ccxlixIn a precursor to the establishment of that body, Governor J. B. A. Robertson convened a meeting of African American and white leaders at the State Capitol to discuss racial problems in Oklahoma, including lynching, civil rights, racial cooperation, and education. Mr. Sawner attended that September 23, 1920, meeting. Dunjee, Roscoe. *The Black Dispatch* (Oklahoma City, Okla.), Vol. 10, No. 26, Ed. 1, Saturday, September 25, 1920. The Gateway to Oklahoma History. http://gateway.okhistory.org:/67531/metadc72818/ (last visited October 15, 2014).

cclSee, *e.g.*, Hannibal B. Johnson, *Black Wall Street—From Riot To Renaissance In Tulsa's Historic Greenwood District* (Austin, TX: Eakin Press 1998).

ccliDunjee, Roscoe. *The Black Dispatch* (Oklahoma City, Okla.), Vol. 5, No. 21, Ed. 1 Friday, April 9, 1920. Oklahoma City, Oklahoma. The Gateway to Oklahoma History. http://gateway.okhistory.org/ark:/67531/metadc/152225/ (last visited October 18, 2014).

ccliiSee, *e.g.*, http://www.naacp.org/ (last visited October 24, 2014). Founded February 12, 1909, the National Association for the Advancement of Colored People is the nation's oldest, largest and most widely recognized grassroots civil rights organization. Early on, the N.A.A.C.P. focused on challenging the Jim Crow laws prevalent throughout the South, succeeding only in a few early cases. A case in point is the N.A.A.C.P.'s 1915 victory over Oklahoma's "grandfather clause," which exempted most white voters from stringent literacy requirements that effectively disenfranchised African Americans. See

Guinn v. United States, 238 U.S. 347 (1915).

ccliiiDunjee, Roscoe. *The Black Dispatch* (Oklahoma City, Okla.), Vol. 5, No. 26, Ed. 1 Friday, December 10, 1920. Oklahoma City, Oklahoma. The Gateway to Oklahoma History. http://gateway.okhistory.org/ark:/67531/metadc/152313/ (last visited October 18, 2014).

cclivDunjee, Roscoe. *The Black Dispatch* (Oklahoma City, Okla.), Vol. 6, No. 7, Ed. 1 Friday, January 21, 1921. Oklahoma City, Oklahoma. The Gateway to Oklahoma History. http://gateway.okhistory.org/ark:/67531/metadc/152318/ (last visited October 17, 2014).

cclvDunjee, Roscoe. *The Black Dispatch* (Oklahoma City, Okla.), Vol. 5, No. 8, Ed. 1 Friday, January 2, 1920. Oklahoma City, Oklahoma. The Gateway to Oklahoma History. http://okhistory.org/ark:/67531/metadc152184/ (last visited October 15, 2014).

cclvi*See* http://www.ame-church.com/ (official website of the African Methodist Episcopal Church) (last viewed July 1, 2010):

> The African Methodist Episcopal Church…is the first major religious denomination in the Western World that had its origin over sociological and theological beliefs and differences. It rejected the negative theological interpretations, which rendered persons of African descent second-class citizens. Theirs was a theological declaration that God is God all the time and for everybody. The church was born in protest against slavery—against dehumanization of African people, brought to the American continent as labor.

For more on the period known as the "nadir" of race relations, *see, e.g.*, Glenda Elizabeth Gilmore, "'Somewhere' in the Nadir of African American History, 1890-1920," Freedom's Story, TeacherServe©, National Humanities Center, http://nationalhumanitiescenter.org/tserve/freedom/1865-1917/essays/nadir.htm (last visited July 29, 2013).

cclvii*See, e.g.*, "Prince Hall Masons (1784 -), http://www.blackpast.org/aaw/prince-hall-masons-1784 (last visited August 15, 2015).

cclviii*The Black Dispatch* hailed Mr. Sawner as "one of the strong Pythians of the state and represented in the Supreme lodge this summer [1917]." Dunjee, Roscoe. The Black Dispatch (Oklahoma City, Okla.), Vol. 4, No. 43, Ed. 1 Friday, November 16, 1917. Oklahoma City, Oklahoma. The Gateway to Oklahoma History. http://gateway.okhistory.org/ark:/67531/metadc152055/ (last visited October 15, 2014).

cclix*See, e.g.*, http://www.freemasons-freemasonry.com/ (last visited June 1, 2010).

> Freemasonry is one of the world's oldest secular fraternal societies. Freemasonry is a society of men concerned with moral and spiritual values. Freemasons are taught its pre-

cepts by a series of ritual dramas, which follow ancient forms, and use stonemasons' customs and tools as allegorical guides. The essential qualification to become Freemason is a belief in a Supreme Being. A Freemason's duty as a citizen must always prevail over any obligation to other Masons, and any attempt to shield Freemasons who has acted dishonourably or unlawfully, or to confer an unfair advantage on other Free Masons is contrary to this prime duty. The Freemasons refer to those who are not Freemasons as 'cowans' because in architecture a cowan is someone apprenticed to bricklaying but not licensed to the trade of masonry.

The first fraternal order to be chartered by an Act of Congress, The Order of Knights of Pythias, is an international, non-sectarian fraternal order established in 1864 in Washington, D.C., by Justus H. Rathbone. Dating back centuries, Odd Fellows (alternatively, "Oddfellows") are friendly societies, nonprofit mutual organizations. Members pool resources and help one another when needs arise, and all income passes back to members in the form of services and benefits. The Oddfellows raised money for both local and national charities, with branches raising money for local causes and Societies raising significant amounts for charities.

[cclx]Dunjee, Roscoe. *The Black Dispatch* (Oklahoma City, Okla.), Vol. 5, No. 29, Ed. 1 Friday, August 16, 1918. Oklahoma City, Oklahoma. The Gateway to Oklahoma History. http://gateway.okhistory.org/ark:/67531/metadc152093/ (last visited October 18, 2014). Mob violence would continue to be a frequent theme for Mr. Sawner and other black leaders. See, e.g., Dunjee, Roscoe. *The Black Dispatch* (Oklahoma City, Okla.), Vol. 5, No. 42, Ed. 1 Friday, September 24, 1920. Oklahoma City, Oklahoma. The Gateway to Oklahoma History. http://gateway.okhistory.org/ark:/67531/metadc152291/ (last visited October 18, 2014).

[cclxi]Dunjee, Roscoe. *The Black Dispatch* (Oklahoma City, Okla.), Vol. 5, No. 36, Ed. 1 Friday, August 6, 1920. Oklahoma City, Oklahoma. The Gateway to Oklahoma History. http://gateway.okhistory.org/ark:/67531/metadc152273/ (last visited October 15, 2014).

[cclxii]Smitherman, Andrew Jackson. *The Tulsa Star* (Tulsa, Okla.), Vol. 9, No. 6, E. 1, Saturday, February 21, 1920. Tulsa, Oklahoma. The Gateway to Oklahoma History, http://gateway.okhistory.org/ark:/67531/metadc72786/ (last visited October 18, 2014).

[cclxiii]"In Memoriam: G. W. F. Sawner", *Chandler News-Publicist Print*, May 2, 1924, at 10.

[cclxiv]Lena Sawner was a staunch supporter of *The Black Dispatch*, and helped the paper gain a foothold in Chandler. Dunjee, Roscoe. The Black Dispatch (Oklahoma City, Okla.), Vol. 4, No. 45, Ed. 1 Friday, November 30, 1917. The

Gateway to Oklahoma History. http://gateway.okhistory.org/ark/67531/metadc152057/ (last visited October 15, 2014).

ᶜᶜˡˣᵛ"Entire State Mourns Death of Pioneer Citizen: Men and Women of Both Races Honor Fallen Leader; Body Enterred [sic] at Newkirk; Masons Have Charge of Funeral", *Black Dispatch*, May 8, 1924, at 1 (*Black Dispatch* archives available at Metropolitan Library System, Oklahoma City, Oklahoma).

ᶜᶜˡˣᵛⁱ"In Memoriam: G. W. F. Sawner," *Chandler News-Publicist Print*, May 2, 1924, at 22 - 23, 44, 41, 48, 21, and 29 – 30, respectively.

ᶜᶜˡˣᵛⁱⁱIn *Lane v. Wilson*, 307 U.S. 268 (1939), Iverson (*a.k.a.* "I.W.") Lane, mayor of the all-black Oklahoma town Red Bird, one of the dozens of Oklahoma all-black towns, challenged Oklahoma's restrictive voter registration requirement. The law in question, like the one declared unconstitutional in 1915, required literacy tests for voter registration. This second law, again like the first, included a "grandfather clause" that exempted most whites from its strictures. The second law, however, gave African American a brief window within which to register without the onerous literacy requirements. The United States Supreme Court found that this second registration law, like the one it had previously held unconstitutional in Guinn v. United States, 248 U.S. 347 (1915), effectively disenfranchised black voters, and thus violated the Fifteenth Amendment.

ᶜᶜˡᵛⁱⁱⁱ"In Memoriam: G. W. F. Sawner," *Chandler News-Publicist Print*, May 2, 1924, at 29.

ᶜᶜˡˣⁱˣ"In Memoriam: G. W. F. Sawner," *Chandler News-Publicist Print*, May 2, 1924, at 35.

ᶜᶜˡˣˣ"Mrs. L. Lena, principal of the Chandler schools and wife of the deceased, was prostrated in the home and it was with difficulty that she was able to sustain herself during the funeral services...." *In Memoriam: G. W. F. Sawner, Chandler News-Publicist Print*, May 2, 1924, at 7.

ᶜᶜˡˣˣⁱ"In Memoriam: G. W. F. Sawner," *Chandler News-Publicist Print*, May 2, 1924, at 57.

ᶜᶜˡˣˣⁱⁱE-mail from Mel Chatman, October 1, 2013. Mrs. Sawner also served as a correspondent of sorts for *The Black Dispatch*, reporting regularly on Chandler news.

ᶜᶜˡˣˣⁱⁱⁱRoscoe Dunjee, *The Black Dispatch*, Oklahoma City, OK, April 30, 1931.

ᶜᶜˡˣˣⁱᵛ*In the Matter of the Estate of G. W. F. Sawner, Deceased*, Case No. 2882, Final Decree and Order Discharging Executrix (Lincoln County District Court, March 26, 1927).

ᶜᶜˡˣˣᵛOn March 21, 1943, almost twenty years after Sawner's death, a middle-aged Mrs. Sawner wed Lewis A. Brown of Chicago, Illinois, in a Justice of the Peace-administered ceremony in her Chandler home. He was 63; she was 58. Marriage Record, Lincoln County, Oklahoma, signed by John W.

Killough, Justice of the Peace, March 22, 1943 (copy of file with the author). Just six years later, on March 1, 1949, twenty-five years after George Sawner's demise, Lena Lowery Sawner joined her first love in death.

[cdxxvii]*See, e.g.*, Michael Cunningham and Craig Marberry, *Crowns: Portraits Of Black Women In Church Hats* (New York, NY: Doubleday 2000)(dust jacket).

[cdxxvii]Victor Brown described Mrs. Sawner as a "student of the English language," who always spoke properly and would not hesitate to correct those who did not. Telephone interview with Victor Brown, former Douglass School student, September 26, 2014.

[cdxxviii]Telephone interview with George Sawner Ellis, November 10, 2014.

[cdxxix]Telephone interview with George Sawner Ellis, October 18, 2013.

[cdxxx]Victor Brown recalled Mrs. Sawner's "memorable and very pleasing" scent. He noted that the aroma stood out above everyone else's, and that he knew it had to be something special. Telephone interview with Victor Brown, former Douglass School student, September 26, 2014.

[cdxxxi]"Principal of first black high school 'exacting'," *The Lincoln County News*, May 9, 1985, at 13.

[cdxxxii]A $30 hat in 1920 would be worth more than $372 in 2015 dollars. See, e.g., http://www.dollartimes.com/inflation/inflation.php?amount=30000&year=1920 (last visited May 30, 2015).

[cdxxxiii]This focus on self-expression through headdresses has its origins in the black church. Early 20th century church services gave black women, many of whom worked as domestic servants or in other subservient roles, a chance to escape, if only momentarily, their drab, dreary workday uniforms. They often donned bright colors and textured fabric, topping their outfits off with flamboyant hats. "When the Apostle Paul declared that women must cover their heads during worship (1 Corinthians 11:15), African American women took his decree, attached feathers and bows to it, and turned it into something beautiful." *See, e.g.*, Faithful Forum, "Why Do Women Wear Hats To Church?" March 23, 2013, http://elev8.com/554605/why-do-women-wear-hats-to-church/ (last visited July 24, 2013). The writer may actually have meant to cite 1 Corinthians 11:5, in the King James Version of the Bible, which provides: "But every woman that prayeth or prophesieth with [her] head uncovered dishonoureth her head: for that is even all one as if she were shaven." 1 Corinthians 11:15, in the King James Version of the Bible, states: "But if a woman have long hair, it is a glory to her: for her hair is given her for a covering."

[cdxxxiv]Telephone interview with Bernice Caldwell, Chandler, Oklahoma, July 15, 2014.

[cdxxxv]Photo courtesy of Mel Chatman.

[cdxxxvi]*See* Chapter 8, *Douglass School & The Sawners (1860 – 1954), Chandler: The Ellis Family Story,* http://www.ellisfamilystory.com/chapter03.html.

cclxxxviiPhoto courtesy of Mel Chatman.

cclxxxviiiPhoto courtesy of Mel Chatman. In a June 27, 1924, letter of condolence (on the occasion of Mr. Sawner's death) from Mrs. Sawner's "Aunt Bell" in Arkansas City, Kansas, the writer includes language corroborating the close relationship between Mrs. Sawner and Nellie ("Nell") Beridon, including: "Hope you and Nell are fine;" and "Love to Nell." *In Memoriam: G. W. F. Sawner, Chandler News-Publicist Print*, May 2, 1924, at 19. An article in *The Black Dispatch* noted "Mr. and Mrs. G. W. Sawner and Miss Nellie Beridon of Chandler, are visiting this week with Mr. and Mrs. Beridon [in Chilesville]." Dunjee, Roscoe. *The Black Dispatch* (Oklahoma City, Okla.), Vol. 7, No. 33, Ed. 1 Thursday, July 20, 1922. Oklahoma City, Oklahoma. The Gateway to Oklahoma History. http://gateway.okhistory.org/ark:/67531/metadc152394/ (last visited October 20, 2014). Ms. Beridon attended Wilberforce University in Ohio. Dunjee, Roscoe. *The Black Dispatch* (Oklahoma City, Okla.), Vol. 7, No. 41, Ed. 1 Thursday, September 14, 1922. Oklahoma City, Oklahoma. The Gateway to Oklahoma History. http://gateway.okhistory.org/ark:/67531/metadc152402/ (last visited October 20, 2014). She had a brother, Clarence. Dunjee, Roscoe. *The Black Dispatch* (Oklahoma City, Okla.), Vol. 7, No. 36, Ed. 1 Thursday, August 10, 1922. Oklahoma City, Oklahoma. The Gateway to Oklahoma History. http://gateway.okhistory.org/ark:/67531/metadc152397/ (last visited October 20, 2014).

cclxxxixBernice Caldwell, a Douglass School student during the Lena Sawner era, recalls Mrs. Sawner as a community leader, consummate educator and motivator, and an elegant lady. Telephone interview with Bernice Caldwell, Chandler, Oklahoma, July 15, 2014.

ccxcInterview with Kevin Sharp, great nephew of Douglass School alumnus, Booker Smith, July 24, 2014, Tulsa, Oklahoma. The quoted language reflects an interpretation of the likely exchange. No transcript exists.

ccxciLetter from J.B.A. Robertson to the Honorable E.D. Cameron, State Superintendent, February 8, 1909, on file at the LCHS Museum of Pioneer History.

ccxcii*See, e.g.*, Hannibal B. Johnson, *Black Wall Street—From Riot To Renaissance In Tulsa's Historic Greenwood District* (Austin, TX: Eakin Press 1998).

ccxciiien.wikipedia.org/wiki/James_B._A._Robertson (last visited August 13, 2013).

ccxcivLetter from J.H. Bayes to the Honorable E.D. Cameron, State Superintendent, February 8, 1909, on file at the LCHS Museum of Pioneer History; Letter from H.G. Stettmund, House of Representative, State of Oklahoma, First Legislature, to the Honorable E.D. Cameron, February 6, 1909, on file at the LCHS Museum of Pioneer History.

ccxcvRidley, Elmira S. *The Oklahoma Guide* (Guthrie, Okla.), Vol. 25, No. 3, Ed. 1 Thursday, June 15, 1916. Chandler, Oklahoma. The Gateway to Oklahoma History. http://gateway.okhistory.org/ark:/67531/metadc154861/(last visited October 16, 2014).

ccxcvi*See* certificate of appointment on file with the LCHS Museum of Pioneer History.

ccxcvii Liz Golliver, "Chandler woman empowered African American community," *The Lincoln County News*, January 29, 2015, at 1, 8. The article continued:

> During a difficult time of mandated segregation Lena Sawner succeeded in becoming an accepted member of society in Lincoln County. She encountered dual difficulties of being a black [person] and a woman, but dealt with it judiciously and firmly by continuing to reach her goals. [Mrs. Sawner] served as principal of Douglass School for approximately 30 years. As a teacher, [Mrs.] Sawner was a near perfect role model. Her diction and use of the English language were flawless. She walked in a proud and dignified manner, becoming the center of attention wherever she entered a room. The female students admired the expensive Parisian perfume she always wore. She was a role model of good grooming, always meticulously and expensively dressed, not to embarrass the children, but to prove to them that black people can succeed if they follow the values she demanded of herself.

ccxcviii The Lowerys' son, William H. Lowery, died in the fall of 1911.

ccxcix Richmond, Indiana, is a small Wayne County town in east central Indiana bordering on Ohio that was once home to various Native American tribes.

ccc During the height of Reconstruction, the federal government stepped in to realign and reincorporate these secessionist Southern states. The eleven Confederate states rejoined the Union, set up governments that acknowledged federal supremacy, and redefined the role of the formerly enslaved Africans whose bondage had fueled Southern economic and political power. C.V. Woodward, *Reunion And Reaction: The Compromise Of 1877 And The End Of Reconstruction*, (Boston, MA: Little, Brown and Company 1951); John Hope Franklin, *Reconstruction After The Civil War* (Chicago, IL: University of Chicago Press 1961).

ccci One example of the promise of Reconstruction was the Freedmen's Savings and Trust Company. The federal bank, established in Washington, D.C., in 1865, did business exclusively with African Americans, boasting some forty branches and total deposits of $3,300,000. Frederick Douglass, the bank's short-serving and final president, called it "the black man's cow and the white man's milk. It ultimately succumbed to the nationwide depression commencing in 1873, and failed in the following year, the year of Mrs. Sawner's birth." Tom Cowan, Ph.D. & Jack Maguire, *Timelines Of African*

American History: 500 Years Of Black Achievement (New York, NY: Roundtable Press 1994) at 102.

ccciiiSee, e.g., E.B. Reuter, *The Mulatto In The United States* (Boston, Ma: Richard G. Badger 1918); Gary B. Nash, *Red, White, And Black: The Peoples Of Early America* (Upper Saddle River, NJ: Prentice-Hall 1974); J.C. Furnas, *Goodbye To Uncle Tom* (New York, NY 1956).

cccivAuthor unknown (credited to "Columnist"), "Alabama.; 'Nigger Day' in a country town...." *New York Times*, Nov. 30, 1874, p. 1; available at http://query.nytimes.com/gst/abstract.html?res=FA0C1EFC3C59117B-93C2AA178AD95F408784F9(last visited July 8, 2013).

cccivA letter penned by James Jacks, president of the Missouri Press Association, spurred the 1896 creation of The National Association of Colored Women (later, the National Association of Colored Women's Clubs) with his slanderous labeling of black women as prostitutes, thieves, and liars. *See, e.g.,* http://afroamhistory.about.com/od/segregation/p/National-Association-Of-Colored-Women.htm; "The ballot and black women," Daily Kos, August 21, 2011, http://www.dailykos.com/story/2011/08/21/1008952/-The-ballot-and-black-women# (last visited September 26, 2013);.

cccvOklahoma's fourth and largest land run, the Cherokee Outlet Opening, began on September 16, 1893. Thousands of seekers, spurred as much by economic necessity as by opportunity, endured an ill-conceived and poorly executed process in hopes of securing homesteads. The seven-million-acre Cherokee Outlet, reserved for the Cherokee Nation after its removal from the southeastern part of the United States pursuant to the Treaty of New Echota, initially began to erode after the Civil War. The United States declared the eastern third of the Cherokee Outlet surplus land, and then began to move smaller Native American tribes onto that land. Simultaneously, railroads, cattlemen, and home-seekers jostled for pieces of the remaining real estate. The Cherokee Nation ceded two other land masses, the Neutral Lands in southeastern Kansas and the Cherokee Strip along the southern border of Kansas, pursuant to the post-Civil War Treaty of 1866 with the federal government. Alvin O. Turner, "Cherokee Outlet Opening," *Oklahoma Historical Society's Encyclopedia of Oklahoma History & Culture,* http://digital.library.okstate.edu/encyclopedia/entries/C/CH021.html (last visited November 20, 2013).

cccviUntitled article, *Newkirk Democrat*, October 31, 1894, at 3.

cccviii"Last Rites For Mrs. L.L. Sawner Here Saturday: Burial Newkirk," [NEWSPAPER NAME], [DATE OF ARTICLE]. Chandler historian Mel Chatman and others, including the author, have attempted to verify that Mrs. Sawner attained an A.B. Degree from The University of Chicago, but have been unsuccessful.

cccviiiPhoto courtesy of Mel Chatman.

cccixPhoto courtesy of Mel Chatman.

cccxJohn R. Lovett, Oklahoma Historical Society's Encyclopedia of Oklahoma History & Culture, http://digital.library.okstate.edu/encyclopedia/entries/P/PR010.html (last visited July 13, 2014).

cccxi*See, e.g.*, History of Photography, Cameras, "When did cameras start being used by the general public?," http://www.quora.com/When-did-cameras-start-being-used-by-the-general-public (last visited July 14, 2014):

> On 8 February 1900, Kodak shipped the first Brownie camera, a very simple to use device that sold for $1 with film rolls that sold for 15 cents. Sales figures vary depending on the source, but consensus is that over one hundred thousand units were shipped in the first year. The ease of use and affordability meant that anyone could take photographs. The first models were essentially a stamped metal frame with a tiny lens, spring loaded shutter released by a single switch, a winding mechanism and a place to load the film. All of this was housed in a cardboard box covered in faux leather. Film could be loaded in daylight and was developed by Kodak, so owners didn't have to invest in a darkroom. Brownies popularized the "snapshot", a hunting term that meant shooting without special care to aim first.

cccxiiPhoto courtesy of Mel Chatman.

cccxiii*See, e.g.*, Jennifer Rosenberg, 1900s Timeline: Timeline of the 20th Century, http://history1900s.about.com/od/timelines/tp/1900timeline.htm (last visited November 16, 2014).

cccxiv"A Brief Overview of Progressive Education," http://www.uvm.edu/~dewey/articles/proged.html (last visited September 9, 2013).

cccxvAmerican Montessori Society, https://www.amshq.org/Montessori-Education/History-of-Montessori-Education.aspx (last visited September 9, 2013).

cccxixDuring this period, "normal schools" (teacher training institutes) began to fall out of favor. Universities expanded their teacher education offerings, focusing more on preparation in academic content and somewhat less on pedagogy. See, e.g., Arthur Levine, "The New Normal of Teacher Education," *The Chronicle Of Higher Education*, May 8, 2011, http://chronicle.com/article/The-New-Normal-of-Teacher/127430/ (last visited September 3, 2014).

cccxviiFor the sake of comparison and perspective, what cost $325 in 1900 would cost $9,103.55 in 2014, http://www.westegg.com/inflation/infl.cgi (last visited May 26, 2015).

cccxviii*See generally*, Deeptha Thattai, "A History of Public Education in the United States," http://www.servintfree.net/aidmn-ejournal/publications/2001-11/PublicEducationInTheUnitedStates.html (last visited September 9, 2013).

cccxixDuring the country's early, agrarian years, subscription schools predominated. For a fee, usually about a dollar, parents enrolled their children in schools that operated roughly three months out of the year. As public schools expanded, so, too, did the push for segregated educational facilities in parts of the nation.

cccxxPeggy Whitley, 1900-1909, *American Cultural History*, Lone Star College-Kingwood Library, Kingwood, Texas, http://wwwappskc.lonestar.edu/popculture/decade00.html (last visited August 4, 2013).

cccxxi*See* Chapter 8, *Douglass School & The Sawners (1860 – 1954)*, Chandler: *The Ellis Family Story*, http://www.ellisfamilystory.com/chapter03.html.

cccxxii*See, e.g.*, One-Room Schoolhouse Center, http://oneroomschoolhousecenter.weebly.com/index.html. Where parents could muster the funds to construct a facility and hire a teacher, modest one-room schoolhouses often emerged. These humble learning centers schools, frequently built on surplus land proximate to the homes of pupils, served children of various ages and often became hubs of the communities they served. Students often sat in classic wooden desks. Spelling bees, literary recitations, ciphering sessions around arithmetic problems, and reading selections from McGuffey Readers helped impart the educational fundamentals. One-room schoolhouses and, later, larger consolidated schools, generally educated students through grade seven. Students desiring a secondary education and possessed of the financial wherewithal to attain it sometimes engaged private tutors or moved to larger cities.

Oklahoma education scholar Frank A. Balyeat noted:

> Parents sent whatever texts they or their older children had used 'back in the States.' Nothing could be done but to use them, varied as they were. Gradually, though, Ray's arithmetic, McGuffey's readers and spellers, Barnes' histories and geographies, and Steele's physiology became fairly uniform. No library or other supplementary materials were known for several years, and then meager and highly prized. Books loaned by the rare and small home libraries sometimes enriched the school's study materials.

F. A. Balyeat, "Rural School Houses in Early Oklahoma," http://digital.library.okstate.edu/chronicles/v022/v022p315.pdf, at 322 – 323 (last visited October 4, 2013).

cccxxiiiThe Allen Toles African American One-Room Schoolhouse in Chickasha, Oklahoma, an example of a classic one-room school for black children, remains. Allen Toles, an African American farmer, built the school in 1910 near Verden, a small town in western Grady County abutting the Caddo

County line, nearly halfway between Chickasha and Anadarko on present-day U.S. Highway 62/State Highway 9. Toles built the school for his children and those of other local black families. Admirers fondly dubbed Allen Toles "a room with a vision." Preservationists moved the school to Chickasha, a larger town in Grady County, in 2004, and it earned a spot on the National Register of Historic Places in 2005. Allen Toles' African American One-Room Schoolhouse, http://www.travelok.com/listings/view.profile/id.14401 (last visited August 15, 2014). Muskogee offers another example of a remaining one-room schoolhouse. On July 20, 2013, the Three Rivers Museum in Muskogee's historic Depot District acquired the Oak Grove Separate School, a one-room schoolhouse that served African American children in the nearby community of Okay from 1917 – 1950. The owners of the property on which the schoolhouse sat donated the nearly one-hundred- year-old structure to the museum. David Harper, "School on the Move: Museum Acquires Historic Schoolhouse—Firsthand look at history," *Tulsa World*, July 21, 2013, at A11.

cccxxiv The Coalition for Community Schools defines a community school as follows:

> A community school is both a place and a set of partnerships between the school and other community resources. Its integrated focus on academics, health and social services, youth and community development and community engagement leads to improved student learning, stronger families and healthier communities. Community schools offer a personalized curriculum that emphasizes real-world learning and community problem-solving. Schools become centers of the community and are open to everyone – all day, every day, evenings and weekends.

> Using public schools as hubs, community schools bring together many partners to offer a range of supports and opportunities to children, youth, families and communities. Partners work to achieve these results: Children are ready to enter school; students attend school consistently; students are actively involved in learning and their community; families are increasingly involved with their children's education; schools are engaged with families and communities; students succeed academically; students are healthy - physically, socially, and emotionally; students live and learn in a safe, supportive, and stable environment, and communities are desirable places to live.

Coalition for Community Schools, http://www.communityschools.org/aboutschools/what_is_a_community_school.aspx(last visited July 22, 2013).

cccxxv Ulam, P. L. *The Chandler Publicist* (Chandler, Okla.), Vol. 15, No. 28, Ed. 2 Friday, November 6, 1908. Chandler, Oklahoma. The Gateway to Oklahoma History. http://gateway.okhistory.org/ark:/67531/metadc151447/ (last visited October 19, 2014).

cccxxvi*See* Chapter 8, Douglass School and Mrs. L. Lena Sawner (1874 – 1949), *Chandler: The Ellis Family Story*, http://www.ellisfamilystory.com/chapter08.html.

cccxxviiFrank A. Balyeat, "Segregation in the Public Schools of Oklahoma Territory," *The Chronicles Of Oklahoma*. http://digital.library.okstate.edu/chronicles/v039/v039p180.pdf, at 186 - 188 (last visited July 18, 2013).

cccxxviii*In the Matter of the Estate of G. W. F. Sawner, Deceased,* Case No. 2882, Final Decree and Order Discharging Executrix (Lincoln County District Court, March 26, 1927) (Lot 70 in the Lincoln County property listing in the will of George Sawner is property located on Manvel Avenue in Chandler.).

cccxxixGilstrap, H. B. *The Chandler News* (Chandler, Okla. Terr.), Vol. 13, No. 40, Ed. 1 Thursday, June 23, 1904. Chandler, Oklahoma Territory. The Gateway to Oklahoma History. http://gateway.okhistory.org/ark:/67531/metadc116055/ (last visited October 16, 2014).

cccxxxFrank A. Balyeat, "Segregation in the Public Schools of Oklahoma Territory," *The Chronicles Of Oklahoma*. http://digital.library.okstate.edu/chronicles/v039/v039p180.pdf, at 188 (last visited July 18, 2013).

cccxxxiArticle XIII, Sec. 3, Constitution of the State of Oklahoma (1907).

cccxxxiihttp://abhmuseum.org/2012/09/education-for-blacks-in-the-jim-crow-south/ (Griot: Russell Brooker, Ph.D.; Copy Editors: Adekola Adedapo and Fran Kaplan, Ed.D.; Photo Editor: Fran Kaplan, Ed.D.) (last visited June 12, 2014):

Why Education for African American Children Was Inferior

- Southern schools were racially segregated. Blacks and whites had to attend different schools. The separate school systems were not equal. Schools for white children received more public money.

- Fewer African Americans were enrolled in school. Black children were often pulled out of school because they were needed on the farm. Many of their parents were sharecroppers. To plant and harvest enough crops, sharecroppers' children had to work alongside their parents.

- Even if they weren't needed on the farm, the white owner of their farm might pull black children out if he decided they were needed for work. Or he might simply believe that African American children did not deserve an education.

- There were not as many public schools available for

blacks. If a town did not have enough money for two separate schools, they built only one school – for white children. This was especially true in the rural towns, because most rural towns had little money.

- City school systems had more money than rural ones. However, at that time in the South, most African Americans lived in rural areas, on farms. On the other hand, many white children lived in cities and could attend well-funded city schools. In rural areas, schools for both black and white children were scheduled around the cotton growing season. These schools were open fewer days than city schools. As a result, many black children went to school only two or three months out of the year.

- Among the African Americans who did attend school, most were in the fourth grade or lower. Many left school after fourth grade. Therefore it would be a long time before there would be a large number of blacks going to college.

The Conditions in the Schools Where Black Children Studied

- Many school buildings for African Americans had leaking roofs, sagging floors, and windows without glass. They ranged from untidy to positively filthy, according to a study issued in 1917.

- If black children had any books at all, they were hand-me-downs from white schools.

- Black schools were overcrowded, with too many students per teacher. More black schools than white had only one teacher to handle students from toddlers to 8th graders. Black schools were more likely to have all grades together in one room.

- There were not enough desks for the over-crowded classrooms.

- Black teachers did not receive as much training as white teachers. On top of that, the salary for black teachers was so low that it was hard to find fully qualified ones.

There were limits on what blacks could be taught in school. White school leaders did not want black children to be exposed to ideas like equality and freedom. Carter G. Woodson told how some black children in Southern schools were not allowed to use books that included the Declaration of Independence or the U. S. Constitution. These documents state that government should get its power from the consent of the governed. Reading them would confirm for African Americans that they were being denied the rights due to all citizens of the United States.

cccxxxiiiO.A.N.T. dissolved in 1958 following a 1955 merger with the Oklahoma Education Association. Before its dissolution, O.A.N.T. honored Mrs. Sawner in 1946 for her forty years of teaching in Oklahoma schools. By the time O.A.N.T. feted her, Mrs. Sawner had held every executive office in that organization. Langston University also recognized her for her contributions to the Negro 4-H program. 4-H stands for Head, Hands, Heart, and Health, and is the youth development program of the nation's 109 land-grant universities and the Cooperative Extension System. *See, e.g.,* Melvin R. Todd, "Oklahoma Association of Negro Teachers," *Oklahoma Historical Society's Encyclopedia of Oklahoma History & Culture,* http://digital.library.okstate. edu/ENCYCLOPEDIA/entries/O/OK017.html (last visited September 24, 2014), citing Leonard B. Cayton, *A History of Black Public Education in Oklahoma* (Ph.D. dissertation, University of Oklahoma 1976). Evelyn R. Strong, *The Historical Development of the Oklahoma Association of Negro Teachers: A Study in Social Change, 1893-1958* (Ph.D. dissertation, University of Oklahoma 1961).

cccxxxivRoscoe Dungee, *The Black Dispatch* (Oklahoma City, Okla.), Vol. 5, No. 45, Ed. 1 Friday, December 5, 1919. Oklahoma City, Oklahoma. The Gateway to Oklahoma History. http://gateway.okhistory.org/ark:/67531/metadc152172/ (last visited October 17, 2014).

cccxxxvPicture available at docsouth.unc.edu/neh/simmons/simmons.html (courtesy of the University of North Carolina at Chapel Hill) (last visited September 25, 2014).

cccxxxviwww.ioffer.com/i/segregation-drinking-fountain-colored-white-i... (cast iron segregation wall sign from side of Montgomery, Alabama building, dated July 14, 1931) (last visited August 21, 2013).

cccxxxii*See, e.g.,* James E. Smallwood, *Segregation,* http://digital.library.okstate. edu/encyclopedia/entries/S/SE006.html

cccxxxiiiSara Evans, "Women in American Politics in the Twentieth Century," The Gilder Lehrman Institute of American History, American History Online, http://www.gilderlehrman.org/history-by-era/womens-history/essays/women-american-politics-twentieth-century (last visited July 9, 2013):

> In 1900 women's legal standing was fundamentally governed by their marital status. They had very few rights. A married woman had no separate legal identity from that of her husband. She had no right to control her biological reproduction (even conveying information about contraception, for example, was illegal), and no right to sue or be sued since she had no separate standing in court. She had no right to own property in her own name or to pursue a career of her choice. Women could not vote, serve on juries,

or hold public office. According to the Supreme Court, they were not 'persons' under the Fourteenth Amendment to the Constitution, which guarantees equal protection under the law.

[cccxxxix]*See, e.g.,* "A History of Teaching in America—As Told By Those Who Know," http://www.wakingbear.com/archives/a-history-of-teaching-in-america-as-told-by-those-who-know.html last visited September 3, 2014).

[cccxl]*See, e.g.,* Veronica H. Shipp, "Fewer Black Female Teachers: Progress or Problem?" *Women's Studies Quarterly,* Vol. 28, No. 3/4, Keeping Gender on the Chalkboard (Fall - Winter, 2000) (New York, NY: The Feminist Press at the City University of New York), at 202 – 210, also available online at http://www.jstor.org/stable/40005485.

[cccxli]"Only A Teacher, Teaching Timeline, 1890s – 1910s, Women Teacher's Rebellion," http://www.pbs.org/onlyateacher/timeline.html (last visited June 26, 2015).

[cccxlii]Carolyn A. Dorsey, "The African American Educational Experience," included in Arvarh E. Strickland and Robert E. Weems Jr., *The African American Experience, An Historiographical And Bibliographical Guide,*http://testaae.greenwood.com/doc_print.aspx?fileID=GR9838&chapterID=GR9838-834&path=books/greenwood (last visited July 15, 2013).

[cccxliii]W.E.B. *Dubois, The Souls Of Black Folk* (New York, NY: First Vintage Books/The Library of America Edition 1990) (introduction by John Edgar Wideman), at 29.

[cccxliv]*See, e.g.,* "Booker T. & W.E.B.: The debate between W.E.B. Du Bois and Booker T. Washington," http://www.pbs.org/wgbh/pages/frontline/shows/race/etc/road.html (last visited July 21, 2015); Robert A. Gibson, "Booker T. Washington and W. E. B. DuBois: The Problem of Negro Leadership," Yale—New Haven Teachers Institute, http://www.yale.edu/ynhti/curriculum/units/1978/2/78.02.02.x.html (last visited July 15, 2015); W.E.B. Du Bois, *The Souls Of Black Folk,* (New York, NY: First Vintage Books/The Library of America Edition 1990), Chapter III, "Of Mr. Booker T. Washington and Others"; "Structured Academic Debate, Booker T. Washington and W.E.B. Du Bois, http://www.blackpast.org/classroom/structured-academic-debate-booker-t-washington-and-w-e-b-dubois (last visited July 15, 2015).

[cccxlv]Mel Chatman, Chandler historian, retrieved these documents from the Sawner home in Chandler several years ago. E-mail from Mel Chatman to author, November 18, 2014. Copies of the documents are on file with the author.

[cccxlvi]Examination for County Certificate, April 20, 27, 28, 1928, Questions First Day Program (on file with author). Test questions included:

Agriculture
- How are plants improved?

- What are the manufacturing organs of the plant?
- Why do we inoculate soil for legumes?

Reading

- Give the complete titles and authors of ten works that you have read during the past year; label in this list two novels, an essay, a play, a short story, a lyric or narrative poem. Designate one of these that you like and tell why.

Orthography

- What are diacritical marks? Why used?
- Give two rules for spelling and illustrate each.

Physiology

- What are the chief chemical compounds of the body?
- Define metabolism.
- Describe the central nervous system.

Oklahoma History

- Give the location of the Five Civilized Tribes before their removal to Oklahoma.
- Who were the Boomers?
- What was the Dawes Commission?

Music

- Name by syllables the tones of the major diatonic scale.
- Illustrate on the staff all the orders of notes and rests, naming each. Also illustrate the sharp, the flat, the natural.

Penmanship

- Make one-half line of direct continuous ovals two spaces high. Fill the remaining half with straight line drill one space high and the retraced ovals one space high.

Home Economics

- What colors make the best finish for the walls of a school room? Why?
- Give five suggestions for the daily care of clothing.

Theory and Practice

- What do you understand to be meant by the re-organization and re-direction of rural education?
- How do you account for the recent great interest in the educational delinquents, defectives and those having special educational needs?

Grammar

- "Lord lead us not into the paths of iniquity." Is this prayer grammatical?
- Besides being the subject of a verb or the object of a preposition, a noun may have other relations to other words. Make a list of the possible relations of nouns.

Geography

- What is longitude?
- How often does high tide occur?

- Which can hold more moisture, warm or cold air?

cccxlviiMel Chatman and Jan Vassar, *"The 'Negro Problem' in Lincoln County, Oklahoma (1889 – 1954)"* (unpublished manuscript based on interviews with Lincoln County pioneers and historical information and documentation relevant to Lincoln County), 2005.

cccxlviiiPhoto courtesy of Mel Chatman. According to George Ellis, Wade and Jim Ellis considered Francis Harold to be an exceptionally good math teacher who was very critical to their success. It should also be noted that George Alexander and Roberta Ellis were secretly married. Prevailing law forbade the employment of spouses as teachers in the same school system. Correspondence with Mel Chatman, February 10, 2015.

cccxlix*See* Chapter 8, Douglass School and Mrs. L. Lena Sawner (1874 – 1949), *Chandler: The Ellis Family Story,* http://www.ellisfamilystory.com/chapter08.html.

ccclhttp://www.waymarking.com/waymarks/WM9ZP8_Chandler_High_School_Chandler_OK (last visited August 7, 2013).

cccliCorrespondence from Jan Vassar, Chandler historian, to the author, July 10, 2014; "Historic Context for the Julius Rosenwald Fund in Oklahoma," Oklahoma State Historic Preservation Office, Cynthia Savage, Architectural Historian (August 1997), http://www.okhistory.org/shpo/thematic/rosenwaldfund.pdf (last visited July 18, 2014)(In 1926, Dunbar Consolidated School #1 at Wellston increased to a six-teacher facility from its original 1921 three-teacher facility as a result of a Rosenwald grant.) A "Rosenwald School" is a school the construction of which was partially funded by philanthropist Julius Rosenwald's foundation, the Rosenwald Foundation, a primary mission of which included enhancing educational facilities for African American public schools, mainly in the South.

ccclii*See* Chapter 8, Douglass School & The Sawners (1860 – 1954), *Chandler: The Ellis Family Story,* http://ellisfamilystory.com/chapter08.html#E (last visited November 16, 2014).

cccliiiU.S. High School Graduation Rates, reproduced from Kenneth A. Simon and W. Vance Grant. Digest of Educational Statistics, Office of Education, Bulletin 1965, No. 4 (Washington, D.C., U.S. Government Printing Office, 1965), available at http://www.safeandcivilschools.com/research/graduation_rates.php (last visited July 11, 2014).

ccclvi*See* Appendix D.

ccclv*Chandler: The Ellis Family Story,* www.ellisfamilystory.com (last visited July 11, 2014).

ccclviTelephone conference with Mel Chatman, August 26, 2013 (regarding intergeneration impact Lena Sawner had on the Ellis family).

ccclvii"Aged Citizen Passes To His Reward," *The Chandler News-Publicist,* November 2, 1928; "The Tomb," *Lincoln County Republican,* November 1, 1928; "Mrs. Priscilla Lowery Answers Last Call," *The Chandler News-Publicist,* October 23, 1931.

ccclviii"Mrs. Priscilla Lowery Answers Last Call," *The Chandler News-Publicist,* October 23, 1931.

ccclixMrs. Sawner's service to the American Red Cross in Lincoln County is but one example of many community contributions:

> Chandler, Okla., Feb. 12, 1918
>
> The Chandler Colored Women of Lincoln [C]ounty are rendering a large service to the American Red Cross thru the leadership of Madam L. Lena Sawner. The Chandler chapter has 180 members and already they have shipped to Lincoln [C]ounty boys at Chillicothe, Ohio, three different shipments of ear muffs, scarfs, sweaters and wristlets. Classes in knitting, sewing[,] surgical dressing and first aid to the injured are held every week. Thru the efforts of the Chandler chapter practically all of the Negro women on Lincoln [C]ounty have been drafted into this great relief work. The officers of the Chandler chapter are: Mrs. L. Lena Sawner, Chairman; Mrs. Mollie Evans, Vice Chairman; Mrs. Lonnie Wall, Secretary; N. R. Battle, Treasurer.

Dunjee, Roscoe. *The Black Dispatch* (Oklahoma City, Okla.), Vol. 5, No. 4, Ed. 1 Friday, February 15, 1918. The Gateway to Oklahoma History. http://gateway.okhistory.org/ark:/67531/metadc152068/ (last visited October 16, 2014). Mrs. Sawner's much-touted community educational efforts began early in her career. *The Chandler News* reported that both Sawners participated in the literary and entertainment program sponsored by the Colored Teachers' Union on April 28, 1906. Mrs. Sawner presented a paper, "Sketch of the Life and Work of Booker T. Washington," and Mr. Sawner delivered an address to the teachers. Gilstrap, H. B. *The Chandler News* (Chandler, Okla. Terr.), No. 15, Vol. 28, Ed. 1 Thursday, April 5, 1906. Chandler, Oklahoma Territory. The Gateway to Oklahoma History. http://gateway.okhistory.org/ark:/67531/metadc160417/ (last visited October 16, 2014).

ccclxThe town's namesake likewise lived the life of a servant leader. George Chandler occupied the post of First Assistant Secretary of Interior in the administration of President Benjamin Harrison (1889 – 1893) when early settlers named the townsite in his honor. Dr. B.B. Chapman, Oklahoma State University, "Biography of George Chandler," http://www.skypoint.com/members/jkm/oklincoln/geo_chandler.html (last visited July 23, 2013).

ccclxiMel Chatman and Jan Vassar, *The 'Negro Problem' in Lincoln County, Oklahoma (1889 – 1954)* (unpublished manuscript based on interviews with Lincoln County pioneers and historical information and documentation relevant to Lincoln County), 2005.

ccclxii Among the vocational options for Douglass students was "New Farmers of America," a sort of farming apprentice program similar to Future Farmers of America, under the direction of Louis E. Burton. Students assisted black farmers with tasks as varied as livestock inoculations, calving, dehorning, hog castrations, and bovine slaughter. Douglass also prized its onsite cannery with modern pressure cookers where, in addition to vegetables, students preserved beef and poultry. The school sported workshops with saws, electrical equipment, and carpentry tools, as well as a home economics cottage, a chemistry room, and stations for the instruction of shorthand and typing. Telephone interview with Victor Brown, former Douglass School student, September 26, 2014. According to George Sawner Ellis, the home economics cottage opened sometime after 1934. Notes from George Sawner Ellis, January 26, 2015 (on file with author).

ccclxiii *Remember The Titans*, directed by Boaz Yakin (Hollywood, CA: Walt Disney Pictures and Jerry Bruckheimer Films, 2000). The film is based on the true story of African American coach Herman Boone, portrayed by Denzel Washington. The story follows Coach Boone as he tries to introduce a racially diverse team at the T. C. Williams High School in Alexandria, Virginia, in 1971.

ccclxiv Telephone conference with Mel Chatman, August 3, 2015.

ccclxv *See, e.g.*, http://www.history.com/topics/dust-bowl (last visited June 8, 2015). The "Dust Bowl" refers to the 1930s drought-stricken, depression-ridden Great Plains region America. The 150,000-square-mile area included the Oklahoma and Texas panhandles and neighboring sections of Kansas, Colorado, and New Mexico. Little rainfall, light soil, and high winds, combined to wreak havoc on the area. Drought struck from 1934 to 1937. The soil lacked the stronger root system of grass as an anchor, so the winds easily picked up loose topsoil and swirled it into dense dust clouds, called "black blizzards." Recurrent dust storms choked cattle and pasture lands and drove some sixty percent of the population away from the region, first to agricultural areas, and then to cities, primarily in the far western United States.

ccclxvi Photos courtesy of Mel Chatman.

ccclxvii "Principal of first black [high school] 'exacting'," *The Lincoln County News*, May 9, 1985, at 13.

ccclxviii Leslie Pinckney Hill, The Teacher, *The Book Of American Negro Poetry* (James Weldon Johnson, ed., San Diego, CA, New York, NY, and London, England: Harcourt, Brace & Company 1933, 1922), at 156.

ccclxix Federal Writer's Project, United States Work Projects Administration (USWPA); Manuscript Division, Library of Congress, WPA Slave Narrative Project, Oklahoma Narratives, Volume 13, Digital ID, mesn 130/150145, http://memory.loc.gov/cgi-bin/ampage?collId=mesn&fileName=130/mesn130.db&recNum=149&itemLink=D?mesnbib:12:./temp/~ammem_

7Jzp:: (last visited July 14, 2015).

ccclxxFederal Writer's Project, United States Work Projects Administration (USWPA); Manuscript Division, Library of Congress, WPA Slave Narrative Project, Arkansas Narratives, Volume 2, Part 2, Digital ID, mesn 022/086082, http://memory.loc.gov/cgi-bin/ampage?collId=mesn&fileName=022/mesn022.db&recNum=87&itemLink=D?mesnbib:1:./temp/~ammem_7Jzp:: (last visited July 14, 2015).

ccclxxi*See, e.g.*, Alabama Archives, Slave Code of 1833, provided:

- Section 31: Any person or persons who attempt to teach any free person of color, or slave, to spell, read, or write, shall, upon conviction thereof by indictment, be fined in a sum not less than two hundred and fifty dollars, nor more than five hundred dollars.
- Section 32: Any free person of color who shall write for any slave a pass or free paper, on conviction thereof, shall receive for every such offense, thirty-nine lashes on the bare back, and leave the state of Alabama within thirty days thereafter....
- Section 33: Any slave who shall write for any other slave, any pass or free-paper, upon conviction, shall receive, on his or her back, one hundred lashes for the first offence, and seven hundred lashes for every offence thereafter....

http://www.archives.state.al.us/teacher/slavery/lesson1/doc1-9.html (last visited July 17, 2013).

ccclxxiiArvarh E. Strickland and Robert E. Weems Jr., *The African American Experience: An Historiographical and Bibliographical Guide* (Carolyn A. Dorsey, The African American Educational Experience), http://testaae.greenwood.com/doc_print.aspx?fileID=GR9838&chapterID=GR9838-834&path=-books/greenwood (last visited September 24, 2013).

ccclxxiiiManassas Industrial School and Jennie Dean Memorial, http://www.hallowedground.org/African-American-Heritage/Manassas-Industrial-School-and-Jennie-Dean-Memorial (last visited July 22, 2013).

ccclxxiv"Blessings of Liberty and Education," Frederick Douglass (Manassas, Virginia, September 03, 1894) http://teachingamericanhistory.org/library/document/blessings-of-liberty-and-education/ (last visited July 22, 2013).

ccclxxvPhoto from: http://www.nrcc.org/2013/06/19/8-interesting-facts-about-frederick-douglass/ (last visited August 8, 2013).

ccclxxvii*See, e.g.*, African American Timeline, 1801 – 1900, Education, http://www.blackpast.org/?q=1900-14 (last visted July 14, 2013).

ccclxxviiiCourtney Ann Vaughn-Roberson, "Sometimes Independent but Never

Equal: Women Teachers, 1900-1950: The Oklahoma Example," *Pacific His-torical Review*, Vol. 53, No. 1 (University of California Press: Feb. 1984), pp. 39-58, at p. 39 (available at http://www.jstor.org/stable/3639378).

cclxxviiiOne wonders whether such close, nurturing relations between edu-cator and student would be acceptable or even possible in the modern era. Much-publicized scandals over issues of harassment and improper relation-ships, coupled with the general litigiousness of society, would seem to sug-gest not.

ccclxxixIn 1927, though, Lincoln County schools adopted newly established state educational guidelines and accreditation policies that disallowed skip-ping grades.

ccclxxx*Carter G. Woodson, The Mis-Education Of The Negro* (Nashville, Tennes-see: Winston-Derek Publishers, Inc. 1990, originally published in 1933), at 56. Dr. Carter G. Woodson (1875 – 1950) was an African American historian, author, and journalist. He founded the Association of the Study of Negro Life and History. Dr. Woodson, the so-called "Father of Black History," is considered one of the first to conduct a scholarly effort to popularize the val-ue of African American history. He stressed the importance of a people—all people—having an awareness of an appreciation for their contributions to humanity. Dr. Woodson was a founder of the Journal of Negro History.

ccclxxxiTelephone interview with George Sawner Ellis, October 18, 2013.

ccclxxxii*See, e.g.,* Ancient History Sourcebook: Code of Hammurabi, c. 1780 BCE, http://www.fordham.edu/halsall/ancient/hamcode.asp(last visited August 26, 2013) ("[B]y far the most remarkable of the Hammurabi records is his code of laws, the earliest-known example of a ruler proclaiming pub-licly to his people an entire body of laws, arranged in orderly groups, so that all men might read and know what was required of them. The code was carved upon a black stone monument, eight feet high, and clearly intended to be reared in public view.")

ccclxxxiiiFrench, Mrs. W. H. *The Chandler Publicist* (Chandler, Okla. Terr.), Vol. 4, No. 51, Ed. 1 Friday, June 2, 1905. Chandler, Oklahoma Territory. The Gateway to Oklahoma History. http://gateway.okhistory.org/ark:/67531/metadc151045/ (last visited October 19, 2014).

ccclxxxivCorrespondence from Chandler historian Jan Vassar, March 8, 2015 (on file with author).

ccclxxxv*The Chandler News* (Chandler, Okla.), Vol. 13, No. 36, Ed. 1, Thursday, May 26, 1904. Chandler, Okla. The Gateway to Oklahoma History. http://gateway.okhistory.org/ark:/67531/metadc116052/ (last visited February 17, 2015, 2014).

ccclxxxvi"Douglass School Closing Program," Lincoln County Republican, June 2, 1921.

ccclxxxvii*Douglass High School Commencement Exercises,* (unidentified newspaper, circa 1918; on file with LCHS Museum of Pioneer History).

ccclxxxviii*Douglass High School Commencement Exercises,* (unidentified newspaper, circa 1918; on file with LCHS Museum of Pioneer History).

ccclxxxix*The Chandler News* (Chandler, Okla.), Vol. 13, No. 36, Ed. 1, Thursday, May 26, 1904. Chandler, Okla. The Gateway to Oklahoma History. http://gateway.okhistory.org/ark:/67531/metadc116052/ (last visited February 17, 2015, 2014).

cccxc"Lena Sawner, Chandler, Okla.: Successful Commencement At Chandler, Oklahoma—The Commencement Exercises Were Best Ever Witnessed at This Excellent School," (unidentified newspaper circa 1918; on file at LCHS Museum of Pioneer History).

cccxciThis image comes courtesy of V. Diana Kinsey, LCHS Museum of Pioneer History. The loving cup, presented by Chandler school patrons in honor of Mrs. Sawner's twenty years of service at Douglass School, cost more than $100. Dunjee, Roscoe. *The Black Dispatch* (Oklahoma City, Okla.), Vol. 7, No. 25, Ed. 1 Thursday, May 25, 1922. Oklahoma City, Oklahoma. The Gateway to Oklahoma History. http://gateway.okhistory.org/ark:/67531/metadc152386/ (last visited October 19, 2014).

cccxcii*See, e.g.,* LeoNora M. Cohen, Oregon State University, School of Education, Section III—Philosophical Perspectives in Education (1999), available at http://oregonstate.edu/instruct/ed416/PP3.html (last visited September 4, 2014) (citing four principal philosophical perspectives in education:

1. Perennialism: Focusing on student learning of the great ideas of Western civilization;
2. Essentialism: Focusing on a common core of student knowledge transmitted in a systematic, disciplined way;
3. Progressivism: Focusing on the whole child rather than substantive content or the teacher; and
4. Reconstructionism/Critical Theory: Focusing on a substantive curriculum that highlights social reform as the aim of education.

cccxciiiThese principles were distilled from the recollections of the Ellis family. The children of Whit and Maggie Ellis all attended Douglass School and went on to remarkable life work and achievements, as illustrated in Appendix D. See *Chandler: The Ellis Family Story,* http://www.ellisfamilystory.com/.

cccxivTelephone interview with Bernice Caldwell, Chandler, Oklahoma, July 15, 2014. In 1908, W. D. Bentley, a pioneer of university extension work in Oklahoma, worked with farmers and ranchers in Tishomingo on harvest improvements. Bentley enrolled fifty boys from across Johnston County to be part of a Boy's Corn Club in 1909. Thus began 4-H in Oklahoma. See Oklahoma Historical Society's Encyclopedia of Oklahoma History & Culture, Oklahoma 4-H, http://digital.library.okstate.edu/encyclopedia/entries/f/

fo054.html, last visited July 14, 2014.

ccxcvhttp://www.4-h.org/ (last visited September 4, 2014).

ccxcviTelephone interview with Bernice Caldwell, Chandler, Oklahoma, July 15, 2014.

ccxcviiThis "Boarding Round" compensation system for school teachers was common in the latter half of the nineteenth century. Local community schools taught basic academic skills and morality. Those communities compensated teachers with, primarily, room and board. This arrangement facilitated positive teacher/community relations and encouraged moral rectitude among teachers. The system comported with the barter economy prevalent during that period. *See, e.g.,* "History of Teacher Pay," Consortium for Policy Research in Education, at the University of Wisconsin-Madison, http://cpre.wceruw.org/tcomp/general/teacherpay.php(last visited October 10, 2014).

ccxcviiiTelephone interview with Mel Chatman, grandson of Whit and Maggie Ellis, October 16, 2014.

ccxcixMel Chatman, *Chandler: The Ellis Family Story,* chapter 5, http://www.ellisfamilystory.com/contents.html (last visited October 22, 2014).

cdMel Chatman, Chandler: *The Ellis Family Story,* chapter 5, http://www.ellisfamilystory.com/contents.html (last visited October 22, 2014); Roscoe Dunjee, "Eight Brothers—Eight Black Dispatch Agents," *The Black Dispatch,* February 19, 1936, at 1.

cdiIn a 1920 article, *The Black Dispatch* recounts one example of Mrs. Sawner's busy travel schedule: "Mrs. L. Lena Sawner, principal of the Chandler Schools, has returned from a visit to Kansas City, St. Louis and Chicago. She was a pleasant caller at [T]he Black Dispatch office Monday. She will attend the Pythian meeting at Tulsa next week and then go to Colorado for the remainder of the summer." Dunjee, Roscoe. *The Black Dispatch* (Oklahoma City, Okla.), Vol. 5, No. 33, Ed. 1 Friday, July 16, 1920. Oklahoma City, Oklahoma. The Gateway to Oklahoma History. http://gateway.okhistory.org/ark:/67531/metadc152264/ (last visited October 15, 2014). That same paper, in a 1919 article, reported the following: "Mrs. L. Lena Sawner, one of Oklahoma's most prominent ladies and principal of the city schools of Chandler, Okla., has returned from an extended visit to Atlantic City, Buffalo, New York and Chicago." Dunjee, Roscoe. *The Black Dispatch* (Oklahoma City, Okla.), Vol. 5, No. 33, Ed. 1 Friday, September 12, 1919. Oklahoma City, Oklahoma. The Gateway to Oklahoma History. http://gateway.okhistory.org/ark:/67531/metadc152153/ (last visited October 16, 2014).

cdiiThurgood Marshall later represented Ada Lois Sipuel Fisher in the desegregation case that changed admissions policy at the University of Oklahoma and set the stage for nationwide school desegregation. *Sipuel v. Board of Regents of Univ. of Okla.,* 332 U.S. 631 (1948) (per curiam). Mr. Marshall later served a stint as the first African American Solicitor General and, still later, he became Justice Marshall, the first African American United States Supreme Court Justice.

ᶜᵈⁱⁱⁱFor example, *The Black Dispatch* reported that Mrs. Sawner hosted "a beautiful lawn party" for Douglass alumni in 1919. Dunjee, Roscoe. *The Black Dispatch* (Oklahoma City, Okla.), Vol. 5, No. 19, Ed. 1 Friday, June 6, 1919. Oklahoma City, Oklahoma. The Gateway to Oklahoma History. http://gateway. okhistory.org/ark:/67531/metadc152133/ (last visited October 15, 2014). The same paper reported that Mrs. Sawner hosted the Endowment Board of the Court of Calanthe, State of Oklahoma, on April 15, 1921, in "the beautiful and palatial home of Mr. and Mrs. G. W. F. Sawner," and that Mrs. Sawner "proved a delightful hostess to the Board." She served a "delicious dinner in the home, after which a brisk drive was taken over the most excellent Lincoln County roads." Dunjee, Roscoe. *The Black Dispatch* (Oklahoma City, Okla.), Vol. 6, Ed. 1 Friday, April 22, 1921. Oklahoma City, Oklahoma. The Gateway to Oklahoma History. http://gateway.okhistory.org/ark:/67531/ metadc152329/ (last visited October 15, 2014). For the full history of The Grand Court Order of Calanthe, organized in Houston, Texas, on May 30, 1897, see http://www.grandcourt.org/history.html (last visited October 23, 1014). The organization arose out of the need to provide African Americans with burial insurance. The core principles of The Grand Court Order of Calanthe, fidelity, harmony, and love, derive from Greek iconography. According to Greek legend, Damon and his friend, Pythias, lived in Syracuse in the 4th century, B.C. Pythias was sentenced to death, and Damon took his place in prison while Pythias put his affairs in order. Just prior to the time for the scheduled execution, Pythias returned, thus preventing the execution of Damon. The king was so impressed with this gesture of loyalty that he pardoned Pythias, husband of Calanthe. The Grand Court of Order of Calanthe organized initially with twenty men and women called "flat rate members" who all paid the same amount of dues. During the second administration (1902 - 1925), The Grand Court Order of Calanthe became a fraternal benefit society in order to increase death benefits, improve services for members, and enhance community engagement. The group launched a juvenile department in 1907, and during the Great Depression, thousands of members received home finance loans. Mrs. Sawner also the Executive Committee of the State Teachers' Association. Dunjee, Roscoe. *The Black Dispatch* (Oklahoma City, Okla.), Vol. 5, No. 46, Ed. 1 Friday, October 22, 1920. Oklahoma City, Oklahoma. The Gateway to Oklahoma History. http:// gateway.okhistory.org/ark:/67531/metadc152301/ (last visited October 16, 2014). She entertained guest from far and wide on the occasion of her husband's fifty-ninth birthday. Dunjee, Roscoe. *The Black Dispatch* (Oklahoma City, Okla.), Vol. 5, No. 7, Ed. 1 Friday, March 14, 1919. Oklahoma City, Oklahoma. The Gateway to Oklahoma History. http://gateway.okhistory. org/ark:/67531/metadc152122/ (last visited October 16, 2014). *The Chandler Publicist* reported that guests at one of the many social gatherings Mrs. Sawner hosted at the Sawner home dubbed her "the queen of entertainers." French, Mrs. W. H. *The Chandler Publicist* (Chandler, Okla. Terr.), Vol. 10, No. 49, Ed. 1 Friday, April 4, 1904. Chandler, Oklahoma Territory. The Gateway to Oklahoma History. http://gateway.okhistory.org/ark:/67531/metadc150978/ (last visited October 19, 2014).

[cdiv]Benny Kent, "Early Days" (newsreel footage of Oklahoma taken, roughly, between 1900 and 1937) (on file with the author).

[cdv]*Colored Schools Meet in 3rd Annual Contest, Chandler News-Publicist*, April 7, 1923.

[cdvi]According to some accounts, these instruments were lent to white students at Chandler High School. Telephone interview with Bernice Caldwell, Chandler, Oklahoma, July 15, 2014. George Sawner Ellis, however, believes that the instruments were given to Chandler High School after Mrs. Sawner's tenure, in part because no Douglass High School band ever evolved. Some Douglass School parents protested, citing the preexisting funding inequities between the white and black public schools. Indeed, Jasper Henderson, a parent of several children who had picked cotton to earn money to buy the instruments, confronted Mrs. Sawner's successor, Edgar Thomas Busby, over the issue. Principal Busby accused Henderson of assault. Some of the instruments mysteriously disappeared before the few remaining instruments reached Chandler High School. George Sawner Ellis recalled another "issue" surrounding the donated instruments: "While Chandler was known to be willing to accept Blacks as humans, and even respect them and allow them to vote, I don't believe many CHS [Chandler High School] parents were willing to [allow their children to] blow into the same horns that had been blown into by Blacks." Notes from George Sawner Ellis, January 26, 2015 (on file with author).

[cdvii]*See* Chapter 8, *Douglass School & The Sawners (1860 – 1954)*, Chandler: The Ellis Family Story, http://ellisfamilystory.com/chapter08.html#E (last visited November 16, 2014).

[cdviii]"Principal of first black [high school] 'exacting'," *The Lincoln County News*, May 9, 1985, at 13.

[cdix]"Last Rites For Mrs. L.L. Sawner Here Saturday: Burial Newkirk,"_____ (March __, 1949).

[cdx]Telephone interview with Victor Brown, former Douglass School student, September 26, 2014. Brown attended Douglass School beginning in the 1944 - 1945 school year, several years after Mrs. Sawner resigned as principal for health reasons. He attended Chandler High School after desegregation, beginning in the 1955 – 1956 school year, and graduating with the Chandler High School Class of 1957. Post-retirement, Mrs. Sawner remained a sage in the Chandler community such that even those who never knew her as Douglass principal nonetheless knew her as a community leader of enormous influence.

[cdxi]*In Memoriam, Lena L. Sawner* (Died March 1, 1949) (funeral program).

[cdxii]*Dred Scott v. Sandford*, 60 U.S. 393 (1857).

[cdxiii]*Plessy v. Ferguson*, 163 U.S. 537 (1896).

[cdxiv]On July 26, 1948, President Harry S. Truman signed Executive Order 9981: "It is hereby declared to be the policy of the President that there shall be equality of treatment and opportunity for all persons in the armed services without regard to race, color, religion, or national origin." The order established the President's Committee on Equality of Treatment and opportunity in the Armed Services. Executive Order 9981," July 26, 1948, Harry S. Truman Library and Museum, http://www.trumanlibrary.org/ (last viewed August 8, 2013).

[cdxv]In the 1948 case *Shelly v. Kraemer*, the United States Supreme Court, led by Chief Justice Fred Vinson, unanimously decided a court may not constitutionally enforce a "restrictive covenant" which prevents people of a certain race from owning or occupying property. The decision thus outlawed the widespread use of these private, racially restrictive real estate clauses that worked to keep neighborhoods rigidly separated by race, locking out African Americans from all social strata. *Shelly v. Kraemer*, 334 U.S. 1 (1948).

[cdxvi]*Brown v. Board of Education of Topeka*, 347 U.S. 483 (1954).

[cdxvii]As quoted in *Wesley Henderson, Under Whose Shade: A Story Of A Pioneer In The Swan Valley Of Manitoba* (Nepean, Ontario: Wes Henderson & Associates 1986), http://thinkexist.com/quotation/the_true_meaning_of_life_is_to_plant_trees-under/216838.html (last visited June 4, 2015). Nelson Henderson was a second-generation farmer from Manitoba, Canada.

[cdxviii]Chandler historian Mel Chatman believes the Sawners should be largely credited with creating the harmonious racial climate in Chandler. This climate remained many years after their deaths, and enabled the African Americans who followed them to be successful. It also created high-level black/white working relationships and a sense of mutual respect seldom found in any other part of the state. Mr. Chapman also believes that Mrs. Sawner played a sort of "black godfather-type" (godmother-type, in this case) role, and must have been involved with unofficially resolving a number of sensitive black/white issues outside the formal legal system. Telephone conference call? with Mel Chatman, June 9, 2015.

[cdxix]The United States Army's 1951 troop desegregation initiative came on the heels of a successful gap-filling experiment under which the Army filled all-white units with black replacement soldiers during the Korean War. Some of those African American replacements hailed from Oklahoma and fought in the 45th Infantry Division, though not as Oklahoma Army National Guard ("Guard") enlistees. The Army summarily discharged them upon the signing of the Korean War armistice on July 27, 1953. The Guard received its desegregation edict shortly before barrier-breaker Lewis signed on in 1958.

This Day in History, July 27, 1953: "After three years of a bloody and frustrating war, the United States, the People's Republic of China, North Korea, and South Korea agree to an armistice, bringing the Korean War to an end. The armistice ended America's first experiment with the Cold War concept of 'limited war.'" http://www.history.com/this-day-in-history/armistice-ends-the-korean-war (last visited June 10, 2015); Army & Air National Guard Oklahoma Frontline, "First African-American to join the Oklahoma National Guard dies," May 20, 2015, http://www.oklahomafrontline.com (last visited June 9, 2015).

[cdxx]NewsOK, "First black man to join the Oklahoma National Guard dies," http://newsok.com/first-black-man-to-join-the-oklahoma-national-guard-dies/article/5420956 (last visited June 9, 2015). Upon learning of Lewis's death, Major General Robbie Asher, adjutant general for Oklahoma, noted: "Sgt. 1st Class Lewis was instrumental in bringing about critically important change in the Oklahoma Army National Guard. Because he was as World War II veteran, and many of his new peers and superiors in the Guard were not, it didn't take long for him to earn their utmost respect. And, I've heard he demanded it. Sgt. 1st Class Lewis was a groundbreaker, a vital piece in the Guard's history in our state. We are a better organization today because he answered the call and paved the way for others." Army & Air National Guard Oklahoma Frontline, "First African-American to join the Oklahoma National Guard dies," May 20, 2015, http://www.oklahomafrontline.com (last visited June 9, 2015).

[cdxxi]Army & Air National Guard Oklahoma Frontline, "First African-American to join the Oklahoma National Guard dies," May 20, 2015, http://www.oklahomafrontline.com (last visited June 9, 2015).

[cdxxii]NewsOK, "First black man to join the Oklahoma National Guard dies," http://newsok.com/first-black-man-to-join-the-oklahoma-national-guard-dies/article/5420956 (last visited June 9, 2015).

[cdxxiii]Berton Z. "Lee Lee" Lewis, http://www.parksbrothers.net/obituaries/Berton-Z-Lewis/ (last visited June 10, 2015).

[cdxxiv]"Race has been a crucial line of division in American society since the settlement of the American colonies in the beginning of the 17th century. . . [T]he salience of race in American life remains powerful. In part because of historic memory, and in part because of current reality, race continues to affect outlook, perception, and experience." *Gratz, et al. v. Bollinger, et al.,* No. 97-75321(E.D. Mich.); *Grutter, et al. v. Bollinger, et al.,* No. 97-75928 (E.D. Mich. 1997), Expert report of Professor Eric Foner (executive summary) in a University of Michigan affirmation action case that eventually made its way to the United States Supreme Court, http://www.vpcomm.umich.edu/admissions/legal/expert/foner.html (last visited October 8, 2013). *See also, Gratz v. Bollinger,* 539 U.S. 244 (2003), wherein the Supreme Court ruled the University of Michigan's undergraduate policy of affirmative action ad-

missions policy unconstitutional. The Court found the University's point system's "predetermined point allocations" that awarded 20 points to underrepresented minorities "ensures that the diversity contributions of applicants cannot be individually assessed" and was therefore unconstitutional.

[cdxxv]James Weldon Johnson (1871 – 1938), author, educator, lawyer, diplomat, songwriter, and civil rights activist, wrote the black national anthem, "Lift Every Voice and Sing," as a poem in 1899 in honor of Abraham Lincoln's birthday. By the 1920s, the hymn, with music written by Johnson's brother, John Rosamond Johnson (1873 – 1954), had become a standard in black churches and schools, protesting Jim Crow and celebrating black faith in an America true to her lofty ideals.

[cdxxvi]http://www.cyberhymnal.org/htm/l/i/liftevry.htm (last visited August 21, 2013).

[cdxxvii]Michio Kaku noted:

> Beyond work and love, I would add two other ingredients that give meaning to life. First, to fulfill whatever talents we are born with. However blessed we are by fate with different abilities and strengths, we should try to develop them to the fullest, rather than allow them to atrophy and decay. We all know individuals who did not fulfill the promise they showed in childhood. Many of them became haunted by the image of what they might have become. Instead of blaming fate, I think we should accept ourselves as we are and try to fulfill whatever dreams are within our capability.
>
> Second, we should try to leave the world a better place than when we entered it. As individuals, we can make a difference, whether it is to probe the secrets of Nature, to clean up the environment and work for peace and social justice, or to nurture the inquisitive, vibrant spirit of the young by being a mentor and a guide.

http://www.goodreads.com/quotes/tag/meaning-of-life (last visited January 26, 2015).

[cdxxviii]http://blogs.villagevoice.com/forkinthero ad/king1.jpg, last visited July 11, 2014. On August 19, 1958, Clara Luper led thirteen children into Katz Drug Store in downtown Oklahoma City, Oklahoma. They seized upon the then-empty lunch counter, placed their orders, and waited. Waitresses refused to serve them. They waited. Still, no service. They eventually left, only to return the next day, and then the next. They got served. These acts of civil disobedience, these sit-ins, spread to other restaurants in downtown Oklahoma City. In about four years, virtually all of them had been integrated. *See, e.g.,* Devona Walker, "50 years ago, children helped change nation when they sat down," http://newsok.com/50-years-ago-children-helped-change-nation-when-they-sat-down/article/3285497 (last visited July 11, 2014).

[cdxxix]www.huffingtonpost.com/2013/08/20/march-on-washington-50th-ann . . . (last visited August 29, 2013).

[cdxxx]architecture.about.com/od/greatbuildings/ig/Monuments-and-Memo . . . (last visited August 29, 2013).

[cdxxxi]http://www.findagrave.com/ (George W.F. Sawner, Find A Grave Memorial #67654200, added March 30, 2011; Lena L. Sawner, Find A Grave Memorial #52433567, added May 15, 2010)(last visited August 6, 2013).

[cdxxxii]This summary is based on an e-mail from Jan Vassar to Mel Chatman, October 6, 2014.

[cdxxxiii]The historic Sac and Fox Reservation, 1867 - 1891, consisted of 480,000 acres. Pursuant to the United States' allotment policy implemented principally through the Dawes Act, the federal government broke up tribal land holdings into individual allotments in the early 1900s. The Sac and Fox Nation is headquartered in Stroud, Oklahoma. *See, e.g.,* http://www.waymarking.com/waymarks/WM9WQH_Sac_and_Fox_Reservation_Lincoln_County_OK (last visited September 12, 2014).

[cdxxxiv]http://www.okcemeteries.net/lincoln/dudley/dudley.htm (last visited August 25, 2014).

[cdxxxv]Photo courtesy Mel Chatman.

[cdxxxvi]Fallis, OK—Ghost Town, http://www.abandonedok.com/fallis/ (last visited August 24, 2014).

[cdxxxvii]*Oklahoma Historical Society's Encyclopedia of Oklahoma History & Culture,* William D. Welge, "Moon, Frederick Douglass (1896 – 1975)," http://digital.library.okstate.edu/encyclopedia/entries/M/MO011.html (last visited August 24, 2014).

[cdxxxviii]http://www.blackpast.org/aah/blayton-sr-jesse-b-1879-1977 (last visited August 24, 2014).

[cdxxxviii]http://www.blackpast.org/aaw/pitts-riley-leroy-1937-1967 (last visited August 24, 2014).

[cdxl]Jan Vassar, *Oklahoma Historical Society's Encyclopedia of Oklahoma History & Culture,* "Fallis," http://digital.library.okstate.edu/encyclopedia/entries/F/FA008.html (last visited August 24, 2014). Jan Vassar and others continue research on whether the editor of the Fallis Blade was indeed an African American. All information to date points in that direction: He and Edward P. McCabe were friends. He lived in Guthrie, at least briefly. He reported on news of particular interest to African Americans. When he left Oklahoma, he moved to a southern black town. E-mail from Jan Vassar to Mel Chatman, September 12, 2014 (on file with author).

cdxliA Rosenwald school is one built with capital funding, in whole or in part, from the Rosenwald Fund, the philanthropic vehicle for Julius Rosenwald, a wealthy Sears, Roebuck & Company executive. Rosenwald created the fund in 1917 to assist with the education of African Americans, largely in the South. The foundation became a substantial benefactor of African American institutions, primarily through bricks-and-mortar grants to schools. *See, e.g.,* Cynthia Savage, Architectural Historian, Oklahoma State Historic Preservation Office, "Historic Context for Rosenwald Fund in Oklahoma" (Oklahoma City, Oklahoma: Oklahoma State Historic Preservation Office: August 1997).

cdxlihttp://www.davenportok.org/ (last visited August 19, 2014). Located on Historic Route 66 and nestled in the hills of eastern Lincoln County, adventurous spirits settled Davenport in the second great land run, the 1891 Sac and Fox Opening. Davenport celebrates Nettie Davenport Day on the Saturday before Mother's Day, a tribute to the town's pioneer heritage that honors the community's first postmistress and namesake. Farmland and ranches dominate the rustic landscape in the small community located between Chandler and Stroud on old Route 66. Davenport is within an hour's commute of Oklahoma's two large metropolitan cities, Oklahoma City and Tulsa. According to Chandler historian Jan Vassar, Davenport was a sundown town. E-mail from Jan Vassar to Mel Chatman, September 12, 2014 (on file with author).

cdxliihttp://www.davenportok.org/ (last visited August 19, 2014). Located on Historic Route 66 and nestled in the hills of eastern Lincoln County, adventurous spirits settled Davenport in the second great land run, the 1891 Sac and Fox Opening. Davenport celebrates Nettie Davenport Day on the Saturday before Mother's Day, a tribute to the town's pioneer heritage that honors the community's first postmistress and namesake. Farmland and ranches dominate the rustic landscape in the small community located between Chandler and Stroud on old Route 66. Davenport is within an hour's commute of Oklahoma's two large metropolitan cities, Oklahoma City and Tulsa. According to Chandler historian Jan Vassar, Davenport was a sundown town. E-mail from Jan Vassar to Mel Chatman, September 12, 2014 (on file with author).

cdxliiiThis summary is based on an e-mail from Jan Vassar to Mel Chatman, October 6, 2014.

cdxlivPhoto courtesy Mel Chatman.

cdxlvPhoto courtesy of Bobby Baker and his sister, Arlene Baker Sully, who grew up in Key West.

cdxlviMel Chatman and Jan Vassar, *The 'Negro Problem' in Lincoln County, Oklahoma (1889 – 1954)* (unpublished manuscript based on interviews with Lincoln County pioneers and historical information and documentation relevant to Lincoln County), 2005.

cdxlviihttp://www.okcemeteries.net/lincoln/keywest/keywest.html   (last visited August 25, 2014).

cdxlviiiPhoto courtesy of Mel Chatman.

cdxlixPhoto courtesy of Mel Chatman.

cdlPhoto courtesy Peggy Bobo.

cdliGalilee is not considered a separate informal black community as is Payson, principally because evidence indicates it had fewer than fifteen residences, a key definitional criterion for designation as an informal black community.

cdliiPhoto courtesy Mel Chatman.

cdliii*Escape from Alcatraz*, http://www.sfgenealogy.com/sf/history/sfoeat02.htm (last visited August 12, 2014).

cdliv*Escape from Alcatraz* (1979), http://www.moviefone.com/movie/escape-from-alcatraz/23326/main?flv=1 (last visited September 11, 2014).

cdlvPhoto courtesy Ethel Grey Wilson.

cdlviPhoto courtesy Ethel Grey Wilson.

cdlviihttp://www.okcemeteries.net/lincoln/sweethome/sweethome.htm (last visited August 25, 2014).

cdlviiiChandler resident David Alsip and former Chandlerite Wayne Pounds made the discovery. Pounds knew about the grave and had searched for it for years. Liz Golliver, "Grave of African American Civil War Hero possibly found near Sweet Home," *The Lincoln County News*, September 11, 2014.

cdlixPhoto courtesy Mel Chatman.

Index

243

About The Author

Hannibal B. Johnson, a Harvard Law School graduate, is an author, attorney, and consultant. He is a recognized expert on diversity and inclusion, with more than twenty years consulting with for-profit and nonprofit groups across the country, as well as writing and lecturing on the topic.

Johnson teaches at Oklahoma State University and the University of Oklahoma. His several books include *Tulsa's Historic Greenwood District, Black Wall Street: From Riot to Renaissance in Tulsa's Historic Greenwood District, Up from the Ashes*, and *Acres of Aspiration: The All-Black Towns in Oklahoma*, which chronicle the African American experience in Oklahoma and its indelible impact on American history. His book, *Apartheid in Indian Country?: Seeing Red Over Black Disenfranchisement*, recounts the history of the Freedmen, persons of African ancestry who lived among the Five Civilized Tribes.

Johnson has led the boards of local, state, and national nonprofits, and has received numerous honors and awards for his professional and community endeavors.

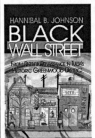

CPSIA information can be obtained
at www.ICGtesting.com
Printed in the USA
FFOW04n1045080518
46450094-48354FF